HEGEL'S PHILOSOPHY AND FEMINIST THOUGHT

Breaking Feminist Waves

Series Editors:
LINDA MARTÍN ALCOFF, Hunter College and CUNY Graduate Center
GILLIAN HOWIE, University of Liverpool

For the last twenty years, feminist theory has been presented as a series of ascending waves. This picture has had the effect of deemphasizing the diversity of past scholarship as well as constraining the way we understand and frame new work. The aim of this series is to attract original scholars who will offer unique interpretations of past scholarship and unearth neglected contributions to feminist theory. By breaking free from the constraints of the image of waves, this series will be able to provide a wider forum for dialogue and engage historical and interdisciplinary work to open up feminist theory to new audiences and markets.

LINDA MARTÍN ALCOFF is Professor of Philosophy at Hunter College and the City University of New York Graduate Center. Her books include *Visible Identities: Race, Gender and the Self* (2006); *The Blackwell Guide to Feminist Philosophy* (co-edited with Eva Kittay, 2006); *Identity Politics Reconsidered* (co-edited with Moya, Mohanty, and Hames-Garcia, Palgrave 2006); and *Singing in the Fire: Tales of Women in Philosophy* (2003).

GILLIAN HOWIE is Senior Lecturer in Philosophy at the University of Liverpool. She has edited *Gender, Teaching and Research in Higher Education* (2002); *Gender and Philosophy* (2003); *Third Wave Feminism* (Palgrave, 2004); *Menstruation* (Palgrave, 2005); *Women and the Divine* (Palgrave, 2008); and the forthcoming *Fugitive Ethics: Feminism and Dialectical Materialism*. She is the founder and director of the Institute for Feminist Theory and Research.

Titles to date:

Forthcoming:

HEGEL'S PHILOSOPHY AND FEMINIST THOUGHT

Beyond Antigone?

Edited by

*Kimberly Hutchings
and
Tuija Pulkkinen*

First published in 2010 by
PALGRAVE MACMILLAN®
in the United States—a division of St. Martin's Press LLC,
175 Fifth Avenue, New York, NY 10010.

Where this book is distributed in the UK, Europe and the rest of the world,
this is by Palgrave Macmillan, a division of Macmillan Publishers Limited,
registered in England, company number 785998, of Houndmills,
Basingstoke, Hampshire RG21 6XS.

Palgrave Macmillan is the global academic imprint of the above companies
and has companies and representatives throughout the world.

Palgrave® and Macmillan® are registered trademarks in the United States,
the United Kingdom, Europe and other countries.

ISBN: 978–0–230–62145–9

Library of Congress Cataloging-in-Publication Data

Hegel's philosophy and feminist thought : beyond Antigone? / edited
by Kimberly Hutchings, Tuija Pulkkinen.
p. cm.—(Breaking feminist waves)
ISBN 978–0–230–62145–9 (hardback)
1. Hegel, Georg Wilhelm Friedrich, 1770–1831. 2. Feminist theory. I.
Hutchings, Kimberly, 1960– II. Pulkkinen, Tuija.

B2948.H35445 2010
193—dc22   2009052994

A catalogue record of the book is available from the British Library.

Design by Newgen Imaging Systems (P) Ltd., Chennai, India.

First edition: August 2010

10 9 8 7 6 5 4 3 2 1

Printed in the United States of America.

CONTENTS

SERIES FOREWORD

Breaking Feminist Waves is a series designed to rethink the conventional models of what feminism is today, its past and future trajectories. For more than a quarter of a century, feminist theory has been presented as a series of ascending waves, and this has come to represent generational divides and differences of political orientation as well as different formulations of goals. The imagery of waves, while connoting continuous movement, implies a singular trajectory with an inevitably progressive teleology. As such, it constrains the way we understand what feminism has been and where feminist thought has appeared, while simplifying the rich and nuanced political and philosophical diversity that has been characteristic of feminism throughout. Most disturbingly, it restricts the way we understand and frame new work.

This series provides a forum to reassess established constructions of feminism and of feminist theory. It provides a starting point to redefine feminism as a configuration of intersecting movements and concerns—with political commitment but, perhaps, without a singular centre or primary track. The generational divisions among women do not actually correlate to common interpretive frameworks shaped by shared historical circumstances, but rather to a diverse set of arguments, problems, and interests affected by differing historical contexts and locations. Often excluded from cultural access to dominant modes of communication and dissemination, feminisms have never been uniform nor yet in a comprehensive conversation. The generational division, then, cannot represent the dominant divide within feminism, nor a division between essentially coherent moments; there are always multiple conflicts and contradictions, as well as differences about the goals, strategies, founding concepts, and starting premises.

Nonetheless, the problems facing women, feminists, and feminisms are as acute and pressing today as ever. Featuring a variety of disciplinary and theoretical perspectives, *Breaking Feminist Waves* provides a forum for comparative, historical, and interdisciplinary work, with special attention to the problems of cultural differences, language and representation, embodiment, rights, violence, sexual economies, and political action. By rethinking feminisms' history as well as its present, and by unearthing neglected contributions to feminist theory, this series intends to unlock conversations between feminists and feminisms and to open up feminist theory and practice to new audiences.

—Linda Martín Alcoff and Gillian Howie

Preface and Acknowledgments

The creation of this book has been a long but enjoyable process. The earliest phases included two conferences, one held in Jyväskylä in 2003 and the other in Berlin in 2006, on the theme of Hegel and feminist philosophy. We would like to thank all of the participants in both of those conferences for providing the initial inspiration for this book. Greatest thanks are due to all of the contributors to the book, who have supported the project throughout. We thank Palgrave Macmillan for their support in the publication process and Elizabeth O'Casey and Tuija Modinos for their help in editing and formatting the final version of the manuscript. We have been given permission to publish two of the chapters in the book that have previously appeared, in whole or in part, elsewhere. We are grateful to Judith Butler and to Taylor and Francis Ltd. respectively for giving the following permissions:

Chapter 6, Judith Butler, "Longing for Recognition," was first published in *Studies in Gender and Sexuality* 1 (3), 2000, then as Chapter 6 of *Undoing Gender* (New York and London: Routledge, 2004, 131–151), reprinted here by permission of the author.

Chapter 7, Karin de Boer, "Beyond Tragedy: Tracing the Aristophanian Subtext of Hegel's *Phenomenology of Spirit*," appeared in a different version as "The Eternal Irony of the Community," *Inquiry* Vol. 52 No. 4, 2009: 311–334, reprinted here by permission of the publisher, Taylor and Francis Ltd.

Kimberly Hutchings and Tuija Pulkkinen
November 2009

Contributors

Nancy Bauer is Associate Professor and Chair of Philosophy at Tufts University, where she teaches courses in feminist philosophy, philosophy and film, phenomenology and existentialism, philosophy of the ordinary and ethics. She is the author of *Simone de Beauvoir, Philosophy and Feminism* (2001) and is presently completing the book *How to Do Things with Pornography*, which is a meditation of philosophy's powers to criticize the culture from which it springs. Her writings are concerned with the attenuation of philosophy's social relevance in the wake of its professionalization in the twentieth century.

Karin de Boer is Lecturer in Philosophy at the University of Groningen (The Netherlands). Her areas of interest include Kant, Hegel, Heidegger, tragedy, metaphysics, and contemporary French thought. She is the author of *Thinking in the Light of Time: Heidegger's Encounter with Hegel* (2000) and *On Hegel: The Sway of the Negative* (forthcoming 2010), as well as numerous articles on modern and contemporary continental philosophy.

Judith Butler is Maxine Elliot Professor of Rhetoric and Comparative Literature, University of California, Berkeley. She writes on contemporary politics, cultural and literary theory, philosophy, psychoanalysis, feminism, and sexual politics. She is the author of several books including *Subjects of Desire: Hegelian Reflections in Twentieth-Century France* (1987), *Gender Trouble: Feminism and the Subversion of Identity* (1990), *Antigone's Claim: Kinship between Life and Death* (2000), *Undoing Gender* (2004), and *Frames of War: When Is Life Grievable?* (2009).

Tina Chanter is Professor of Philosophy and Interim co-director of the Women's and Gender Studies Program at DePaul University, Chicago. She is author of *Ethics of Eros: Irigaray's Re-writing of the Philosophers* (1995), *Time, Death and the Feminine: Levinas with Heidegger* (2001), *Gender* (2006), and *The Picture of Abjection: Film Fetish and the Nature of Difference* (2008). She is editor of the Gender theory series at the State University of New York Press (SUNY). She is also editor of *Feminist Interpretations of Emmanuel Levinas* (2001), co-editor of *Revolt, Affect, Collectivity: The Unstable Boundaries of Kristeva's Polis* (2005), and co-editor of *Sarah Kofman's Corpus* (2008). She is currently writing *Antigone's Affects: Political Legacies*.

Joanna Hodge is Professor of Philosophy, Manchester Metropolitan University, and President of the British Society for Phenomenology. She works on phenomenology, feminist critique, and transcendental aesthetics. She is the author of *Heidegger and Ethics* (1995) and *Derrida on Time* (2007). Current projects include a genealogy of affectivity and a study of the problem of evil.

Kimberly Hutchings is Professor of International Relations at the London School of Economics. She is the author of *Kant, Critique and Politics* (1996), *International Political Theory: Re-thinking Ethics in a Global Era* (1999), *Hegel and Feminist Philosophy* (2003) and *Time and World Politics: Thinking the Present* (2008). She co-edited *Cosmopolitan Citizenship* with Roland Dannreuther (1999) and was a founding editor of the journal *Contemporary Political Theory* (2002–2004) and associate editor of *European Journal of International Relations* (2004–2008). Her research interests include Hegel's philosophy, feminist philosophy, and international ethical and political theory. Her book *Global Ethics: An Introduction* is forthcoming in 2010.

Rakefet Efrat-Levkovich was awarded her PhD *summa cum laude* in Philosophy from Ben Gurion University in Israel in 2007, for her thesis *The Significance of Sexual Difference in and for Hegel's Phenomenology of Spirit*. She has published articles on feminist philosophy and women's poetry and teaches feminism at Ben Gurion University. Her interests include feminist philosophy, psychoanalysis, Hegel, Levinas, Kristeva, and Irigaray and she currently writes on the philosophical relation between doubt, melancholia, femininity, and language.

Susanna Lindberg is Associate Professor of Philosophy at the University of Helsinki and a postdoctoral researcher in the Academy of Finland and the University of Helsinki. She is the author of *Filosofien ystävyys* (1998) and has published widely on Heidegger and Hegel, including the forthcoming *Les Irréconciliables: Heidegger contre Hegel* (L'Harmattan, 2010) and *Être comme phusis, être comme vie* (2010) and, as editor, *Mikä mimesis: Philippe Lacoue-Labartheen filosofinen teatteri* (2009) and *Tulkintoja Hegelin hengen fenomenologiasta* (forthcoming). She has also translated Blanchot, Nancy, and Derrida into Finnish. Her current work deals with ideas of "life" and the "elemental" in German idealism, contemporary phenomenology, and deconstruction.

Tuija Pulkkinen is Professor of Women's Studies at the University of Helsinki. Her publications include *Valtio ja vapaus* (The State and Liberty/Freedom) (1989), *The Postmodern and Political Agency* (2000) and she has co-edited *Käsitteet liikkeessä. Suomen poliittisten käsitteiden historia* (Concepts in Motion. The History of Political Concepts in Finland) (2003), and *Ashgate Research Companion on the Politics and History of Democratization in Europe* (2008). She is an editor of the journal *Redescriptions.* Pulkkinen is the leader of the Research Group "Politics of Philosophy and Gender" within the Academy of Finland Centre of Excellence in Research of Political Theory and Conceptual Change. She is currently working on a research project on the politics of philosophy within contemporary feminist theory.

Alison Stone is Senior Lecturer in Philosophy at Lancaster University. Her interests include Hegel's philosophy, especially his metaphysics and philosophy of nature, feminist philosophy, Irigaray, and German Romanticism. She is the author of *Petrified Intelligence: Nature in Hegel's Philosophy* (2004), *Luce Irigaray and the Philosophy of Sexual Difference* (2006), and *An Introduction to Feminist Philosophy* (2007).

Laura Werner is Postdoctoral fellow at the Committee on Social Thought at the University of Chicago. She has published *The Restless Love of Thinking: The Concept* Liebe *in G.W.F. Hegel's Philosophy* (2007) as well as articles on feminism and the history of philosophy, Hegel's thought, and the philosophy of literature and film. She has co-edited *Visions of Value and Truth: Understanding Philosophy and Literature* (2006) and *Feministinen Filosofia* (2005). She is currently doing research on the connection of active sexual desire and virility to political rights in Europe around 1800.

CHAPTER ONE

Introduction: Reading Hegel

Kimberly Hutchings and Tuija Pulkkinen

HEGEL: DEAD OR ALIVE?

But every exegesis of Hegel's writings which tries to catch hold of him and keep him risks gripping his neck and closing around him like a rope. Hegel's reader becomes his gallows, his sarcophagus: his reading becomes a sepulchre of stone on Hegel's name.[1]

Werner Hamacher raises the question of whether it is possible to read Hegel without catching and keeping and thus murdering and burying him. It is a question that resonates through the history of the reception and interpretation of Hegel's thought from his most immediate successors to the present.[2] As many commentators have pointed out, Hegel's work is open to being read in so many different ways that any given interpretation, however historically sensitive or philosophically sophisticated, can be accused of silencing (murdering, burying) other Hegels.[3] The question of reading Hegel is at the heart of this book in a double sense. On the one hand, the book seeks to demonstrate how approaches to reading Hegel inspired by feminist and queer thought (of different kinds) generate vivifying rather than killing interpretations of Hegel's work. On the other hand, the book is concerned with the *value* of reading Hegel from perspectives that take the philosophical significance of gender and sexuality seriously.[4] The book will show that in the years since the publication of the last Anglophone edited collection of essays on Hegel and feminist thought, *Feminist Interpretations of G. W. F. Hegel*,[5] the feminist interrogation of Hegel has moved beyond its initial predominant focus on the pros and cons of Hegel's explicit treatment of women, sex, and gender in his texts. Contemporary feminist scholars are building on their philosophical insights into the meanings of sex, gender, and sexuality to illuminate Hegel's philosophical method and central concepts, and drawing creatively on Hegel's thought for feminist theory.

Competing interpretations of Hegel's texts—and arguments about what is or isn't philosophically valuable (alive or dead) in his work, including which texts are of most importance—have been ongoing since his death.[6] The early disputes, labeled in retrospect as being between "right" and "left" Hegelianisms, set the scene for the contentiousness of Hegel's legacy. In recent Anglophone scholarship, we find debates between metaphysical and non-metaphysical, idealist and realist, liberal and communitarian readings of Hegel's work.[7] Frederick Beiser, commenting on the "puzzling" renaissance of interest in Hegel's philosophy, presents the choice of the Hegel scholar as lying, uninvitingly, between anachronism and antiquarianism.[8] Either scholars read Hegel as if he were concerned with the same philosophical questions that confront the contemporary epistemologist or political theorist, or they read Hegel historically and contextually in terms of his own time and the philosophical questions he and his contemporaries were addressing. In the first case, Beiser suggests, Hegel is not really being read at all, but rather being invented in the image of his reader. In the second case, he argues, it is difficult to see the relevance of Hegel's thought to contemporary concerns.

Beiser's assessment of, as it were, the twin dangers confronting Hegel scholarship relies on assumptions about what kind of work counts as Hegel scholarship and about what doing philosophy means. On this account, Hegel scholarship includes exegetical work that aims to grasp Hegel's meaning, as well as work that identifies elements of Hegel's arguments that can be drawn on to resolve contemporary philosophical problems. Contemporary philosophical problems are understood as located within predominantly anti-metaphysical twentieth-century traditions of analytical and critical thought. Since Beiser argues that Hegel's meaning can be grasped only *metaphysically* (reflecting the philosophical concerns of Hegel's own time),[9] he questions the validity of non-metaphysical (philosophical in contemporary terms) readings of Hegel, in which the ongoing relevance of Hegel's work is claimed.[10] Instead, Beiser holds out for an approach to Hegel scholarship that puts the contextual reading of Hegel first and only then moves on to the question of Hegel's contemporary relevance.[11]

Beiser objects to cherry picking from Hegel's texts, and to readings that strip aspects of his (Hegel's) work from their overall systematic context, but he does so on the grounds that such readings obscure Hegel's *real* meaning, that is to say, the substantive claims that properly historical scholarship should be able to discover. Although many scholars would no doubt disagree with Beiser's particular views about exemplars of anachronistic readings of Hegel, his argument is a plausible one if one assumes that Hegel's texts embody an admittedly difficult but nevertheless decipherable, coherent, univocal, *fixed* set of meanings. The vast majority of current Anglophone scholarship on Hegel, whether anachronistic or antiquarian in Beiser's terms, shares his presumption that Hegel's work has a determinate content.[12] And yet both past and present of Hegel scholarship may also be taken to suggest something different: that is, that Hegel's meaning is incapable of being expressed in singular terms, that it is inherently open to being read in a variety of different ways, and that it can offer a productive sounding board for philosophical inquiries emanating from radically different philosophical perspectives and traditions, metaphysical, non-metaphysical and anti-metaphysical. Katerina Deligiorgi argues that the ongoing *timeliness* of Hegel's philosophy is to be found in the ways in which rival interpretations play into contemporary philosophical conversations.[13] Good historical contextualization does not resolve the question of Hegel's meaning but rather deepens and broadens the range of significance it can have for contemporary scholars. Deligiorgi suggests that contemporary readings of Hegel, rather than being either anachronistic or antiquarian, are philosophically creative and productive in their very disagreements about Hegel's meaning.

Beiser and Deligiorgi offer contrasting views about the philosophical significance and value of diverse interpretations of Hegel's thought. In both cases, however, their account of interpretation keeps in place the authority of Hegel's voice as author of his texts. In this way, they both follow the predominant traditions of Hegel interpretation in German and English, which, whether they are respectful or dismissive of Hegel's philosophy, focus on the explicit (often, of course, explicitly self-subverting) messages of the text. In the meantime, within the context of French philosophy, rather different approaches to reading Hegel have developed. These are interpretations that are heavily influenced by the poststructuralist critical readings of Hegel's work.[14] For poststructuralist thought, Hegel's work exemplifies what philosophy should and indeed could not be, that is to say, *absolute*. Deconstructive readings of Hegel demonstrate this through showing how the apparent completion and closure of Hegel's system could be unraveled by paying attention to the margins of his texts and to the reliance of his arguments on concepts that exceed and undermine his claim to comprehensive philosophy. However, in reading Hegel aporetically, poststructuralist interpretations of Hegel also open up a new range of interpretive possibilities. Thinkers such as Nancy and Malabou have, in recent years, offered new readings of Hegel that run counter to the idea of Hegel as the philosopher of violent closure.[15] And they do so by following a deconstructive strategy of reading, one that draws attention to themes and tropes in Hegel's work that have been marginal to the concerns of mainstream German and English language scholarship.

In crude terms, the above discussion has suggested that there are three different modes of reading Hegel that continue to be central to contemporary Hegel scholarship: *closed*, *open*, and *deconstructive*. The first, closed, mode is one that seeks to locate definitive answers to philosophical questions about, for instance, the foundations of valid knowledge claims or the nature of the good state in Hegel's texts. The second, open, mode, accepts the plurivocity of Hegel's philosophy and draws on Hegel's arguments as a resource for articulating and potentially transforming the terms of contemporary philosophical dilemmas. The third, deconstructive, mode finds the interpretive key to his work in those passages that unsettle the claims foregrounded by Hegel's authorial voice. There is no necessary connection between any of these modes of reading and any particular substantive (negative or positive) interpretation of Hegel's work. This means that debates and areas of common ground proliferate within as well as between these different routes to engaging with Hegel's texts.

FEMINIST READINGS OF HEGEL

Hegel has relatively little to say explicitly about sex, gender, and sexuality. What he does say promotes a gendered division of labor that effectively excludes women from life beyond the household. In this respect, Hegel's views fit with the gender ideology emerging at the time of the French Revolution—an ideology in which women were connected closely with "love" and "family" and simultaneously excluded from the emerging process of political democratization.[16] On a closed reading Hegel's treatment of sex, gender, and sexuality is, from a feminist point of view, uninteresting and, therefore, easily debunked or dismissed.[17] And it appears to offer little to feminist philosophy in terms of casting light on the place of sex, gender, and sexuality in posing and answering philosophical questions about epistemology, ontology, ethics, aesthetics, or politics.

In contrast, open and deconstructive readings of Hegel have played a significant part in the development and articulation of feminist philosophies. Most importantly, Simone de Beauvoir and Luce Irigaray, two major icons of feminist thought, both elaborated significant parts of their project through engaging with readings of Hegel. Beauvoir exemplifies a reading that uses Hegel against himself, embracing his account of self-consciousness, history, and modernity, whilst rejecting his overt exclusion of women from history.[18] And Irigaray, drawing on the liminality of the figure of Antigone in Hegel's *Phenomenology*, deconstructs the claim to universality of Hegel's system and thereby opens up the project of a philosophy of sexual difference.[19] In the former case, feminist philosophy draws selectively on Hegelian insights; in the latter, feminist philosophy is defined through its exclusion of Hegel.

The work of these two groundbreaking feminist philosophers is largely representative of the pathways taken in the first generation of explicit feminist engagement with Hegel's philosophy. Whether appropriating or rejecting Hegel, these were readings primarily concerned to *use* Hegel's work for feminist purposes. In doing so, however, they simultaneously demonstrated how raising questions about sex, gender, and sexual difference in Hegel's work opens up interpretive possibilities unexplored or underexplored in predominant traditions of Hegel scholarship. Feminist thinkers accomplished this in two predominant ways: first, by refocusing attention on certain passages within Hegel's texts, notably his story of the formation of self-consciousness, in particular the "struggle for recognition" in the *Phenomenology*, his diverse treatments of *Antigone* (in the *Phenomenology* and the *Aesthetics*), and his discussions of sexual difference in the *Philosophy of Nature* and of the sexual division of labor in modernity in *Elements of the Philosophy of Right*; second, in the wake of the clash between Beauvoir's and Irigary's response to Hegel's work, by focusing on the meaning and implications of Hegel's phenomenology and logic as modes of philosophical inquiry, which might or might not be antithetical to feminist thought in principle.

For example, the feminist focus on the significance of the figure of Antigone, inspired by Irigaray's argument, has become the starting point for a range of debates about the role played by Antigone within Hegel's *Phenomenology*, and about the ethical and political significance of Antigone for feminism. This work has put Hegel's concepts of spirit, nature, the state, tragedy, men, women, and ethical life under a spotlight, one that has generated a range of views about what these terms mean for Hegel, and how they operate within the overall argument of the *Phenomenology* and the rest of Hegel's philosophy. Does Hegel's treatment of Antigone confirm or disturb his distinction between nature and spirit? Does Hegel's reference to women as the "eternal irony" of political community contradict his own historicism? What is the significance of Hegel's insistence on the mutual guilt of Antigone and Creon and of his departure in this respect from the Sophoclean text?[20] At the same time, Hegel's treatment of Antigone has provided sometimes a vehicle and sometimes a reference point for debate over the ethical and political implications of different modes of feminist thought. Does Antigone demonstrate the fallacy of masculinist philosophy's exclusion of women from history and the public sphere? Does she represent a heroic "other" to masculinist political community and, therefore, the antithesis between feminist political aspirations and the masculinist state? Or is she the site of a crisis of representation that troubles any feminist aspiration to a purer politics? What begins as a feminist critique of Hegel becomes a proliferation of arguments about Hegel and feminist thought and about how they may illuminate each other.[21]

Feminist readings of Hegel's mode of philosophical inquiry demonstrate a similar kind of fecundity. Approaching Hegel's work from a feminist perspective has generated fresh insights into how his argument proceeds in his different texts, its historicism, and its dialectical, dynamic conceptual structure. A crucial aspect of this has been feminist demonstrations of how Hegel's treatment of gender and women exposes the fault lines of his supposedly immanent analysis—for example, the way in which his elucidation of the ethical life of the modern state depends on a trans-historical commitment of women to the sphere of natural connection.[22] However, the process of identifying gaps and tensions within Hegel's phenomenological and logical work does not necessarily lead to a rejection of dialectical thinking or historicism in feminist philosophy. Some sexual difference and deconstructive feminist readings of Hegel are highly suspicious of his philosophical method (for want of a better term) and use it as a foil for articulating alternative ways of thinking.[23] But many feminist readings of Hegel's philosophy identify his mode of philosophical thought as productive for feminism.[24] In this respect, the engagement with Hegel becomes internal to feminist debates and spirals in unexpected directions.[25]

The contributions to this book develop and challenge lines of debate prompted by the feminist interrogations of Hegel sketched out above. The book is divided into two main parts. In Part One, "Feminist Encounters with Hegel," the chapters are all concerned with the relation between interpretations of Hegel's philosophy and broad questions of ontology, epistemology, and ethics in feminist philosophy. Writing from a variety of feminist and queer viewpoints, the authors explore and challenge the substance-subject of Hegelian ontology, the systematicity of Hegel's thought, the role of race and tragedy in Hegel's aesthetics and philosophy of history, and his accounts of ethical subjectivity and recognition. In Part Two, "Re-Reading Hegel's Method," each chapter offers an innovative reading of Hegel's philosophical procedure, through focusing on the parts of his work in which he considers gender and sexuality. In doing so, they each cast fresh light on Hegel's meaning and its implications for feminist thought.

CHAPTER OUTLINE

The book begins with two chapters that offer contrasting views on the appropriate response to Hegel's philosophy from a gendered perspective and yet share a great deal in terms of the philosophical and political prescriptions that follow from their arguments. In "Differing Spirits," Tuija Pulkkinen offers a critique of feminist thinkers who have developed conceptions of the feminist subject based on the treatment in Hegel's *Phenomenology* of the struggle for recognition (Beauvoir) or the figure of Antigone (Irigaray). Pulkkinen argues that these readings of Hegel are mistaken in two senses. First, they are mistaken because they read Hegel through the prism of phenomenology and existentialism and thereby reduce the Hegelian substance-subject to the human subject. Second, they are mistaken because these readings reproduce foundationalist accounts of the human subject. In contrast, Pulkkinen argues for a non-foundational reading of Hegel's thought and for the potential value of this mode of thinking for feminist philosophy. Such a mode of thinking, she claims, provides an alternative to predominant subject-centered traditions of feminist thought, and also to recent feminist moves toward a Spinozan or Deleuzian "substance" thinking. Pulkkinen's argument is an example of an "open" reading of Hegel, but it is notable that it also draws on the influence of deconstruction, with Pulkkinen acknowledging the influence of Derrida, Nancy, and Malabou in her work.

Derrida is also central to Joanna Hodge's argument in "Queering Hegel." However, whereas Pulkkinen embraces a particular reading of Hegelianism and finds Hegelian thought to be compatible with deconstruction and politics "to come," Hodge deploys Derrida's "queering" of Hegel in *Glas* to develop a "queering theory kit." Her kit destabilizes a variety of patriarchal families: the lineages headed by good fathers in the Western philosophical tradition, the heterosexual "normal" family produced by capitalist modernity, and the holy family of Christianity. Hodge's reading is a deconstructive one and, as such, debunks Hegel the systematic philosopher. In contrast to Pulkkinen, Hodge does not engage with Hegelian ontology. Nevertheless, she follows Derrida and Nancy in drawing attention to the way in which "queering" operates internally within Hegel's text: "the queering of Hegel may take place already in the pages of Hegel himself, since his exposition must subvert what the conceptual order proposes." In some ways, therefore, she shares ground with Pulkkinen, both in her argument for the openness of Hegel's texts and prescriptively in the anti-foundationalist, anti-utopian methodological and political implications of queering. Pulkkinen and Hodge read Hegel in ways that deliberately pick apart different aspects of his arguments. For Pulkkinen, her reading remains faithful to Hegel, even as it rejects Hegel's explicit claims about the ontological subject, gendered subjects, or the state, because it acknowledges Hegel's own account of the substance-subject of spirit as historically self-moving. Hodge is not interested in faithfulness to Hegel but sees queering as a mode of engaging with philosophical texts that open up new possibilities for thought, ones that challenge existing patriarchal order in a variety of ways.

In "Antigone's Liminality" Tina Chanter approaches Hegel's work from a different kind of critical perspective. For Chanter, Hegel's work exemplifies the oppressive exclusions inherent in philosophy and art in the Western tradition, with which, she argues, certain feminist appropriations of Hegel's reading of Antigone have been complicit. Based on a close reading of Hegel's *Aesthetics*, Chanter demonstrates how, in his treatment of Greek tragedy, Hegel excludes the subject of slavery as proper to the tragic form. Although Hegel explicitly condemns slavery, within his accounts of history and tragedy it becomes something that "must sometimes be borne" and, therefore, something that is implicitly validated as a moment in the onward march of spirit toward an end that has yet to be reached. For Chanter, the focus of feminist critics on Antigone as the figure for the exclusion of the *feminine* from the public realm has neglected the equally significant suppression of class and race within the Hegelian account of the philosophy of history and the philosophy of art. The figure of Antigone can certainly be read as symbolic of the feminine, but she should also be read as the aristocrat, one whose brother is not a slave, one who is allowed to speak within the tragic genre, on Hegel's account, in a way that the slave cannot. In this respect she also, therefore, affirms the ongoing Eurocentrism and colonialism of the Western philosophical tradition. In Chanter's view, this confirms the dangers for feminist philosophy of following a Hegelian pathway in aesthetics, the philosophy of history, or in politics.

Kimberly Hutchings's chapter complements Chanter's in its focus on Hegel's treatment of the story of *Antigone*. In Hutchings's case, however, the focus is on ethics rather than aesthetics, and on parallels that can be drawn between interpretations of the significance of certain passages in Hegel's *Phenomenology* and the contemporary ethics of Irigaray and Butler. In contrast to Chanter, Hutchings reads Hegel's treatment of the character of Antigone in terms of the cue provided by Hegel's insistence on the guilt of both Antigone and Creon. For Hutchings it is not the purity or heroism of Antigone in Hegel's account that is ethically significant. Rather, it is the ways in which she troubles the idea of moral self-certainty characteristic of modern conceptions of ethical subjectivity, expressed by Hegel in the figures of the "hard heart of judgment" and the "beautiful soul." In spite of their dismissals of Hegel's reading of Antigone, Hutchings argues that the ethical thought of both Irigaray and Butler can also be understood in terms of the implications of a Hegelian critique of moral self-certainty.

Judith Butler's chapter is also concerned with the conceptualization of the self, but her focus is on engaging with Jessica Benjamin's critical psychoanalytic theory and the account of sexuality and gender underpinned by it. Butler explores Benjamin's reliance on a dyadic model of recognition, which derives from a particular reading of Hegel. And she counters Benjamin's recognitive model of the subject with an alternative Hegelian account of self: "It is, then, one perspective on rationality derived from Hegel which claims that the self seeks and offers recognition to another, but it is another which claims that the very process of recognition reveals the self is always already positioned outside itself." In her argument, Butler pits these two different readings of the significance of the struggle for recognition for individual self-consciousness against each other. For her, the alternative Hegelian account of the self as "Ek-static" is a more productive starting point for understanding the relation between sexuality and gender than that provided by the dyadic model of recognition.

In Part Two of the book, the chapters by Karin de Boer, Rakefet Efrat-Levkovich, Susanna Lindberg, Laura Werner, and Alison Stone all offer interpretations of Hegel's texts that have been inspired, in different ways, by thinking about the significance of sex and gender in Hegel's philosophy. On the basis of close readings, the writers excavate clues as to how to read the movement of Hegel's argument within specific texts. De Boer's contribution is iconoclastic in feminist terms.

It offers a counter to the focus of feminist readings on the significance of the *Antigone* both for Hegel's philosophy and for feminist
philosophy more broadly. De Boer argues that most feminist interpretations of the sections of the *Phenomenology* on Greek ethical life
are mistaken. This is, first, because most of the text does not actually
concern the interpretation of *Antigone* and, second, because it is an
error to think that Hegel is using *Antigone* to express his own views
on issues of gender. In a close reading of the relevant passages, de
Boer demonstrates the transitions in Hegel's discussion from a focus
on divine law to the emergence of the family in Greek ethical life. In
the famous passage in which women are described as the "eternal
irony" within the political community, de Boer argues that Aristophanes
rather than Sophocles is the reference point for Hegel's discussion.
She points out that in order to comprehend this passage, the peculiar
method of Hegel's *Phenomenology* must be taken seriously: "The
Phenomenology considers any particular mode of thought in such a
way that its self-comprehension turns out to be untenable." De Boer
concludes that feminist philosophy might take Aristophanes' comedies as a more productive starting point for thinking about gender
equality than either Greek tragedy itself or Hegel's masculinist treatment of the lessons of Greek ethical life.

Efrat-Levkovich is also concerned with the question of how to read
a puzzling transition within the *Phenomenology*, in her case the point
at which the initial focus on consciousness in relation to *objects* gives
way to the appearance of *self*-consciousness. On the basis of a close
reading of the parallels between Hegel's treatment of sense-certainty
and desire, she argues that the feminine has a much more fundamental place in Hegel's thought than is usually imagined. Her reading
counters interpretations that associate the appearance of the feminine
in the *Phenomenology* only with the much later section concerning
Greek ethical life and the contrast between human and divine law.
Instead, she argues that the feminine plays a crucial part within the
Hegelian system in epistemological and temporal terms right from
the beginning. Essentially the feminine corresponds to the pre-social,
pre-historical phase of knowing (explored in the first four chapters of
the *Phenomenology*), which is the condition of the possibility of spirit.
Efrat-Levkovich identifies Hegel's account of *ahistorical* time with
practices of memory, desire, fantasy, and recollection, which become
internalized in the masculine subject's (*historical*) time as a condition
of the possibility of his agency. In the revelation of this hidden subtext of the early chapters of the *Phenomenology*, she argues, the dependence of the masculine on the denial of the feminine is confirmed,

even as the distinctions between ahistorical and historical, masculine and feminine are problematized.

The question of women's time is also a theme in Lindberg's reading of Hegel. In her case, her interpretation takes its starting point from the work of philosophers such as Nancy and Malabou. She argues that these thinkers focus our attention on a philosophical question crucial also to German idealism. This is a question of the *presentation* of truth, which is never simply neutrally revealed but has always to be *figured*. Lindberg examines Hegel's use of figuring as a method of thought, particularly how woman *figures* in Hegel's texts, which means examining what kind of work is done by the figure of woman in Hegel's presentation of truth. She points to two kinds of work accomplished by the figure of woman in Hegel, "lifework" and "psycho-technique," figured as giving birth and the funerary work of mourning, remembering, and burying. Through a careful tracing of the appearances of woman in Hegel's work, Lindberg shows how woman presents the work of mediation—as a movement of transition, between nature and spirit. Essentially woman plays the role of the transcendental imagination—not in time, but making time possible.

Werner's argument focuses on how we need to understand Hegelian categories of "actuality" and "reality," "identity" and "difference," in order to understand Hegel's construction of gender difference and its political implications, in which women are banished from the public sphere. She argues that Hegel constructs gender difference conceptually, first, from the standpoint of absolute spirit, as *actual* difference between men and women, and second, from the standpoint of everyday experience, as *real* or concrete differences. This differentiation, she argues, conforms neither to the classical nature/culture divide in modern philosophy nor to the sex/gender differentiation in feminist thought. The concrete differences Hegel ascribes to men and women are evinced equally in the sphere of material bodies and social and political life, but neither of these spheres is the cause of the other. If one wants to challenge Hegel's account of gender difference, therefore, it is necessary to understand and challenge the conceptual distinctions and logical strategies through which it is grounded.

While Werner's argument offers an analysis of how Hegel grounds his understanding of gender difference conceptually, Stone addresses the gendered nature of the "concept" in Hegel. Stone focuses on Hegel's *Philosophy of Nature* as the key to his organicist account of the modern state and the gendered divisions on which it is based. She argues that Hegel's philosophy as a whole can be understood through the sexual symbolism of Hegel's metaphysics, manifested in the

Philosophy of Nature in the relation between "matter" and "form." The undifferentiated unity of "matter" is symbolically female, the "being-outside-of-itself" of the symbolically male "concept." In the *Philosophy of Nature*, nature is understood in terms of the progressive return of the "concept" to itself from its being-outside-of-itself in matter. This corresponds, Stone argues, to the pattern set up in Hegel's theory of the state in which women's confinement to the family and men's entry into political life from the family mark a stage in the (male) concept's progressive return-to-itself as spirit, out of (female) matter. For Stone, the sexual symbolism of Hegel's account needs to be understood in terms of his entrenchment within the history of Western philosophy and a conceptual structure in which female/woman is abjected from the realm of thought. She argues that feminist appropriations of Hegel such as that of Beauvoir reproduce rather than challenge this conceptual structure and suggests that Irigaray's work provides a more productive feminist response to Hegel.

The final chapter in the book is very different from the previous ones in both content and form. It focuses on the contemporary, the urgent, and the political and takes the form of a discussion and debate. The question is: *What relevance does Hegel's philosophy have for contemporary feminism?* The discussants are three authors of previous chapters, Hutchings, Pulkkinen, and Stone, and they are joined for this discussion by Nancy Bauer. For all four thinkers there are reasons why Hegel's work remains relevant to contemporary feminism. They differ, however, in their readings of Hegel and, therefore, in their accounts of where the relevance of his work resides. In this respect, the final chapter points up the overall message of this book. There is no single Hegel, just as there is no single feminist philosophy. For this reason the feminist conversation with Hegel will always be productive in a variety of ways, both in terms of how it illuminates Hegel's thought and in terms of the philosophical and political implications drawn for feminism.

Notes

1. Werner Hamacher, *Pleroma—Reading in Hegel,* trans. Nicholas Walker & Simon Jarvis (London: Athlone Press, 1998), 16.
2. John Toews, "Transformations of Hegelianism, 1805–1846," in *The Cambridge Companion to Hegel,* ed. Frederick C. Beiser (Cambridge: Cambridge University Press, 1993).
3. See Katerina Deligiorgi, "Introduction: On Reading Hegel Today," in *Hegel: New Directions,* ed. K. Deligiorgi (Chesham: Acumen, 2006); and F. C. Beiser "Introduction: The Puzzling Hegel Renaissance," in

The Cambridge Companion to Hegel and Nineteenth-Century Philosophy, ed. F. C. Beiser (Cambridge: Cambridge University Press, 2008).

4. The contributions to this book are not written from a uniform feminist perspective and do not operate with a uniform understanding of terms such as "sex," "gender," and "sexuality." Not all of the contributors would define themselves as writing feminist philosophy in any straightforward sense. But what all of the ensuing essays have in common is that they read Hegel in the light of interpretations of his work that take feminist concerns seriously.

5. Patricia Jagentowicz Mills, ed. *Feminist Interpretations of G. W. F. Hegel* (University Park, PA: Pennsylvania State University Press, 1996). Other examples of bringing Hegel and feminist philosophy into conversation can be found in: Jennifer Ring, *Modern Political Theory and Contemporary Feminism* (Albany: State University of New York Press, 1991); *Owl of Minerva* 24(1)1992: 41–69; Harry Brod, *Hegel's Philosophy and Politics: Idealism, Identity and Modernity* (Boulder, CO: Westview Press, 1992); Jeffrey A. Gauthier, *Hegel and Feminist Social Criticism: Justice, Recognition and the Feminine* (Albany: State University of New York Press, 1997); Stella Sandford and Alison Stone, eds., *Hegel and Feminism,* Special Issue of *Women's Philosophy Review* 22, 1999; Kimberly Hutchings, *Hegel and Feminist Philosophy* (Cambridge: Polity Press, 2003).

6. See Toews, op. cit., See Deligiorgi, op. cit., for a particularly fresh and insightful overview of different ways in which "what is living and what is dead" in Hegel's thought have been identified at different historical moments. The phrase "what is living and what is dead" was coined by Croce, cited by Deligiorgi, "On Reading Hegel Today," 2.

7. A useful bibliography of Anglophone Hegel scholarship in the last fifteen years can be found in *The Cambridge Companion to Hegel and Nineteenth Century Philosophy,* ed. Beiser, 419–422. The 1993 and 2008 *Cambridge Companions* together provide a good sense of the issues and debates characteristic of mainstream Anglophone Hegel scholarship in the last three decades.

8. Beiser, "Puzzling Hegel Renaissance," 6–8. Beiser's own solution to this dilemma is to pursue the antiquarian line of scholarship as a prerequisite for engaging with Hegel philosophically.

9. See Beiser, "Introduction: Hegel and the Problems of Metaphysics," in *Cambridge Companion to Hegel* (1993); and "Puzzling Hegel Renaissance," 5.

10. Beiser has in mind here interpreters such as Taylor, Hartmann, Pinkard, Pippin and Brandom. See Charles Taylor, *Hegel* (Cambridge: Cambridge University Press, 1975); Klaus Hartmann, "Hegel: A Non-metaphysical View," in *Hegel,* ed. Alisdair MacIntyre (New York: Doubleday, 1972); *Hegel Reconsidered,* ed. Terry Pinkard (Dordrecht: Kluwer, 1994); Robert Pippin, *Hegel's Idealism: The Satisfactions of Self-consciousness* (Cambridge: Cambridge University

Press, 1989); Robert Brandom, *Tales of the Mighty Dead* (Cambridge, MA: Harvard University Press, 2002).

11. Beiser, "Puzzling Hegel Renaissance," 8–14.

12. This is particularly the case with Hegel's ethical and political thought, which has been the object of particular attention in recent years. See Frederick Neuhouser, *Foundations of Hegel's Social Theory* (Cambridge, MA: Harvard University Press, 2000); Alan Patten, *Hegel's Idea of Freedom* (Oxford: Oxford University Press, 1999); Paul Franco, *Hegel's Philosophy of Freedom* (New Haven, CT: Yale University Press, 1999); Dudley Knowles, *Hegel and the Philosophy of Right* (London: Routledge, 2002).

13. Deligiorgi, "On Reading Hegel Today," 7–9.

14. Derrida is the primary exemplar of a post-structuralist reader of Hegel, see Jacques Derrida, *Glas,* trans., John P. Leavey and Richard Rand (Lincoln: University of Nebraska Press, 1990); *Hegel after Derrida,* ed. Stuart Barnett (London: Routledge, 1998).

15. Jean-Luc Nancy, *The Speculative Remark (One of Hegel's Bon Mots),* trans., Céline Suprenant (Stanford: Stanford University Press, 2001); Jason Smith and Steven Miller, trans., *Hegel: The Restlessness of the Negative* (Minneapolis and London: University of Minnesota Press, 2002); Catherine Malabou, *The Future of Hegel: Plasticity, Temporality, Dialectic,* trans. Lisabeth During (London and New York: Routledge, 2005).

16. Although Seyla Benhabib accuses Hegel of anachronism in his treatment of women (see "On Hegel, Women and Irony," *Feminist Interpretations*), historical scholarship suggests that he was, in fact, in tune with his times. See Tuija Pulkkinen, "The Gendered 'Subjects' of Political Representation," in *The Ashgate Research Companion to the Politics of Democratization in Europe,* eds. K. Palonen, T. Pulkkinen, and J. Rosales (Farnham/ Burlington: Ashgate, 2008); Denise Riley, *"Am I That Name?" Feminism and the Category of "Women" in History* (Houndmills: Macmillan, 1988); Stephanie Coonzt, *Marriage, a History: How Love Conquered Marriage* (London: Penguin Books, 2005); Werner in this volume.

17. See Carla Lonzi, "Let's Spit on Hegel," in *Feminist Interpretations.*

18. Simone de Beauvoir, *The Second Sex,* trans. H. M. Parshley (Harmondsworth: Penguin Books, 1988).

19. Luce Irigaray, *Speculum of the Other Woman,* trans. G. C. Gill (Ithaca: Cornell University Press, 1985).

20. See Irigaray, op. cit.; Patricial Jagentowitz Mills, "Hegel's *Antigone,*" in *Feminist Interpretations;* Judith Butler, *Antigone's Claim: Kinship between Life and Death* (New York: Columbia University Press, 2000); Chanter and Hutchings in this volume.

21. See Irigaray, op. cit.; Christine Battersby, *The Phenomenal Woman* (Cambridge: Polity Press, 1998), 103–124; Hutchings, op. cit.,

80–111; Mills "Hegel's *Antigone*" op. cit., Butler op. cit.; Chanter, Hutchings and de Boer in this volume.

22. See Stone in this volume.

23. See, for example, Irigaray op. cit.; Rosalyn Diprose, *The Bodies of Women* (London: Routledge, 1994); Chanter, Efrat-Levkovich and Stone in this volume.

24. This includes readers critical of other aspects of Hegel's argument such as Mills and Benhabib op. cit., as well as readers who identify more fully with Hegelianism, see Hutchings, *Hegel and Feminist Philosophy*, and Hutchings and Pulkkinen in this volume.

25. One of the most interesting, and influential examples of this is the work of Butler, which incorporates explicitly Hegelian and anti-Hegelian moments. On the one hand, Butler lines up with deconstructive critics of Hegel as the philosopher of totality, see *Subjects of Desire: Hegelian Reflections in Twentieth-Century France* (2nd Edition, New York: Columbia University Press, 1999) and *Antigone's Claim* op. cit.; on the other hand, Butler uses Hegelian categories to capture the idea of a non-totalizing ethical universality, see Butler, "Restaging the Universal: Hegemony and the Limits of Formalism" and "Competing Universalities," in *Contingency, Hegemony and Universality: Contemporary Dialogues of the Left* by Judith Butler, Ernesto Laclau and Slavoj Žižek (London: Verso, 2000).

PART ONE

Feminist Encounters with Hegel

CHAPTER TWO

Differing Spirits—Reflections on Hegelian Inspiration in Feminist Theory

Tuija Pulkkinen

Hegel's central notion "spirit" (*Geist*) has been ascribed distinctly different meanings depending on how his philosophy has been interpreted. I see Hegel's philosophy, first and foremost, as metaphysics and as an ontological doctrine in which he posits a substance in the form of a subject. The primary use for the term "spirit," in this view, is that it is Hegel's name for the all-inclusive ontological substance-subject. The rest of the spirit vocabulary, such as "the objective spirit," which refers to social life, and the "subjective spirit" or "finite spirit," which refer to human beings, repeats the self-reflexive structure of the absolute spirit.

In contrast to this is Alexander Kojève's influential reading of Hegel's *Phenomenology of Spirit*, which has established a very different interpretation. Instead of being an ontological premise, in Kojève's reading, the spirit as a subject comes close to being identified with humanity and human consciousness. Kojève's approach is tied to his close connection to the modern phenomenological and existential tradition of Husserl and Heidegger. It bypasses Hegel's ontology and concentrates instead on another kind of approach in which the human serves as the ontologically relevant foundation, the channel to all being as appearance.

The effects of the Kojèvian reading of Hegel in the history of feminist interpretations of Hegel have not yet been sufficiently explored. A good number of significant feminist theorists, such as Simone de

Beauvoir, Luce Irigaray, and Judith Butler, have integrated major aspects of Hegelian philosophy in their thought, and it is interesting to note that most of this has been done with Kojève's interpretation in the background. In this chapter I will argue that taking Hegel's ontology more seriously—as I regard Catherine Malabou and Jean-Luc Nancy as doing—produces different options for feminist thought. Most importantly, however, I will suggest that recognizing or giving recognition to Hegel's philosophy as an ontological effort makes it possible to reject the ontological approach itself and yet learn from aspects of this particular ontology in contrast to others.

While rejecting both foundational projects, the Hegelian subject ontology, and its humanized phenomenological Kojévian reading, feminist thinkers can still profit from what Hegel presents of the thought process of the substance-subject spirit. In addition to what Kimberly Hutchings has argued about the value of the Hegelian model of thinking in non-exclusive opposites for feminist thought, I suggest that the ontology itself, particularly the inconclusiveness of the life of absolute spirit in Hegel's ontology, signals a model for thinking and operates as inspiration for feminist thought, discernible, for example, in Judith Butler's work. Here, Hegelian ontology provides an inspiration for looking at gender not in terms of material ontology or the human condition, but as constantly transforming in the middle of a thought/matter process of materialization.

DIFFERING SPIRITS

The absolute spirit in Hegel's system is an ontological claim that also includes an epistemological stand. The absolute as the substance is everything there is, and this everything is, ultimately, a subject that thinks, moving from concept to concept. In other words, all that is, is a self-reflexive thinking process, which is simultaneously all reality shaping itself and on its way to fuller self-recognition of itself as a conceptual process. It follows, among other things, that Hegelian logic is not a method, but a part of one and the same process of spirit proceeding in concepts, a process that is simultaneously the historical becoming of all that there is. As Catherine Malabou notes, more recent French interpretations, such as that of Bernard Bourgeois, are exceedingly clear on this point and have considerably clarified the discussion on the historical becoming and the logical truth; historicity and eternity in Hegel's thought.[1]

Hegel's epistemological position, his "philosophy," or "scientific philosophy" can be described initially by following, for example,

Jean-Luc Nancy, who writes that "philosophy is not one more representation, not one more knowledge...Neither is it a reflection upon knowledges as if these latter...must be submitted to another knowledge and another evaluation...."[2] In Nancy's presentation, Hegel's "philosophy consists in not adopting any point of view —in not even being a 'view' at all, if there is no more 'view' once one penetrates the thing, or grasps it."[3] Nancy differentiates Hegel's grasping (*greifen—Begriff*) of "the thing" from other philosophical projects that take the thing as merely being. It is not mere *being* but its *doing* that is at stake in Hegel. The thing is an act or, as Nancy says, creation without a creator,[4] and "philosophy" grasps this thing.

Nancy's chosen vocabulary in his redescription of Hegel includes terms such as "facts," "vitality," "life," "giving," and "penetration," as well as "manifestation," and "decision." The *factum* is the "thing itself" that the thought penetrates and that philosophy grasps. In Nancy's presentation the thing itself is vitality, which is "the character of bearing itself outside itself, manifesting itself." The thing gives itself. And it is here that the decision to philosophize comes into play.[5] As Nancy's text tends toward phenomenological-existential vocabulary, he continues about the philosophical decision, "which is always the decision of the identity of being and thought" that "it is the decision of a world without secret, or a world whose whole secret lies in its *logos* or its revelation."[6]

I would prefer to speak of Hegel's decision to write philosophy in terms of a particular type of ontology. This is an ontology that refuses the Kantian unknown thing in itself (*das Ding an sich*) and insists on the ultimate identity of the known and the knower within the acting substance, which is simultaneously the ongoing creation of all and, therefore, the absolute. The epistemology that the system suggests is a description of the process in which absolute substance/subject reflects itself and unfolds itself in the process of speculation, which is simultaneously the history and the grasping of it in concepts and which is provided by the finite spirit in the form of philosophy.

Hegel's description of this state of affairs is not completely devoid of hubris (of the philosopher and philosophy): philosophy is the form of knowledge that best reflects and comes closest to the real process of absolute thought, the substance that is thought, in its essence. Nevertheless, Hegel's text is also a description of knowing/being, which is crucially and fundamentally, always and permanently, a noncomplete process. Here, Nancy's characterization of the "restlessness" of the spirit catches the essential within Hegelian thought.[7] The creation of the spirit of itself, as well as its self-reflection and recognizing itself, is constantly ongoing; there is no endpoint or closure in this process of change.

In comparison to modern phenomenology and existentialism, the human being, or the transcendental human consciousness, "the finite spirit" in Hegel's terms is not the point of departure for ontology. On the contrary, the absolute subject/substance divides itself and externalizes itself in order to grasp itself in the medium of the finite spirit and in the history of human consciousness. Hegel's dialectical philosophy is systematically non-transcendental in a Kantian and Husserlian sense: it does not aim to explore the conditions of consciousness and the conditions of human existence.

KOJÈVE AND THE PHENOMENOLOGICAL READING OF HEGEL

Kojéve lectured on the *Phenomenology of Spirit* at the École des Hautes Études from 1933 to 1939,[8] and a whole generation of young French intellectuals followed his Heidegger- and Marx-inspired Hegel lectures, which later decisively shaped their own work. Among them were Jacques Lacan, Jean-Paul Sartre, and Maurice Merleau-Ponty, among others.[9] Simone de Beauvoir did not attend the lectures herself, but she also operates with Kojèvian interpretations of Hegel.[10] The effect of Kojève's lectures on his contemporaries' understanding of how to read Hegel is hard to overestimate. As a redescription of Hegel's philosophy, Kojève's interpretation had a powerful impact, reaching well into the present. The most significant aspect of this impact is that Kojève's reading of Hegel's entire project is strongly based on the *Phenomenology of Spirit,* which for him constitutes the key work in Hegel's corpus.

The centrality of the *Phenomenology of Spirit* in Kojève's reading is usually acknowledged, but it is rarely pointed out that by the same token the Hegelian "spirit"/"subject" in Kojève's presentation is rendered what Hegel himself calls "the subjective spirit," or alternatively, "the finite subject." To a degree, this transformation happens simply because other parts than the "Phenomenology of Spirit" in the Hegelian system are left out of Kojève's spotlight. More seriously, it is obvious that Kojève's reading represents Hegel as a philosopher essentially engaged with thinking of the human subject, human consciousness, and the history of humanity.

The *Phenomenology of Spirit* is Hegel's early version of what later became a part of his entire philosophical system. In a subsequent complete presentation of Hegel's system in the *Encyclopaedia of the*

Philosophical Sciences (1830), one subsection is entitled "Phenomenology of Spirit." The entire system consists of three main sections called "Logic," "The Philosophy of Nature," and "The Philosophy of Spirit."[11] "The Philosophy of Spirit" is divided into three parts: "The Subjective Spirit," "The Objective Spirit," and "The Absolute Spirit." Each of them is further subdivided, and "The Phenomenology of Spirit" is the second subsection of the three that make up "The Subjective Spirit."

The other two parts of "The Subjective Spirit" are "Anthropology" and "Psychology." In the middle section, "The Phenomenology of Spirit," the central term is "consciousness" (*Bewusstsein*) as distinct from the term "soul" (*Seele*), which is central in the first part (Anthropology), and "the subject" (*Subjekt*), which is central in the third part (Psychology). The subchapters of the "The Phenomenology of Spirit" part are (1) Consciousness as such (senses, perception, awareness); (2) Self-consciousness (desire, recognizing self-consciousness, general/universal self-consciousness); and (3) Rationality/Reason(ing).[12]

Although the earlier book *Phenomenology of Spirit*, published in 1807, is not exactly identical in content with the later subsection "Phenomenology of Spirit" in the Encyclopaedic system, and although it also comprises issues later developed under the headings "Objective" and "Absolute Spirit,"[13] it is clear that phenomenology is only one small part of Hegel's philosophy, the part that is concerned mostly with human mental functions. Hegel's thought elsewhere, in other parts of the same system, comprises much more than the human. In other parts of the system, Hegel is concerned with nonhuman life and nonliving nature, as well as other nonhuman things.

Kojève's reading can be seen as a form of politics of philosophy. It is well known that Kojève highlighted Marxian themes in his reading of Hegel, such as the theme of work and its role in human history. However, an even more ambitious and influential redescription and a grand act of the politics of philosophy is that Kojève reads the Hegelian spirit and subject in a manner that glues it together with Husserl's phenomenological consciousness, particularly with the existentialist, humanistically interpreted *Dasein* of Heidegger.[14] Kojève rarely mentions Heidegger in the lectures, but many central themes in the book—such as man's struggle for transformation through work, freedom, death, and time, as well as many terms, such as finitude, mortality, world, and *Dasein*—very clearly connect with Heidegger's texts.[15] At the very end of the book Kojève even writes that Heidegger's *Sein und Zeit* adds nothing to the anthropology of Hegel's phenomenology,[16] a statement that shows the degree to which Kojève sees the two projects as being identical.

Most commonly, Kojève is seen to introduce the theme of the dialectic of the master and the slave firmly into the French conception of Hegel. He is also seen to firmly implant the idea of the end of history as being Hegelian. It is more rarely noted, however, that his major, and I would think the most influential, contribution was the phenomenologizing of Hegelian ontology.

Already, Kojève's choice of the particular section in Hegel's work that is called "phenomenology" points to his initial interest, as well as the fact that this is the section in which the main concept is "consciousness," a term so central in Husserl's work. In Kojève's reading, Hegel appears as if his philosophical project was to uncover finite consciousness and, in the last instance, the human as the foundation of ontology.[17] Kojéve is also explicit in his merging of Hegel with modern phenomenology:

> The Hegelian *method*, therefore, is not at all "dialectical": it is purely contemplative and descriptive, or better, *phenomenological* in Husserl's sense of the term.[18]

For example, what happens to the theme of recognition (*Anerkennung*) in Kojève's reading of Hegel is noteworthy. One of the central themes in Hegel's ontology is the recognition of spirit of itself in all its externalizations. Spirit recognizes itself in inorganic nature and organic nature, as well as in human consciousness, social life, history, and thought, reaching ultimately, within philosophy (scientific philosophy), its most evident self-identity: it recognizes itself as all this and ultimately as *thought* in Hegel's ontology. Instead, in Kojève's interpretation, the theme of recognition is developed in terms of the human condition of people being dependent upon social recognition. The most essential feature of a human being, in the Kojèvian interpretation of Hegel, is the desire for social recognition.[19] In this redescription, Hegel's huge ontological-epistemological process of the recognition of the spirit of itself turns into a theory of the essential characteristics of a universalized human being. This involves another kind of foundational project in contrast to Hegel's: not the positing of a substance, as Hegelian ontology does, but instead grounding being in the human.

Kojève's philosophical-political move (associating Hegel's project with those of Husserl and Heidegger) is remarkable, particularly when it is taken into consideration that Hegel's phenomenology is not phenomenology in Husserl's or Heidegger's sense. The human, whether as a species or as a singular existence, is not the core issue in Hegelian thought, at least not to the same degree as it is in the modern phenomenological tradition.[20] Hegel's "subject" and "spirit" do not primarily refer to a generalized human consciousness, nor do they refer to the human psyche; they do not primarily express transcendental conditions of consciousness, nor the *Dasein* between birth and death. Hegel's phenomenology of spirit is one part of his philosophical system, which aspires to be a presentation of all there is, and is a metaphysical project of positing an ontology. Hegel precisely does *not* do this through the exploration of the conditions of transcendental consciousness, nor human consciousness, nor existence; he does not do it in the style of transcendental philosophy: instead, Hegel posits substance. And his peculiarity, of course, is that he posits substance as subject, as spirit. The substance-subject is sheer (self-reflecting) activity and a perpetual motion in concepts: it is thought.

Many notions of the harmfulness or usefulness of Hegelian thought for feminist purposes rest on humanist considerations that rely on the Kojèvian reading of Hegel's spirit. I would like to reflect on whether Hegel's philosophy, seen not in this Kojèvian light, but as metaphysical thought, has any significance for contemporary feminist thought. If we take seriously that Hegel's subject is not the human, but substance, does this render his work more or less interesting for feminists? Are there features in the way he constructs the activity of thought in his substance-subject that would benefit feminist thought? Are there other dimensions in his thought that would be more beneficial?

Kojève's phenomenological-existential approach has had a major impact on feminist readings of Hegel, starting from Beauvoir.[21] It is relevant in this context that the focus of this interpretation is on human consciousness, human mortality, and the general conditions of the human species' existence as the foundation for being. Sex is easily considered one of the general conditions of human existence, and even the central condition for the continuous existence of the human species. A theorist interested in gender is likely to highlight this aspect, although it was never much developed in Husserl, Heidegger, or Kojève.[22] It fits readily into the agenda of feminist thinkers working within the heritage of the phenomenological-existential tradition. Since the phenomenological-existential approach invites particularly intensive interest in the foundations of the human condition, when division into two (reproductive) sexes is identified as being such a condition, this shows in the work of feminist thinkers who have been influenced by the Kojévian reading of Hegel.[23] The idea of sexual difference as ontological difference is a convincing step in phenomenological ontology, which grounds being in the human. In this context the feminist position consists of positing that the human is not one, but two.

When gender is approached through an ontology that takes the human as an exemplary being, gender is conceived of as a foundational issue, not related to a particular time or place, but as a basic and static human condition. A very different approach could follow from a Hegelian open-ended ontology. In Hegel, the timelessly generalized human being and the conditions of its being there are not the center of interest, and the human is not made absolute and thereby standardized to the same extent as it is in phenomenology. Taken seriously, Hegelian ontology creates possibilities for highlighting the perspective of constant change, including that with respect to gender. Even more importantly, it is relevant for feminist thinking that in Hegelian thought, without the Kojèvian interpretation, the interest is not in the stable features of the human; instead, human beings are always conceived of as already being within a culture, and in the eternally changing process of cultures and history in the infinite and unconcluded process of the spirit.

OPTIONS FOR A HEGELIAN INSPIRATION IN FEMINIST THOUGHT

As the Hegelian spirit/subject is most often considered to be human, finite spirit, and rarely an infinite spirit—that is to say, substance as subject—it is difficult to work out what Hegelian ontology actually would or could mean for feminist thinking. This has not been advocated as a project—unlike, for example, the Spinozist ontology of Deleuze, the feminist potential of which has been explored intensely by some contemporary feminist theorists, such as Elizabeth Grosz and Rosi Braidotti.[24] One way of exploring a different Hegelian inspiration for feminism would be through the notion of "plasticity," suggested by Catherine Malabou in her reading of Hegel. In introducing this concept, Malabou is acting in a sense as a Hegelian philosopher, as if expressing in concepts the consciousness of spirit of itself. She creates concepts to grasp the very Hegelian substance-subject, which, in her redescription, is plasticity. Building on other contemporary studies, such as Bernard Bourgeois's work on the relationship of Hegel's logic and historical presentation/becoming, Malabou describes the spirit as activity and redescribes it in terms of plasticity: "... the very plasticity of substance itself, its capacity both to receive form and to give form to its own content."[25] She suggests that the self-determination of the spirit can be phrased as the "originary operation of plasticity,"[26] which in terms of time is speculation, not predication.

The implications for gender of Malabou's highlighting of the notion of plasticity are interesting. Her redescription includes Aristotelian notions of "giving form" and "receiving form," which, in the tradition of both philosophy and feminist thought, have been heavily marked with gender: giving form has been associated with idea and male, and receiving form has been associated with material and female. Their mutual exclusivity, which has been intensely maintained in the tradition, is clearly challenged in the notion of plasticity, the capacity of a substance both to receive form and to give form to its own content. Although Malabou has not elaborated extensively on the theme of gender in this context,[27] her notion certainly offers such opportunities.

Malabou's redescription of Hegel's subject differs from many others in that she does not read Hegel through the phenomenological human perspective. Instead, Malabou, exploring the time structures of Hegelian texts, considers the peculiar experience of reading that Hegel's text offers,[28] as well as various subjects in Hegel's text: humanity, God, and the philosopher as "perspectives open to the crossroads of time."[29] Humanity, God, and the philosopher, far from being subjects constituted in advance, turn out to be sites where subjectivity forms itself.[30] Malabous's perspectivist approach is a promising reading of Hegelian ontology, which, most importantly, recognizes the main characteristic of Hegel's thought and deals with it as metaphysics. But it also provides a consideration of the effect of reading Hegel. As a particular type of writing and thinking, Hegel's reading also has an effect and it sets out a model.

Another possible way of approaching Hegel's thought and its "usefulness" for contemporary feminist thought is to pay attention to it as a style of thinking and as a way of proceeding in thought. Kimberly Hutchings precisely considers the model of thinking that Hegel sets out. There are specific thought procedures that can be discerned in the thought process of the substance-subject that Hegel describes, setting aside the ontological claim it makes. For Hutchings, the value of Hegel's thought is in how thought proceeds through moments of identity and difference and allows reasoning in mutually inclusive statements. In her view, this is particularly valuable for contemporary feminist thought, because it makes it possible to supersede traditional conceptual differences such as nature/spirit, body/mind, passive/active. Apart from dichotomous either/or forms, Hegel's thought, Hutchings maintains, enables the form "both A and not A." In other words, Hutchings sees the value of Hegel's thought for feminist theory in Hegel's "identity of identity and difference."[31]

In comparison to Malabou and Hutchings, Judith Butler's engagement with Hegel is often less direct and more diffuse. In her early work, *Subjects of Desire* (1987), Butler engages explicitly with the French readings of Hegel. The rest of her work, although mostly not explicitly on Hegel,[32] still carries traits of the French readings of Hegel. In more subtle ways, inherent in both how she writes and what she writes, Butler's texts also exhibit Hegelian characteristics that not only have been filtered through Kojève's phenomenological-existential reading but also connect with post-structuralist readings engaging critically with the inheritance of phenomenology transmitted through Kojève.[33] In my view, Butler's writing can be seen to reflect Hegelian teachings in multiple ways.

For example, Butler has notoriously been accused of not taking into consideration "the materiality of the body," and as a response, she refers to materialization, her point being that she refuses to maintain the distinction between material and non-material.[34] I would see such a refusal as a Hegelian trace in her work. The process of materialization echoes the spirit of Hegel, which ultimately refuses a division into material and ideal and posits their unity in the absolute spirit and its process. Although Butler never engages in an ontological project—and I would see this as crucial in her approach—reading Hegel might well be the inspiration to overcome this dualism and to speak in terms of processes with respect to such metaphysical concepts as "matter." This is a distinct position in terms of philosophical inspirations within contemporary feminist theory. In comparison to those feminist thinkers for whom positing an ontological position of materialism is crucial, Butler resolutely rejects an ontological approach to materialization and yet seems to insist on language that is reminiscent of the process of absolute spirit as a constant turning of concepts, which simultaneously is the turning of everything else.

Another and even more significant Hegelian inspiration for feminist thought, one particularly present in Butler's work, is provided by the restlessness and non-conclusiveness of the self-speculation process of spirit in Hegel. The implication of Nancy's redescription of Hegel's ontology is the eternal restlessness of thought, its constant laboring through the negative, and its incompleteness. This is thinking that does not set completing itself as its goal. It does not aspire to find the bottom of things, or to establish the conditions for what is or what can be. In this sense, the philosophical attitude it implies—described almost as a cliché, and certainly not often heard of with respect to

Hegel—is non-foundational. Hegel's model in the restlessness of thought, in Nancy's terms, functions as a contemporary non-foundational gesture. But it does this only if Hegel's substance as subject is thoroughly reconsidered: if it is recognized, and not just changed into humanity but also rejected as too much of an ontological claim.

Hegel can also be read with an emphasis on the immanence of reflection within the life of the spirit, which further underscores the non-conclusiveness of the process of thought. Every thinker is always already within the process of thought, dependent upon the previous life of spirit, and there is no possibility of a view from the outside, or a completely new beginning. This again engenders an approach that distinctly differs from any foundational project, ontological as well as transcendental. The interest in such an immanent non-foundational approach is not in finding the basis, the final foundation, or the conditions of existence; instead, the interest lies in generating new conceptualizations in the midst of what occurs, of speculating on one's own time in concepts. Read with an emphasis on the openness of the process and the restlessness of thought, without commitment to ontology, Hegel provides another kind of inspiration for feminist theory. This inspiration comes close to that provided by Jacques Derrida, whose texts are also inhabited by Hegelian spirits and ghosts.

I would read Butler's work as reflecting the inspiration provided by Hegel in both of the above mentioned dimensions: non-conclusiveness and immanence. Butler clearly avoids any ontological approach, instead, reflecting "in the middle of it all" throughout her work, she provides conceptual interventions in the process of history rather than studying its foundation.[35] This contrasts with, for example, Deleuze-inspired feminist theorists Rosi Braidotti and Elizabeth Grosz, who also are interested in processes of transformation, Butler is not primarily concerned to reveal the ultimate reason or the basis of change, such as the matter itself. Such a Hegelian-inspired (non)ontological approach in feminist theorizing differs in comparison to both the ontology-oriented thinking of Deleuzians and the phenomenological idea of sexual difference as ontological difference.

CONCLUSION

Discerning Hegelian inspiration in contemporary feminist thought and suggesting future possibilities for such inspiration increase when Hegel is read as a metaphysical thinker of spirit. My point in underlining the difference in spirits and the role of absolute spirit in

Hegel here is that Hegel's subject-substance ontology can be rejected only when it has actually been recognized. I also want to draw attention to the fact that Hegel's thought includes a multitude of aspects, which can be detached from his ontological claims. In the feminist context, I think it is particularly important to be aware of the limitations of the humanizing Kojévian reading of Hegelian ontology, and to pay attention to the difference between absolute spirit and the human spirit/human psyche in Hegelian thought. Hegel's thought should not be identified with the philosophical project of transcendental consciousness and a philosophy based on a foundational notion of the human. When Hegel is interpreted through Kojèvian lenses, a crucial effect of reading Hegel for feminist thought is the notion that gender, sex, and sexuality should be philosophized as something that ground the human and constitute its condition. If, however, Hegel is read in terms of differing spirits, humans in his thought are considered always already in history, in culture, in the process of absolute spirit, and in a condition of constant change.

Seen through such a reflection, there is also the restlessness of gender, the troubled history of gender, to which Hegel's own description of his time in concepts bears witness. Hegel's own view of gender and the clearly posited masculinity of spirit appear as a problem for any feminist reading his text. He writes,

> Thus one sex is mind in its self-diremption into explicit personal self-subsistence and the knowledge and volition of free universality, i.e. the self-consciousness of conceptual thought and the volition of the objective final end. The other sex is mind maintaining itself in unity as knowledge and volition of the substantive, but knowledge and volition in the form of concrete individuality and feeling.[36]

According to Hegel, the feminine consciousness/spirit does not separate itself; it does not reflect; it does not engender or generate spiritually. The creator of the creation without the creator is masculine, and the feminine is described within the system as non-creativity.

But what does it actually mean that a philosopher writing in the first part of the nineteenth century and trying to describe his time over-ambitiously in its key concepts in the form of an absolute thinking process reflects women in a particular fashion: that they are not capable of thinking, that they are not creative, and that they are not able to change culture although they are necessary for its continuity? I would contend with the view that this reflects the gender order of Hegel's time and the opportunities (not) given to women. I would leave Hegel's view on gender to its time and would also drop off not only his ontology as grand metaphysics but also the project of humanizing Hegel's spirit and subject. Despite this, I would not leave reading Hegel and I would encourage those interested in a feminist perspective to continue learning from Hegel in another spirit. As an inspiration for thought, the Hegelian teachings sketched above offer a considerably different choice in contemporary feminist theorizing compared to other approaches, such as Deleuzian ontology or phenomenological theorizing, which continue to operate within the primary notion of the human condition of two sexes.

NOTES

1. Malabou mentions commentators such as Bernard Bourgeois, Pierre-Jean Labarrière, Gerard Lebrun and Denise Souce-Dagues. Malabou, Catherine, "The Future of Hegel: Plasticity, Temporality, Dialectic," *Hypatia*, 15 (4) Fall 2000: 202. See particularly, Bourgeois, Bernard: *Éternité et historicité de l'esprit selon Hegel* (Paris: Vrin, 1991).

2. Nancy, Jean-Luc: *The Restlessness of the Negative,* trans. Jason Smith and Steven Miller (Minneapolis: University of Minnesota Press, 2002), 32.

3. Ibid., 32.

4. Ibid., 34 Nancy also writes: "It would be right to say that Hegel, after Spinoza and Kant, thinks nothing else than what has become of the creation of the world once there is no longer a creator given, nor one to be invented." Ibid., 33. In a way the Hegelian system displays a pattern parallel to the Christian doctrine of the incarnation of the Holy Spirit (Father—Son—and The Holy Spirit)—in a more or less secular form. See also Malabou, Catherine. *The Future of Hegel. Plasticity, Temporality and Dialectic,* trans. Lisabeth During (London: Routledge, 2005), 79–130.

5. Nancy, *The Restlessness of the Negative*, 33.

6. Ibid., 38.

7. Nancy highlights a passage from Hegel's "Philosophy of Mind" in the *Encyclopaedia*, in which Hegel writes: "Spirit is not an inert being, but on the contrary, absolutely restless [*unruhig*] being, pure activity," cited in Nancy, *Restless of the Negative*, 6. Nancy writes: "This world of movement, of transformation, of displacement, and of restlessness, … this world moves toward no end or result other than itself" (Ibid.) and also "In these two ways—absence of beginning and absence of end, absence of foundation and absence of completion—Hegel is the opposite of a 'totalitarian' thinker." Ibid., 8.

8. The lectures were published by Raymond Queneau in 1947. Kojève Alexandre: *Introduction to the Reading of Hegel. Lectures on the Phenomenology of Spirit,* assembled by Raymond Queneau, ed. Allan Bloom, trans. James H. Nichols, Jr. (Ithaca: Cornell

University Press, 1980). Orig. Kojevé, Alexandre. *Introduction à La Lecture de Hegel* (Paris: Gallimard, 1947).

9. Among them were also Raymond Aron, Georges Bataille, and André Breton. Bauer, Nancy, *Simone de Beauvoir. Philosophy & Feminism* (New York: Columbia University Press, 2001), 87.

10. I think Eva Lundgrén-Gothlin is right when she argues that *The Second Sex* is not only mediated via Kojève's Hegel-interpretation, but Beauvoir also directly operates with Kojèvian interpretations of Hegel, instead of merely being indirectly influenced by it via Sartre. According to her, "Beauvoir turned to what appeared to be the progressive philosophy of her times: a Hegelianism with an existentialist and Marxist bent." Lundgrén-Gothlin, Eva, "The Master-Slave Dialectic in *The Second Sex*," in *Simone de Beauvoir—A Critical Reader*, ed. Elizabeth Fallaize (London & New York: Routledge, 1998), 93–108, and Bauer, Nancy, *Simone de Beauvoir. Philosophy & Feminism* (New York: Columbia University Press, 2001), 87.

11. Confusion has certainly been created among those who read Hegel in English translations, due to the fact that Hegel's term *Geist* (spirit) has been translated to English in two different ways. In the translation of *Die Philosophie des Geistes* section of *Encyclopaedia*, "*Geist*" has been translated as "Mind" ("Philosophy of Mind"), when in the book *Phenomenologie des Geistes*, "*Geist*" has been translated as "Spirit" ("Phenomenology of Spirit"). Hegel, G.W.F. *Hegel's Philosophy of Mind: Being Part Three of the Encyclopaedia of the Philosophical Sciences, 1830*, trans. W. Wallace and A.V. Miller (Oxford: Clarendon Press, 1971) (Orig. Hegel, Georg Friedrich Wilhelm. *Enzyklopädie Der Philosophischen Wissenschaften Im Grundgrisse 1830. Dritter Teil. Die Philosophie des Geistes, Werke 10* (Frankfurt am Main: Suhrkamp, 1970). Hegel, G.F.W, *Phenomenology of Spirit*, trans. A. V. Miller (Oxford: Oxford University Press, 1977). Orig. Hegel, G.F.W., *Phänomenologie des Geistes. Werke 3* (Frankfurt am Main: Suhrkamp, 1970).

12. The "Phenomenology of Spirit" of the *Encyclopaedia* does not include a similar subtext of a hierarchy of civilizations as does the book, *Phenomenology of Spirit*. The hierarchy, according to the line of passivity/activity, is nevertheless present: "the soul" is natural, comprising senses and habit, "the consciousness" is observing, desiring and results in reasoning, whereas the "subject" (the spirit) is, on the one hand, theoretical: imagining, remembering and thinking; and on the other hand practical: so that it comprises feelings, instincts, contingent will, and finally happiness and freedom.

13. This happens particularly in the long preface of the *Phänomenologie des Geistes* book, which connects it with the rest of the system. The preface was written after the book itself. Hegel, G.F.W. *Phänomenologie des Geistes*, 11–67. G.F.W, *Phenomenology of Spirit*.

14. In his lectures Kojève is quite commonly seen to combine Hegel, Marx and Heidegger. For example, Allan Bloom in his introduction to the English translation of the book in 1968 writes, "Anyone who wishes to understand the mixture of Marxism and Existentialism which characterizes contemporary Radicalism must turn to Kojève." Allan Bloom, "Editor's Introduction" in Kojève, *Introduction to the Reading of Hegel*. Bloom also cites Aimé Patri, who writes "M.Kojève is, so far as we know the first ... to have attempted to constitute the intellectual and moral *ménage a trois* of Hegel, Marx and Heidegger, which has since that time been such a great success," vii.

15. Consider, for example, such statements, in Kojève's *Introduction to the Reading of Hegel*, as "Time is Man, and Man is Time," 138; or "Therefore, if Man *is* Concept and if the Concept *is* Time (that is, if Man is an *essentially temporal* being), Man is *essentially* mortal; and he is Concept, that is, absolute Knowledge and Wisdom incarnate, only if he *knows* this. Logos becomes flesh, becomes Man, only on the condition of being willing and able to *die*," 148. Or: "Now the finiteness of being and of reality 'appears' on the human 'phenomenal' level as that thing, which is called *Death*. Consequently to say that man 'reveals' himself as *historical free individual* (or as 'Personality') and that he 'appears' as essentially *mortal* in the strict sense of the term," 242.

16. Kojève, *Introduction to the reading of Hegel*, 259.

17. Kojève also writes very explicitly: "Now, 'Spirit' in Hegel (and especially in this context) means '*human* Spirit,' or Man, more particularly collective Man—that is, the People or State, and, finally, man as a whole or humanity in the totality of its spatio-temporal existence, that is the totality of universal History." Ibid., 138.

18. Ibid., 171. Kojève also mentions that Husserl himself wrongly opposed the Hegelian method and his own. Ibid., 195.

19. "In other words, all human, anthropogenetic Desire—the Desire that generates Self-Consciousness, the human reality—is, finally, a function of the desire for recognition." Kojève, *Introduction to the Reading of Hegel*, 7. Note, that the translation of Heidegger's *Dasein* with "réalité humaine" (human reality), is the term Kojève makes use of in this sentence, as he does throughout the book. He writes: "Without this fight to death for pure prestige, there would never have been human beings on earth ... Indeed, the human being is formed only in terms of a Desire directed toward another Desire, that is—finally—in terms of a desire for recognition." Ibid., 7. Also: "this Time lasts only as long as History lasts—that is, as long as human acts accomplished with a view to social *Recognition* are carried out." Ibid., 135.

20. The issue of the degree to which Husserl and Heidegger study the human as a species is delicate, but needs to be seen in proportion. Both Husserl and Heidegger defended first and foremost the

philosophical mode of inquiry, which in their context was threatened by the "scientific" empirical study of the human by psychology, anthropology and biology. Nevertheless, in terms of the tradition of philosophy, modern phenomenology and existentialism are centered on the conditions of human species in a way no other philosophy before. Husserl studies human consciousness, even if there is a transcendental dimension in his eidetic thought. His ontology is not based on the consciousness of God, although Husserl can also be seen as a religious thinker, but on the human consciousness. In contradiction to eternal being, *Dasein*, which is the basis for ontology in Heidegger, is a finite being, between birth and death, mortal in contradiction to gods, therefore in a Greek and philosophical sense, human. Yet, confusing Husserl's philosophy to problems that could be solved with empirical psychological or cognitive study, as well as reducing Heidegger *Dasein*'s merely to Man, would be wrong, and "humanist" attempts to do this have been a problem. Tom Rockmore (1995), for example, writes extensively on the misinterpretation caused by Koyré's introduction words to the first translation of Heidegger to French, and by the translation of Heidegger's term *Dasein* into *réalité-humaine*, which did not do justice to "Heidegger's insistence on the radical distinction between phenomenological ontology and the sciences of human being: anthropology, psychology and biology." Tom Rockmore, *Heidegger and French Philosophy. Humanism, Antihumanism, and Being* (London: Routledge, 1995), 75.

21. Beauvoir's reading of Hegel through Kojève's Heideggerian approach is visible particularly in the introduction of *The Second Sex*, in Simone de Beauvoir, *The Second Sex,* trans. and ed. H.M. Parshley (New York: Vintage Books, 1989) in which she uses terms such as the Subject, the Absolute, the Other, which she writes capitalizing the terms as if following Hegel's German. She also uses the Heidegger's term *Mitsein* in German and ends her introduction with what I would see as a reference to Heidegger's *Dasein*, which was translated into French by "réalité humaine." She writes: "Nous essaierons de montrer ensuite positivement comment la 'réalité feminine' s'est constituée, pourquoi la femme a été définie comme l'Autre et quelles en ont été les consequences de point de vue des hommes." Simone de Beauvoir, *Le deuxième sexe. 1* (Paris: Gallimard, 1949), 35. The English translation looses the connection to Heidegger's term: "Next I shall try to show exactly how the concept of the 'truly feminine' has been fashioned—why woman has been defined as the other—and what have been the consequences from man's point of view." Beauvoir, *The Second Sex*, xxxv.

22. Derrida's discussion on Heidegger and gender in Jacques Derrida, "*Geschlecht* I: Sexual Difference, Ontological Difference," in *Psyche. Inventions of the Other*, ed. Peggy Kamuf and Elizabeth Rottenberg, 7–26. Stanford: Stanford University Press, 2008 shows the complexity

of the fact that *Dasein*, in Heidegger's own terms, is especially *not* sexed/gendered.

23. Beauvoir writes in the Introduction of *The Second Sex*: "He is the Subject, he is the Absolute—she is the Other" (xxii), and continues: "The category of the Other is as primordial as consciousness itself" (Ibid.). She also states: "The division of the sexes is a biological fact, not an event in human history. Male and female stand opposed within a primordial *Mitsein*, and woman has not broken it. The couple is a fundamental unity with its two halves riveted together, and the cleavage of society along the line of sex is impossible. Here is to be found basic trait of woman: she is the Other in a totality of which the two components are necessary to one another" (Ibid., xxv).

Luce Irigaray, whose ambitious philosophical project is in clear connection to the tradition of phenomenology comes to surprisingly parallel conclusions than Beauvoir about the human couple, the man and the woman, and the sexual difference residing at the heart of the matter. Surprisingly parallel to Beauvoir's stance is also Irigaray's future oriented conclusion about this foundational human condition: her ethico-political vision is based on the mutual recognition of the two different kinds, which together make the human species. Luce Irigaray, *Speculum of the Other Woman* (Ithaca: Cornell University Press, 1989) discusses directly Hegel. The ethico-political vision is elaborated in Luce Irigaray, *Je, tous, nous: Pour une culture de la différence* (Paris: Éditions Grasset & Fasquelle, 1990); Luce Irigaray, *J'aime à toi: Esquisse d'une félicité dans l'histoire* (Paris: Éditions Grasset & Fasquelle, 1992); Luce Irigaray, *An Ethics of Sexual Difference* (London: Athlone Press, 1993); Luce Irigaray, *To Be Two*, trans. Monique M. Rhodes and Marco F. Cocito-Monoc (New York: Routledge, 2001).

24. See Elizabeth Grosz, *Volatile Bodies. Toward a Corporeal Feminism* (Bloomington and Indianapolis: Indiana University Press, 1994); Elizabeth Grosz, *The Nick of Time. Politics, Evolution, and the Untimely* (Durham and London: Duke University Press, 2004), and Rosi Braidotti, *Metamorphoses. Towards a Materialist Theory of Becoming* (Cambridge: Polity Press, 2002).

25. Malabou, *The Future of Hegel*, 207.

26. Ibid.

27. In Noelle Vahanian, "A Conversation with Catherine Malabou," *Journal for Cultural and Religious Theory*, 9 (1)Winter 2008: 1–13. Malabou discusses plasticity, gender, femininity and matter/form distinction, developing plasticity in relation to critique of gender binary and sexual difference, and in terms of individual subjects. Thinking of a relation between self and itself, she talks of "transubjectivation," emphasizing that a Hegelian subject "trans-subjects" itself constantly, 4–5.

28. "Reading Hegel amounts to finding oneself in two times at once: the process that unfolds is both retrospective and prospective. In the

present time in which reading takes place, the reader is drawn to a double expectation: waiting for what is to come (according to a thought that is linear), and while presupposing that the outcome has already arrived (according to the teleological ruse).... Hegelian thought announces the arrival of a new time." Malabou, *The Future of Hegel*, 212.

29. Ibid., 215.
30. Ibid.
31. Kimberly Hutchings, *Hegel and Feminist Philosophy* (London: Polity Press, 2003).
32. Butler has explicitly engaged with Hegel in section 1, "Stubborn Attachment, Bodily Subjection. Rereading Hegel on the Unhappy Consciousness," of *The Psychic Life of Power. Theories in Subjection* (Stanford: Stanford University Press, 1997), 3–62, and in *Antigone's Claim. Kinship between Life and Death* (New York: Columbia University Press, 2000), and in chapter 6, "Longing for Recognition" of *Undoing Gender* (New York: Routledge, 2004), 131–151 (reprinted in this volume), and "Post-Hegelian Queries," in *Giving an Account of Oneself* (New York: Fordham University Press, 2005), 26–40. But also in the rest of her work Hegel is a frequent reference.
33. Butler reflects on her own early work in *Subjects of Desire*, which is based on her dissertation, and the context of its writing, in the preface to the new edition published in 1999. She mentions that she resisted the post-structuralist readings until the completion of the dissertation. She was confined to the conventional phenomenological approach still when writing the book, and engaged fully with the post-structuralist readings only afterword. It is clear that Derrida is not one of the figures of the book, and Foucault has been added only after the dissertation project was over. Judith Butler, *Subjects of Desire. Hegelian Reflections in Twentieth-century France* (New York: Columbia University Press, 1987), vii.
34. Judith Butler, *Bodies That Matter: On the Discursive Limits of Sex* (New York: Routledge, 1993), 4–12. Although the topic in this passage where Butler suggests "materialization" is obviously not on metaphysics or materiality but on the constructivist position to sex and gender, defended against the critics who say that the body has been forgotten, and replaced by mere language, her position of language and its referent, is reminiscent of Hegel's work of the concept, which in a similar way disturbs the division into the concept and its referent, the thought in concepts and the historical occurring. In a similar way as "the constative claim is always to some degree performative" (*Bodies That Matter*, 11), the Hegelian thought in concepts is always an act.
35. Distinctive to Butler is the refusal to look for a foundation in "the human." Butler particularly throughout her work constantly

challenges the notion of "human," and points at its concrete historical construction in particular time and place.

36. Hegel, G.F.W. *Grundlinien der Philosophie des Rechts oder Naturrecht
und Staatswissenschft im Grundrisse*. Werke 7; Hegel, Georg Wilhelm
Friedrich, *Hegel's Philosophy of Right*, transl., T.M. Knox (Oxford:
Oxford University Press, 1967); Hegel, G.F.W. *Elements of the
Philosophy of Right*, transl. H. B. Nisbet (Cambridge: Cambridge
University Press, 1991), § 166.

CHAPTER THREE

Queering Hegel: Three Incisions[1]

Joanna Hodge

The absolute philosopher said, or at least thought of himself, of course, as a thinker, and not as a human being: la verité, c'est moi, *in a way similar to the saying:* l'etat, c'est moi *of the absolute monarch and to the saying* l'être, c'est moi *of the absolute God. The human philosopher on the other hand says: even in thinking and in being a philosopher, I am human, among human beings.*[2]

Exergue

The selection of this citation from Feuerbach is designed to suggest that a certain Young Hegelianism, in its dispute over the Hegelian inheritance with more strictly scholarly readings, has already queered Hegel, long before other more obviously queer candidates for the task and the honor can come on the scene: Michel Foucault, for example, or indeed Judith Butler. The embodiment of the philosopher, the diversity of human embodiments queers the model of abstract absolute reason. The writings of Derrida might seem as unlikely a source for a queering Hegel as those of Feuerbach. Certainly, the trajectory of *Specters of Marx, The State of the Debt, the Work of Mourning and the New International* (1993), of *Politics of Friendship* (1994), and of *Rogues: Two Essays on Reason* (2001)[3] looks rather more like an intervention within and on the margins of political theory and political economy, than like contributions to the increasingly sophisticated discussions of gender and queer theory. The argument to be developed here, however, will follow a return from these more recent writings of Jacques Derrida, to propose a re-reading of *Glas: What Remains of Absolute Knowing* (1974).[4] This is designed to demonstrate the radical nature of Derrida's rethinking of politics, and thereby to demonstrate that this text from 1974 affects at least the first stage of queering Hegel. Such a demonstration is under a certain obligation and owes a debt to the enquiries of Sarah Kofman, who presented an important response to *Glas* in her text "*Ça Cloche*," for whom the bell tolls, read at the first Cerisy conference dedicated to Derrida's writings.[5] Doing justice to Kofman would require embarking on a second and third stage of queering Hegel, reading Hegel more emphatically through Freud than will here be possible, and then reading Hegel through the question to the logic and privileging of fraternal relations and to the name of the father at the heart of philosophy, politics, and high theory, as conducted in the Western intellectual tradition. In the concluding section of these remarks the focus will return to a discussion of the conditions for such a second and third stage of queering Hegel.

The proposed re-reading of *Glas* reveals that in that text Derrida engages in a process of queering the Hegelian text, and indeed Hegel himself, in at least three ways. First, there is a disruption of the line of descent from Hegel, to Marx, to present-day discussion of politics, in favor of a discussion of a bio-politics that considers seriously the arrival of queer identifications for concepts of sovereignty, family, and reason. Although the proposals concerning a thinking of an *à-venir*, as democracy to come, arrive less obliquely in Derrida's more recent work, and although the encounter with Marx is made the focus of attention in the *Specters of Marx* (1993), there already is an encounter with Marx underway in *Glas*. Marx here is the thinker who can reorient the Hegelian enquiries such that they are no longer driven by an ideal of closed teleology but can rather be read to reveal the workings of a fully material series of conflicts and resolutions. Marx and Engels famously propose to invert the hierarchy of Hegel's enquires, setting the dialectic back on its feet, for this dialectical logic no longer works as a set of relations between conceptual structures. It is instead to provide an account of the cunning of reason in history as nothing but the developing conflicts in the materialities at work and worked on by and in human activity. Derrida's diagnoses of an interruptive futurity, as the *à-venir*, are as disruptive of any necessary triumph for the proletariat as of any other necessarily inscribed political theology. These diagnoses move beyond analyses of the topographies of inversion into those of contamination and the cultivation of limits, in the limitrophy announced in *Aporias: Dying Awaiting (One another at) the Limits of truth* (1993), and again in the long series of papers collected under the title *L'animal que donc je suis* (The animal from which I inherit).[6] This insistence on the animality of the human prevents

Marx and Marxism from insisting on the metallic components among the forces of production, to the exclusion of the organic, the infinite variety of ways of being human. It also destabilizes Hegel's attempt to leave animality behind in the transition from the philosophy of nature to the philosophy of spirit.

This *Glas*, this tocsin, or death knell of absolute knowledge echoes the death knell of Capital and of capitalists, sounded by the Proletariat, who Engels and Marx identify in the *Communist Manifesto* (1848) as the gravediggers of the bourgeois. It is, however, also the death knell of any Marxism that supposes that its hour must come. *Glas* is also the death knell that does not ring out as it should but rather clatters out of synchrony with itself. The text is a composition in two columns, the first of which exposes Hegel's text to its autobiographical contingencies, and to Kantian and Marxian conditions and appropriations of it. Alongside that column, the enquiry is also exposed to a guerrilla strategy, a small war, never formally declared and, therefore, never concluded, which turns out to be more large scale than even the conflict between Kant, Hegel, and Marx. In that second column, the manner in which Jean Genet turns his life into a fiction, thereby turning that fiction into a fact of reason, is traced out. This fact of reason, the subversion of all Christian imagery in an explosion of floral homoeroticism, founds a new critique of political reason. Throughout the text, Derrida weaves into a disruption of Hegel's system a further disruption of the Kantian system, of Marx and of Marxism, and of any attempt to write in the name of a completed political reason. There are always more peoples whose oppressions have been concealed in the heroic stories of triumph and tragedy. Retrieving their stories unhinges the story of politics told up until now. Thus the second queering of Hegel is this revealing in his text of a silent silenced place for articulating gay rights and a queer political activism.

The experience of the silenced third party, who disputes the right to inheritance of the privileged audible third, suffices to rock the foundations of absolute knowledge. The manner in which Derrida sets up the responses to Hegel and to Genet, as each responding to the claims of the other, while utterly independent of each other, reveals that a completeness of reason and of history is sustainable as a thought only so long as innovation does not arrive to fracture the completeness of what has so far been schematized. The thought of the a-venir arrives in the wake of the disruption of a transvestite annunciation, where the words and names are reordered to proclaim another kind of death knell, one that has not yet been heard. In the course of *Glas*, Derrida recites the names of various repressed conceptualities and evokes a series of paradoxical logics—the logic of the flower, a logic of citation, a logic of transvestism, and a logic of an orphaned unconscious—without the authority of a paternal name, thus generating a logic of the unconscious, and of its remainders, released from but still aligned to a thinking, with Freud, of the closures of the death drive and the openings of polymorphous perversity. These logics both are and are not fully articulated in the text, since they too remain to arrive out of another kind of logic, one that has not yet been formalized. This third form of queering is then a question of formulating the deviance of deviant logics.

The operations, in the specification of which a queering of Hegel may be demonstrated, are, first, the necessary transposition of the concept of the family, and of love out of the procreative and symbolic context provided for it by Hegel in the *Elements of the Philosophy of Right* (1821), first of all back into its asexual, Christian, Trinitarian ontological origins, which impose a rigid three-place relation on the proliferations of the multiple place relations of natural affection. These then are to be transposed back into the context of the prison communities, lovingly outlined by Jean Genet, in his prison writings, political writings masquerading as novels. This first set of operative variations works through the displacement of concepts. The second set of variations is to be found in the refusal of completion of the speculative movement into the reconciliations promised at the higher level, as proposed by Hegel in that drastic operation called *Aufhebung*. This is a refusal to accept the precedence of speculative proposition over all other forms of expression, or, better, the thought that Genet forms his own speculative proposition. Here there is certain complicity between the writings of Derrida, of those of Jean-Luc Nancy, of Lacoue-Labarthe, and of Lyotard, in the exploration of the necessity and impossibility of Hegel's device. The Hegelian concept can be put to work only if it is articulated through such speculative propositions and, left unconstrained by that enabling constriction, generates the kinds of illegitimate off-spring to which Derrida draws attention in sections of *Glas*.

The third set of variations turns around a return to and rewriting of the fractured and fractious relations between religion and the supposedly secularized state, as founded in the rule of law, which turns out to be irreducibly in debt to theological principles. This is discussed by Derrida in his long treatise, "Faith and Knowledge: The Two Sources of Religion at the Limits of Mere Reason," which starts out as a reflection on the move from Greece to Rome and from Hebrew to Christian religious bondings but is gradually deflected into a reflection on the relation between these two moves, and the excluded third, Islam.[7] Although Greek and Hebrew legacies and origins are for Hegel combined in his version of Christianity, there is currently a confrontation between political theology and religious politics to be negotiated, the latter working as a play of enmity and hostility between the inheritances of Isaac and of Ishmael, the former exposed as the lender of last resort in questions of political legitimacy. The various sections of this chapter will explore how already in Hegel's text, as read by Derrida, and in the texts of his critics Marx and Feuerbach, an unpicking of the supposedly seamless linkages between levels is at work, opening up the vista of a Hegel by no means easily closed off to the politics of diversity, illegitimacy, and interruption that queering initiates. The diagnosis is an elaboration of that of Sarah Kofman, in her essay "*Ça Cloche*":

> What resonates in Derrida's *Glas* is that the question of fetishism is linked to the question of an undecidable oscillation and thus to a speculation, in which one wins and loses at the same time. Beginning with a reading of Freud's text, *Glas* puts forth what may be called a generalization of fetishism, and therefore of undecidability and oscillation as well, as the first step/negation of a deconstruction of phallogocentrism: "My excitement is the oscillation."[8]

This remark and its citation of Derrida's text would, of course, demand an extended commentary and analysis. Later in *Glas*, the following remark is found in the right hand column under the title "Genet's failure":

> The economy of the fetish is more powerful than that of the truth—decidable—of the thing itself, or than a deciding discourse of castration (*pro aut contra*). The fetish is not opposable. It oscillates like a clapper of a truth that rings awry.[9]

This invocation of a clapper of truth is the incision that in this context reveals the inoperative character of any logical operation. This would also be the place to acknowledge the impossible work of translation, undertaken by Richard Rand and John P. Leavey, in their heroic attempts at an Englishing of *Glas*.

THE STATE OF THE FAMILY, THE FAMILY OF THE STATE: HEGEL, FEUERBACH, MARX

The family disintegrates in a natural manner and, essentially, through the principle of personality, into a plurality of families whose relation to one another is in general that of self-sufficient concrete persons and is consequently of an external kind. In other words the moments, which are bound together in the unity of the family as the ethical idea, which is still in its concept, must be released from the concept to achieve self-sufficient reality. This is the stage of difference.[10]

The citation is from Hegel's *Philosophy of Right*, published in 1821 but forming part of the third section of his *Encyclopaedia of the Philosophical Sciences*, the section on the workings of spirit in human institutions. It occurs at the point of transition from family to civil society, and a queer Hegel is going to result from reversing the order here, destabilizing the opposed elements: civil society and the state. A certain relation between state and civil society sets up a certain kind of family unit, with its own discrete stabilities and instabilities, and alternative family units reveal a different constitution of the relation between civil society and state. This series of disruptive moves might be thought to be the mode of analysis offered by Foucault in the works on governmentality and the history of sexuality, and to Foucault might be attributed the honor of first queering Hegel, unless Feuerbach, Engels, and Marx have already performed the task. Questioning the State of the Family starts with a juxtaposition of two families, the terrestrial family, as the property owning, propagating unit, of Hegel's *Elements of the Philosophy of Right*, from which my citation is taken, and the Holy Family, which Ludwig Feuerbach detects lurking behind it and which Engels and Marx take up with such enthusiasm. This Holy Family of Father, Son, and Holy Spirit, on inspection, turns out already to be distinctly queer, which no amount of Marian idolatry can repair. In his *Principles of the Philosophy of the Future* (1843), and other texts, Feuerbach explores the underpinning of the threefold figures of Hegel's thinking not just in the terrestrial family and its legitimation of patriarchal authority but also, of course, in the Holy Family, the title of Engels and Marx's polemical tract from 1844. This then invites a further series of juxtapositions with a third, "pretend" family relation that was invented in a piece of legislation under the UK Conservative Government of Mrs. Thatcher, now Baroness Thatcher of Grantham, in the Local Government Bill (1987), with its only recently repealed Clause 28, forbidding local governments from "promoting homosexuality." This "pretend family relation" was the description given to people living together and perhaps bringing up children, people who had stepped outside the model of married, heterosexual monogamies. It instantly becomes clear, of course, that this captures not just family units headed up by self-declared lesbians and gay men, units that fail to conform to the two-by-two model of mummy, daddy, Janet, and John. This then is my first non-Hegelian conceptual triad: Hegelian family, Holy Family, and Mrs. Thatcher's pretend family relation.

In the course of this chapter, I shall set out a few more non-Hegelian triads that will indicate how the figure of *ex-appropriation* developed by Derrida, by contrast to a metaphysics of the proper, but not only in response to the authority of Hegel's text, provides the basic elements for a queering theory kit. Such a kit, by contrast to a queer theory of contents, provides a stimulus to thought and understanding of these startling conditions we find ourselves in in this new century. The problem with queer theory has been, perhaps, that it has not been queer enough: it has sought to locate a set of enquiries in terms of human identifications, instead of marching cheerfully into the supposedly four-square bastions of classical political and conceptual theory, to reveal the instabilities in evidence there. As Derrida indicates in his *Politics of Friendship* (1994), the political tradition of the Western world is inscribed within a set of masculine homoerotic identifications, the impact of which is hard to shake off. A fourth family, alongside the terrestrial family of Hegel's thought and the Holy Family of young Hegelian polemics, and besides Mrs. Thatcher's attempt to distinguish real from pretend families, is one revealed and imagined by Jean Genet in his descriptions of prison life, mainly, but not only, in the *Miracle of the Rose* (1943). In the context of a reading of Derrida's *Glas*, such a juxtaposition, retrieval, and subversion in Genet's text of elements of Hegel's *Elements of the Philosophy of Right* is only to be expected. Hegel, Feuerbach, and Marx constitute one Holy Trinity of Political Theory, alongside the Greco-Christian trinity: Plato, Aristotle, and Augustine; Hegel, Freud, and Genet constitute a queer third. This then inaugurates queer lineages in the telling of the history of the Western political tradition, a crucial second element in the queering of Hegel, alongside the insistence on human animality.

CONSTITUTING A (CON)TEXT

Marx and Engels' text *The Holy Family, or a Critique of Critical Criticism, against Bruno Bauer and Company* (1844) may be cited as a source and inspiration for the construction of Derrida's *Glas: What Remains of Absolute Knowledge* (1974). The combined moves of ironical inversion and satirical intensification are prominent in both. *Glas* is one of three highly experimental Derridean texts that emphatically follow up the hypothesis from *Of Grammatology* (1967) concerning the end of the book and the beginning of writing. *Glas* (1974) was the first, and it was followed by *Truth in Painting* (1978) and *The Post Card from Socrates to Freud and Beyond* (1980), with its long explicit and implicit discussion of Freud's essay "Beyond the Pleasure Principle" (1921).[11] There would be a possible re-edition of this with the first and second sections printed as parallel columns, such that the diary style reflections might be interrupted by the appended apparently free standing essays. This hypothetical page layout poses the following question: Where are the boundaries of the text? In their extraordinary work of translation of *Glas*, Richard Rand and John P. Leavey, regrettably, lose the subtitle "What Remains of Absolute Knowledge," which underlines the Freudian remainder as disrupting any Hegelian closure. This reserved business then suitably enough once again goes missing, and in English this text is known only by its opaque Gallicism: *Glas*, meaning tocsin, death knell, mourning bell, the single tolling sound marking the beginning of the funeral service and the end of a life. The ending of one life, of one tradition, must, however, mark the beginning of another, on a further side of the break marked by that moment of interruption. The title itself is interrupted by its interrogation: What remains? This provides a clue about how to read the text as continually interrupted by questions that it has not yet managed to formulate.

In French, the subtitle, what remains of absolute knowledge, introduces the figure of *Savoir Absolu*, the SA of the feminine possessive adjective, which is also a *siglum* for the French term for Freud's "id," the *es* in German, that which is not taken up into conscious self-identification. In German and English, it is also the abbreviation or paraph for the *Sturm Abteilung*, the riot squad of the Nazi Party in its formative years. Other possible subtitles then would have been the following: what remains of the *Sturm Abteilung*, the riot squad implicit in political organization; or what remains of the unconscious, of the violence that cannot be sublated into symbolic forms of political order. One tradition of political theory, that of sovereignty, is dead. What remains is that which was not taken up into such theorizing, of which fascism, the riot squad, pretend family relations, and queer identification are no doubt all part. In *The Post Card* (1980), Derrida refers back to the experiments of *Glas*. The text of *The Post Card* juxtaposes a running journal from June 3, 1977, through to August 30, 1979, under the title "*Envois*," to the text "To Speculate—on 'Freud,'" in which Derrida gives a reading of Freud's essay "Beyond the Pleasure Principle" (1921), and to the text responding to Lacan, "The Deliverer of the Letter." The second footnote of the first section of "To Speculate—on 'Freud'" reads,

> These three words refer to the most obsessive motif of *Glas*. Let us say that I am adding or relating a supplementary "judas" from *Glas*. An incision tattooed for example between pages 270/272, left column.[12]

"Judas" is the technical term for a text box inserted into a column of organized prose, as a freestanding item demarcated by spacing from a main text. Commenting on the three or four words "binding, *nexum*, *desmos* or stricture," Derrida continues: "To posit, we asked: what does this amount to, come back to (*a quoi cela revient-il?*)? And to whom? For whom?" Here is marked up a transition from the deceleration of the *restance* of the title of *Glas*, and of the encounter with Hegel, to that of the movement of the *revenance*, of Hamlet's ghost, and of the Freudian encounter. Derrida thus indicates that *Glas* is an open text into which various subsequent and presumably previously written texts may be inserted.

While the text of *Glas* is divided into two columns, these can or perhaps must be read antiphonally, although more at the level of assonance than at the level of meaning. The hypothesis underpinning this odd mode of composition is, however, sufficiently Hegelian, for the content follows form, as form enables the communication of content. In order fully to disrupt the Hegelian processes of completion, it might then be necessary to compose a text that does not conform to the three-part structure: beginning, middle, and end; statement, peroration and argument, and conclusion; hypothesis, accumulation of determinacy, and thesis. Derrida is certainly wary of the philosophical commitments required for such determinacy and starts a long way back in the process of revealing the sleight of hand required to filter out the sources of uncertainty and instability that introduce indeterminacy and prevent the drawing of conclusions. My proposal then is to substitute the writing experiments of Derrida's *Glas* for the certainties of a Feuerbachian humanism, and to see what then becomes of political theory. The hypothesis is that the outcome is a non-familial, DIY queer political theory kit. This is a radicalization of and departure from the proposals made by Richard Beardsworth in his instructive book *Derrida and the Political*.[13] There he locates Derrida's thinking of sovereignty and the undecidability of justice with respect to law, in terms of conflicts between the Hegelian theory of the state and the Kantian theory of right and cosmopolitical intent. However,

Beardsworth then domesticates the impact of Derridean disruption by locating Levinas as the third interlocutor, who, as is well known, emphatically reintroduces patriarchal religion as the source of order and gender privilege in human relations. It, therefore, seems to me healthier to go for the trinity of Hegel, Freud, and Genet, as does Derrida, instead of Kant, Hegel, and Levinas. A floral or organic political reason will function in accordance with a logic of the emblem, and not of the name. By contrast to a logic of the name that implicates a lineage of descent from father to son, the logic of the emblem permits the arrival of Genet's pretend family relations and adopted inheritors, both revealing and disrupting the masculinity and homoeroticism of the political inheritance.

THE WORK OF THE CONCEPT

> *The Idea, which is independent or for itself, when viewed on the point of this unity with itself, is perception or intuition, and the percipient Idea is nature. But as intuition the idea is, through an external "reflection," invested with the one-sided characteristic of immediacy or of negation. Enjoying however an absolute liberty, the idea does not merely pass over into life, or as finite cognition allow life to show in it: in its own absolute truth it resolves to let the "moment" of its particularity, or of the first characterization, and other being, the immediate idea, as its reflected image, go forth freely as nature.[14]*

No paper on Hegel is complete without a quotation from the *Encyclopaedia of the Philosophical Sciences*, so I give you Section 244, as encouragement and warning. It is the last section of the *Encyclopaedia Logic*, on the brink of the transition into the *Philosophy of Nature*. In part two of the *Encyclopaedia*, Hegel will first recognize and then erase the animality of the human. The speculative proposition suggests that if it is rigorously followed through, there is no degree of exteriorization or distance from the work of the concept so great that it cannot in principle be recuperated within a Hegelian discursivity. The tension arising between the discursive order of exposition of the text and the conceptual content of what Hegel is arguing is a matter taken up and microscopically analyzed by Jean-Luc Nancy in his French work *La remarque spéculative. Un bon mot de Hegel*, published in 1973 and recently heroically translated into English by Céline Surprenant as *The Speculative Remark*.[15] These discussions make room for the thought that the queering of

Hegel may have taken place already in the pages of Hegel himself, since his exposition must subvert what the conceptual order proposes. The move that Hegel makes in relation to the family, of the necessary division of the unitary idea of the human into female and male, and into older and younger generations, into mutually competing existent units, will be made again in relation to the sovereignty of the state. This division of sovereignty and the consequent dispersion of rational derivations of the logic of state power into a number of competing instances form the theme that binds together the otherwise distinct trajectories of Hegel's thinking on the state and the realm of the international and Kant's ideas on cosmopolitical intent.

Queering Hegel is a doubly doubled operation, of course. There is a movement of disrupting and displacing of Hegel's various rather wobbly observations about gender, as predicated on a two-place relation, and giving birth to one and only one-third. Instead what is to be thought is a multiplicity of possible outcomes and indeed of orientations, taking up and expanding on Foucault's diagnoses of, for example, the actual and symbolic erasure of hermaphroditism from historical and bio-political registers.[16] This involves, first, historical archival research to prove that the hypostatisations called "family" and "gender distinctions" are artificial and imposed rather than naturally ordained and always confirmed by the detailed evidence. Second, there is also, of course, an operation called deconstruction that stalls a certain cumulative style of argumentation and conceptuality. There is, third, a matter of showing the connections between these two registers of enquiry: about gender and about the nature of concepts, but without reinstalling some Hegelian mediation between an order of the concept, as given in an analysis of being; an order of existence, as analyzed in a philosophy of nature; and an order of their reconciliation, in the register of the spirit. For once the logic of the concept arrives at its most elaborated form, it becomes external to itself in the form of nature, a domain of non-finite differentiation, a bad infinity, to be brought to a stand only in the concepts of life and death, and their interrelation, and retrieved into the movement of non-finite spirit. Hegel proposes the one account of the relation between life and death and thereby generates his theory of spirit. The phenomenology of Heidegger generates another account of the relation between life and death and thereby aids the dissolution of the Hegelian concept. Derrida, in *Aporias: Dying-Awaiting (One another at) the "Limits of Truth"* (1993), opposes the one account of death to the other and thus holds open the Hegelian closure without accepting the Heideggerian account as definitive. In these ways the work of the concept may be retrieved from enclosure in any Hegelian "happy ending."

Marx, however, as noted earlier, has already challenged the separation of spheres whereby the legitimacy of concepts is secured at one level and then read back into the analyses of human society, since the necessity of the order of exposition in the *Elements of the Philosophy of Right* is secured not in that text but in the analyses of the concept provided elsewhere in the Hegelian system. The structures described can be rendered contingent as a result of the text being read in isolation, for the Work of the Concept (*Anstrengung des Begriffs*) is not in evidence in the *Philosophy of Right*. What is presented there are the externalized forms of social order, not the dynamics of a self-realization of spirit. Marx proposes to correct this splitting by reading the dynamics of the negativity of the concept back into the social forms as a conflict between opposed political forces, thus denying that the sources of development can take place on the surmised other level.[17] This is the famous setting of Hegelian dialectic back on its feet: showing how the movements of the concept are generated not by movements of spirit but by movements of human history. It would be possible then to claim that it is Marx who queers Hegel: for neither family nor state nor the relation between the two is to be secured through conceptual transformation as identical to the spirit of a people. The distinction between conceptual movement secured in the self-knowledge of a Trinity, on one hand, and its contamination by the linguistic determinacy of natural languages, on the other—and between the logic of the concept and the pure contingencies of historical process—is undermined. The complexity of the relation between Hegel and Marx may serve as a warning to those who seek too swiftly to disambiguate that between Derrida and Nancy.

Jacques Derrida's relation to the enquiries of Jean-Luc Nancy are, to put it mildly, complex, and it is further complicated by the relation back to Hegel.[18] Derrida reads Nancy emphatically, if elliptically, in the essays forming the second part of *Rogues: Two Essays on Reason* (2003).[19] This text opens by refusing the Hegelian resolution of an implied antithesis between Greek and Modern inceptions of philosophy, to be found by contrasting the theogony of Plato's *Timaeus* to Kant's critical system. Nancy and Derrida are preoccupied with the possibility of a non-Hegelian thematization of freedom and of sovereignty, one not predicated on a conception of subjective autonomy, with its implied commitment to founding identity in a notion of self-sufficiency. However, in a reading of chapter seven of Nancy's *The Experience of Freedom* (1988), "The distribution of freedom: equality, fraternity, justice,"[20] Derrida articulates most strongly his doubt about the use to which Nancy puts the third value, proposed in the name of the French Revolution, fraternity:

> There is never a war or a danger for the arrival of democracy, except where there are brothers. More exactly: not where there are brothers, (there will always be brothers and that is not the evil, there is not evil in that determinacy) but there where the fraternity of brothers makes the law, there where there is imposed the political dictatorship of fraternocracy.[21]

Since for Nancy "fraternity" is the name for a *partage*, or necessary collectivity and divisibility of sovereignty and freedom, as not guaranteed by some natural or rational origin but in the course of discussing this, Derrida is quite uncharacteristically abrasive in marking out a danger, which for Nancy seems not to be so, of excluding the sister and thereby the sister of the sister.

This *partage* is one in which sovereignty is divided among the people not only within the states but also between states, to then be renegotiated through the precarious systems instituted variously as a League of Nations, a United Nations, or a New International. This notion of a New International, first put into circulation by Marx, was redeployed and reaffirmed by Derrida in *Specters of Marx* in 1993, but, in this later text, it is displaced in favor of discussing the function of the term "rogue" or outlaw nation. This possibility of remobilizing a concept of a New International will prove that Derrida has swung from optimism to pessimism, with all the more reason, granted the indifference of a certain G. W. Bush and a certain T. Blair to gaining and holding UN approval for their neo-imperialist ventures. Here once more is a passage concerning the family from the *Elements of the Philosophy of Right*:

> The family disintegrates in a natural manner and essentially through the principle of personality, into a plurality of families whose relation to one another is in general that of self-sufficient concrete persons and is consequently of an external kind. In other words the moments, which are bound together in the unity of the family as the ethical idea, which is still in its concept, must be released from the concept to achieve self-sufficient reality. This is the stage of difference.[22]

This then also applies to the Hegelian concept of the State, and Derrida pursues the implications of this to the point of diagnosing that there are Rogue States because there are no longer any Nation

States that can function effectively as international agency and authority. There is division and destabilization of the notion of the state at this stage of differentiation, and it would be the work of a speculative philosophy to reveal the possibility of a move beyond this stage of difference, of apparently irresolvable conflict, or indeed of *difference*, of historical delay and contingency, to a complete stable concept given without condition. Hegelians are apt to surmise that Derrida's conceptuality is arrested at the stage of the externalization of essence, into an indeterminacy of natural differentiation that is to be located as a stage along the way of the spirit's full articulations necessary for its achievement of completion. This notion of arrested development has an intriguing resonance with surmises of a similar kind with respect to homosexuality as a stage on the way to a fulfilled and fulfilling heterosexuality. Derrideans, on the other hand, can reply that, for the purposes of current analyses of human conditions, this stage of difference, and of *différance*, of internal inconsistencies, of arguments to be applied in one context but not in others, and of repeatedly postponed justifications of State, of International and of other Orders, is exactly apposite for thinking about current conditions.

In an early essay on Levinas and Hegel, discussed vigorously by Beardsworth in *Derrida and the Political*, Derrida himself diagnoses Levinas' response to Hegel, in *Totality and Infinity: An Essay on Exteriority* (1961),[23] as prone to a certain re-appropriation within the Hegelian system, for in that text, Levinas sets up a distinction between the Hegelian totality of absolute knowledge and his own preferred notion of infinity. The former promises completeness and an overview of what there is, and of what can be thought, thereby, in Levinas' view, imposing closure and homogeneity, by contrast to his own preferred model of an open-ended infinity, an acceptance of an absolute, divine command. In his preface, Levinas writes that the visage of being that shows itself in war is fixed in the concept of totality,

> which dominates Western philosophy. Individuals are reduced to being bearers of forces that command them unbeknown to themselves. The meaning of individuals (invisible outside of this totality) is derived from the totality."[24]

In this essay "Violence and Metaphysics: Essay on the Thought of Emmanuel Levinas," first published in 1964 and revised for publication in *Writing and Difference* (1967), Derrida daringly mobilizes a certain Hegel, although not yet a queer Hegel, against a certain Levinas:

> Philosophical language belongs to a system of languages. Thereby, its non-speculative ancestry always brings a certain equivocality into speculation. Since this equivocality is original and irreducible, perhaps philosophy must adopt it, think it, and be thought in it, must accommodate duplicity and difference within speculation, within the very purity of philosophical meaning. No one it seems to us has attempted this more profoundly than Hegel. Without naively using the category of chance, of happy predestination or of the chance encounter, one would have to do for each concept what Hegel does for the German notion of *Aufhebung*, whose equivocality and presence in the German language he calls delightful (*erfreulich*).[25]

Derrida also notes Hegel's interest in a similar equivocation in the German notion of history as *Geschichte*. This remark is then much expanded on by Nancy in his treatment of it in *The Speculative Remark*, which also fills out the account of the raising to another level of the *relève* of *Aufhebung*, given in Derrida's essay "The Pit and the Pyramid."[26] Whereas in Hegel's texts there is one perspective from which the whole system is to be viewed as interlocking and self-completing, the Derridean and Levinasian challenge is to open up any number of lines of sight and angles of approach that do not permit the formation of a single unified coherent account, for meaning depends on what arrives from and in a future that is as yet to be decided, and classical perspective meets and is up-ended by Picasso.

What Remains: Politics of the Unconscious, Politics of Religion

This will be a brief and suitably inconclusive last section. Queering Hegel might be thought to have already taken place when the *Elements of the Philosophy of Right* is read without benefit of the speculative, theo-political principles through which the concepts are supposed to be articulated. Karl Marx does this one way, and Carl Schmitt's political enquiries are notable, precisely because they draw attention to the theological underpinnings of political thought implicit in Hegel's theory of justice. Schmitt proposes a radical break with those underpinnings in the principle of the exceptional circumstance, thus theorizing the anarcho-auto-immunization of Nazi jurisprudence. There are then worse outcomes than those projected by Hegel's political theology, but the gesture Derrida is proposing is that of neither Hegel nor Schmitt. The theological underpinnings of Hegel's analysis of the state are clear enough, and in Hegel's terms the outlaw nation would be the one without such theological under-pinnings. Schmitt's outlaw state is the one that constitutes its own rule of law and asks for no confirmation or affirmation from other states. This then is a new Holy Trinity of political theory, Hegel, Stalin, and Schmitt. In *Glas*, by contrast, Derrida puts up a non-Hegelian triad of Hegel, Freud, and Genet, bringing Hegel into col-lision with readings of Jean Genet's *Our Lady of the Flowers* and *The Miracle of the Rose*, by way of a certain Freudian concern for the effects of the unconscious, although no less important is the Marxian subversion of the Hegelian text, and a reading of the Christian Gospels to subvert the priority assigned to Greek philosophizing in questions of ontology.

Let one remark suffice to suggest the work of reading performed by Derrida in *Glas*. Derrida reiterates Hegel's speculative iteration: "The Father is the Son, the Son is the Father, and the *Wesen*, the essential energy of this copulation, its unity, the *Wesenseinheit* of the first and the second, is the essence of the Christian Last Supper scene," and then presumably, therefore, also for all the many varieties of Communion: high mass, low mass, communication in both kinds, communication in one kind, communication by priestly representa-tives alone.[27] Derrida adduces,

> Consequently even before wondering whether the ontological project, as first a Greek event from which Christianity would have developed an outer graft, one must be certain that for Hegel at least no ontology was possible before the Gospel or outside it.
>
> Then the bond announced between the question of the copula and the question of the family also bears this consequence: if one tries to articulate an apparently "regional" (sociological, psychological, economico-political, linguistic) problematic of the family onto an ontological problematic, the place that we have just now recognized cannot be reversed (*le lieu que nous venons de reconnaître est incontournable.*)[28]

The essential energy of this copulation is not heterosexual and pro-creative; it is rather invested in a serial transmission of meaning and authority from father to son, the son in turn becoming father. This model, of course, is not restricted to Christianity, and thereby in Hegel's terms all systems of religion are compelled to conform to the imagery offered by a Christian imaginary.

In the meantime, it is important to note certain differences between Derrida and Hegel about the nature of conceptuality, so that while it may be the case that Derrida's analyses of the sign, of speech, and of writing are, on one level, recuperable within the Hegelian program, there is an insistence on the *restance*, on the remainder, in Derrida's reading, on that which does not and cannot get taken up into the next level of theorizing, disrupting the Hegelian claim to have retrieved all that has gone before. This underpins the indication here of an irreversibility, in the stress on the irreversibility of the "incontournable." The notion of *restance*, of a remainder resisting recuperation, is marked up in the second part of the title of Derrida's second, queer reading of Hegel, in *Glas: What Remains of Absolute Knowledge* (1974), which retrieves an unconscious displacement working in parallel with and disruptive of the Hegelian recuperations of consciousness. Derrida returns to the workings of the *"inconscient,"* of that which is not conscious, alongside the workings of a *conscience,* in the later text, *Rogues*. It has in French and German, but perhaps not in English, the ambiguous inflection of a doing without knowing, as well that of the more drastic condition of having no activity, no consciousness at all. Derrida thus reads Genet and reveals a certain set of unconscious effects and affects holding the discursivities of Kant, Hegel, and indeed Marx together. These effects may escape the attention of even the most rigorous reading, if that reading is conducted within an English language register. One hypothesis then is that what remains of absolute knowledge will be a necessary disruption of transatlinguisization, the merging of English and American into a polymorphous *lingua franca*, driving out all other languages. This becomes all the more imperative if the role of Freud as contributing to the queering of political theory is to be taken seriously. It may be that for a while these processes of disruption migrated into queer studies, but it may also be that queer studies may have become so respectable and territorialized that their disruptive effect is weakening.

There is a gulf opening up between a world of domesticated queer studies and a world in which homosexuality is still punishable with death. There is another gulf concerning Freud that opens up between an English-speaking world and a German-speaking world. This in part results from the failure in the former to take on board the possibility of an epistemology of unconscious knowledges and affects. These operate for Kant and for Husserl in the notions of a transcendental synthesis, transcendental imagination, and a transcendental unity of apperception, of which empirical selves are unaware, and, for Hegel and Marx, in processes taking place above and beyond individual human intent. Marx and Kant are also points of reference for the articulation of the argument in *Glas*, but a reading of Freud is the most urgently needed in order to do justice to the tolling bell, which both echoes the repetitions of the death drive and marks the commencement of the funeral obsequies, for with the funeral obsequies a new era, indelibly marked by the death of the one to be buried, opens out. The three elements of Derrida's queer Hegel are, first, the insistence on animality, which reveals the *pa*s of the move from nature to spirit and underlines that which remains after or despite the relève (raising to another level) of the *Aufhebung*. Second, there is the insistence on queer lineages and on alternate triads, with no triad more queer than that of Father, Son, and Holy Ghost. Third, there is also the uninterruptable work of disruption of any logic founded in naming and reference by the logic of the flower, of the emblem, of the repetition that repeats the name with a difference.

Notes

1. I should like to dedicate this essay to the memory of my mother, Jane Aiken Hodge (1917–2009), who alas died between penultimate and final drafts.
2. Ludwig Feuerbach, *Principles of the Philosophy of the Future*, trans. Manfred Vogel (Indianapolis, IN: Hackett Publishing Co., 1986) 71–72.
3. Jacques Derrida, *Specters of Marx: The State of Debt, the Work of Mourning and the New International,* trans. Peggy Kamuf (New York and London: Routledge, 1994); *The Politics of Friendship,* trans. George Collins (London: Verso, 1997); *Rogues: Two Essays on Reason,* trans. Michael Naas and Pascale Anne Brault (Stanford: Stanford University Press, 2003).
4. Jacques Derrida, *Glas,* trans. John P. Leavey and Richard Rand (1974; reprint, Lincoln and London: University of Nebraska Press, 1990).
5. See Sarah Kofman's fine essay on the reading of Freud in *Glas*, first presented at the Cerisy conference 1980, "On the Ends of Man," "*Ca Cloche*," translated in *Derrida and Deconstruction Continental Philosophy II,* ed. Hugh Silverman (London and New York: Routledge, 1989), and also given in Kofman, *Selected Writings* (Stanford: Stanford University Press, 2005), 71–98.
6. Jacques Derrida, *Aporias: Dying-Awaiting (One Another at) the "Limits of Truth,"* trans. Thomas Dutoit (Stanford: Stanford University Press, 1994); *L'animal que donc je suis* (Paris: Galilée, 2006).

7. On this see Gil Anidjar's excellent introduction to Jacques Derrida, *Acts of Religion* (London and New York: Routledge, 2002).

8. Derrida, *Glas*, 127; Kofman, "*Ca Cloche*," 82.

9. *Glas*, 227.

10. G. W. F. Hegel, *Elements of the Philosophy of Right*, trans. H. B. Nisbet, ed. Allen Wood, *Cambridge Texts in the History of Political Thought* (Cambridge: Cambridge University Press, 1991), 219. I have in each case where possible given a date for publication in the original language but given the most available translation in English.

11. Jacques Derrida, *The Truth in Painting*, trans. Geoffrey Bennington and Ian McLeod (1978; reprint, Chicago: University of Chicago Press, 1987), and Jacques Derrida, *The Post Card: From Socrates to Freud and Beyond*, trans. Alan Bass (1980; reprint, Chicago: University of Chicago Press, 1987).

12. *Post Card*, 259

13. See Richard Beardsworth, *Derrida and the Political* (London: Routledge, 1996). The quality and impact on me of this study is insufficiently recognized by me in Joanna Hodge, *Derrida on Time* (London and New York: Routledge, 2007).

14. G. W. F. Hegel, *Hegel's Logic*, Being Part One of the *Encyclopaedia of the Philosophical Sciences* (1830), trans. William Wallace (Oxford: Oxford University Press, 1975), 296.

15. Jean Luc Nancy, *The Speculative Remark (One of Hegel's Bon Mots)*, trans. Celine Surprenant (1973; reprint, Stanford: Stanford University Press, 2001) discusses this in some detail.

16. Michel Foucault and Herculine Barbin, *I, Herculine Barbin, Being the Recently Discovered Memoires of a Nineteenth Century French Hermaphrodite* (1977; reprint, New York: Random House Knopf, 1980). The publishers' description of this, plus quote from a review in *Le Monde*, runs:

> From the Publisher: With an eye for the sensual bloom of young schoolgirls, and the torrid style of the romantic novels of her day, Herculine Barbin tells the story of her life as a hermaphrodite. Herculine was designated female at birth. A pious girl in a Catholic orphanage, a bewildered adolescent enchanted by the ripening bodies of her classmates, a passionate lover of another schoolmistress, she is suddenly reclassified as a man. Alone and desolate, he commits suicide at the age of thirty in a miserable attic in Paris.
>
> Here, in an erotic diary, is one lost voice from our sexual past. Provocative, articulate, eerily prescient as she imagines her corpse under the probing instruments of scientists, Herculine brings a disturbing perspective to our own notions of sexuality. Michel Foucault, who discovered these memoirs in the archives of the French Department of Public Hygiene, presents them with the graphic medical descriptions of

Herculine's body before and after her death. In a striking contrast, a painfully confused young person and the doctors who examine her try to sort out the nature of masculine and feminine at the dawn of the age of modern sexuality.

Herculine Barbin can be savored like a libertine novel. The ingeniousness of Herculine, the passionate yet equivocal tenderness which thrusts her into the arms, even into the beds, of her companions, gives these pages a charm strangely erotic... Michel Foucault has a genius for bringing to light texts and reviving destinies outside the ordinary.

Le Monde, July 1978.

17. See Eric Weil, Appendix to *Hegel and the State,* trans. Mark A. Cohen (1950; reprint, Baltimore: Johns Hopkins University Press, 1998), Marx and the Philosophy of Right: "We can therefore say that all the elements of Marx's thought action nexus are present in Hegel. They become scientific concepts and revolutionary elements from the moment Marx applies the concept of negativity developed in the *Phenomenology* to the fundamental structures elaborated in the *Philosophy of Right,* 120."

18. On the relation between Derrida and Nancy, see Jacques Derrida, *Le Toucher, Jean Luc Nancy* (Paris: Galilée, 2000). I give a brief description of their encounters in the 1980s, in Joanna Hodge "Kant *par excellence*" introduction to *Kant after Derrida,* ed. Philip Rothfield (Manchester: Clinamen, 2003). See also: Joanna Hodge, "Why aesthetics might be multiple; On Jean Luc Nancy," *Angelaki: A Journal for the Theoretical Humanities,* 7(1) Spring 2002.

19. *Rogues: Two Essays on Reason* (2001), trans. Michael Naas and Pascale Anne Brault (Stanford: Stanford University Press, 2003). This consists of two essays, one lengthy and in ten parts, called "*La raison du plus fort Υ a-t-il des états voyous?*" with which I am here much concerned.

20. Jean Luc Nancy, *The Experience of Freedom,* trans. Bridget McDonald (1988; reprint, Stanford: Stanford University Press, 1993).

21. *Rogues,* 76.

22. G. W. F. Hegel, *Elements of the Philosophy of Right,* trans. H. B. Nisbet, ed. Allen Wood (1821; reprint, Cambridge: Cambridge University Press 1991), 219.

23. Emmanuel Levinas, *Totality and Infinity: An Essay on Exteriority,* trans. Alphonso Lingis (1961; reprint, Pittsburgh, PA: Duquesne University Press, 1998).

24. *Totality and Infinity,* 21–22.

25. Jacques Derrida, *Writing and Difference,* trans. Alan Bass (1967; reprint, London: Routledge, 1978), 79–153.

26. Derrida, "The Pit and the Pyramid: Introduction to Hegel's Semiology," in *Margins of Philosophy*, trans. Alan Bass (Chicago: University of Chicago Press, 1982), 69–108.

27. For a development of the theme of meals into nausea, see Werner Hamacher, *Pleroma: Reading in Hegel*, trans. Nicholas Walker and Simon Jarvis (1978; reprint, London: Athlone Press, 1998).

28. *Glas*, 56–57.

CHAPTER FOUR

Antigone's Liminality: Hegel's Racial Purification of Tragedy and the Naturalization of Slavery

Tina Chanter

The Sophoclean tragic cycle stands exemplary of Western culture in so many diverse ways, the exemplarity of which has been expounded by various philosophical, psychoanalytic, and literary figures, some of whom—G. W. F. Hegel among them—have themselves founded schools of thought. Yet all too rarely have the exponents of Sophocles' Oedipus or Antigone been willing or able to take on and think through the paradox that these literary, philosophical, psychoanalytic heroes were penned by an aristocratic author whose "leisure" time to conceive, write, and perform his exemplary tragedies was bought at the expense of a system of chattel slavery. The achievements of ancient Athenian society are glorified in a manner that encourages a certain evasion of our own implication in empires built on slavery and colonialism.

Although a good deal of scholarly attention has been devoted to the sense in which Sophocles' Antigone claims Polynices is irreplaceable, such that he is distinguished from a future husband or son of Antigone's, there is very little consideration of the fact that Antigone also distinguishes Polynices from a slave, implying that had he been a slave, rather than her brother, she would not have insisted upon burying him.[1] In differentiating Polynices from a slave, Antigone is contesting Creon's dishonoring of Polynices in death, but she is also appealing to and re-inscribing a distinction between the humanity of the royal aristocracy to which her family belongs and the inferior status of slaves. Antigone does not want to leave the corpse of Polynices to carrion birds but would have no such qualms in doing so had he been a slave rather than her brother.

How, then, is Antigone's effort to discriminate between a slave and a brother to be read, and how are we to account for the consistency with which it has not been read, the extent to which an entire tradition of scholarship has been able to read over it? Could it be that the tradition of German idealism that idealized the Greeks, even while it sought to distinguish itself from them, was unable to attend to this reference to slavery because to do so might have led to introspection about its own complicity with new world slavery? Is the failure to notice or attend to the assumptions Antigone imports into her defense of her brother a direct result of the impossibility of a white, European tradition confronting its own failure to see its endorsement of slavery and colonialism as an indictment of its claims to be civilized?

Recently critics have begun to investigate Hegel with a view to addressing his ideas on slavery and colonialism. He justifies the latter, even as he decries slavery. Not all races, according to Hegel, qualify as world historical; Africans suffered from an undeveloped consciousness.[2] Building on the work of such critics, while taking seriously on the one hand the tradition of post-colonial appropriations of *Antigone*, and on the other hand the paradox that the Oedipal cycle was written during a period when aristocratic, archaic rule was giving way to democratic rule in Athens, and yet the democracy that was emerging based itself upon a slave society, this chapter seeks to revisit some of the received parameters within which critics have interpreted *Antigone*.

By broadening the purview of questions beyond that of family and kinship, we need to ask how these themes have been developed in a particular direction that might have obscured or downplayed other concerns at stake both in Sophocles and in the theoretical tradition to which the Oedipal cycle has given rise. These concerns prove to be entangled with the questions of kinship and gender that have taken precedence in recent debates, questions that have derived in part from the crucial role that the conflict between family and state plays in Hegel's interpretation of *Antigone* as a tragedy. Taking them seriously requires a reconfiguration both of key Hegelian tenets and of the contemporary focus on gender and sexual difference in responses to *Antigone*.

HEGEL'S PROHIBITION OF SLAVERY AS A TRAGIC TOPIC

Hegel's aesthetics has had a determining influence on the critical reception of Greek tragedy, not least his reading of *Antigone*, a play that he considers to be one of the most sublime works of art of all time.[3] From the opening pages of his study, Hegel dismisses the art of "savages" as "effemina[te]" in its indulgence, for failing to accord with "the true ends and aims of life" (1: 3–4; 1: 16). He continues his polemics against "provincial females" for being too ready to sympathize with "misfortune" [*Unglück*] that is merely "external," "finite," and "negative" (2: 1198; 33: 525). The philosophical narrative Hegel provides is sustained by a multiplicity of references designed to establish the superior self-consciousness of spirit in the West. His differentiation of nature from spirit and his accompanying conception of how females differ from males proceed in terms of a relentlessly racialized discourse, and his aesthetics prove to be no exception. So, for example, in accounting for the development of ancient Greek religion, the transition from the old to the new gods is rendered in terms that privilege spirit over nature, and correspondingly privilege Greece over Asia (see 1: 459; 2: 53 and 1: 474; 2: 72–3). Hegel is committed to a nostalgic view of a classical Greece that he construes as the originating force of the modern state, its as yet undeveloped precursor that lacks the differentiated moral and legal complexity it will come to have in his own time. If Hegel confers upon Greek ethical actors a lack of sophistication, he also admires them for their "unity" (ibid.) and disinclination to evade responsibility for their own actions. The heroic character does not have "recourse to everyone else" or "shuffl[e] guilt off himself so far as possible" (ibid.). Neither is there any distinction between "person and family" (ibid.). The individual takes on the inherited guilt of the family and enjoys immediacy in relation to the whole community (see 1: 188–9; 1: 247–8). In short, the ancient Greeks might have lacked the moral sophistication and self-consciousness of modern subjects, but at the same time they did not share the modern trait of evasiveness.

In locating the true origins of dramatic poetry in ancient Greece, rather than in the East (see 2: 1205–6; 3: 534–5), Hegel encounters an especially recalcitrant problem. This requires him on the one hand to maintain that the works of the tragic poets embodied a spirit of freedom, and on the other hand to negotiate the fact that the very society that produced the tragic poets, "where the principle of free individuality makes the perfection of the classical form of art possible for the first time" (2: 1206; 3: 535), was, in fact, structured as a slave society. In order to circumvent the blatant lack of freedom that confronting slavery would entail, Hegel is obliged to produce an argument that explains why slavery constitutes an inappropriate topic for tragedy. In doing so, he embraces tragic poetry as an idealized resolution of collisions, to the point of excluding conflicts that would prove to be unaesthetic. Thus Hegel is able to maintain tragedy as a site of reconciliation by admitting only those conflicts that can be said to be ethical as the locus of collision, thereby purifying in advance the contents of tragedy, such that slavery is excluded as a tragic theme. To include slavery within the orbit of tragedy would be to contaminate it with a contradiction that remains unthinkable and irresolvable by Hegelian logic: slavery becomes the excluded, unthought ground of tragedy, and Antigone is decipherable as a figuring of its exclusion.

Ironically, given his ethical ambivalence with regard to the ancients and the modern—in particular his misgivings about the way in which we moderns shuffle guilt onto others—in determining the scope of tragic content and thereby identifying which conflicts are appropriate to it, Hegel will engage in some particularly evasive reasoning. In order not to compromise the stability of the state, Hegel finds himself issuing the advice that even though it is unjust, slavery must sometimes be borne. At the same time—in a gesture that, even if it has nothing else to recommend, goes at least some way toward acknowledging the potential of art to channel political unrest—Hegel advises that tragedy be sanitized of references to slavery or at least that such references be minimal, that they be fleeting (see 1: 191; 1: 251 and1: 205; 1: 268). The grounds on which he makes such a recommendation, however, are internally contradictory. Yet Hegel, the master dialectician, does not prove himself inclined to follow out the consequences of this particular contradiction.

It is well known that Hegel requires of his tragic heroes that their claims are ethically justified, yet at the same time guilty. Less attention has been paid, however, to the convoluted logic that allows Hegel to condemn slavery (while recommending that such admittedly unjust practices must sometimes, of necessity, be borne) and at the same time to exclude such practices as possible topics of tragedy. Hegel restricts the content of tragedy to a range of "substantive and independently justified powers that influence the human will" (2: 1194; 3: 521). When such powers come into conflict with one another due to the passionate and single-minded adherence of tragic heroes to a fixed aim with which the characters completely identify themselves, a tragic collision ensues. Hegel regards as the "chief conflict" that which arises between family love and political life, which Sophocles treats the "most beautifully" and which is embodied above all in his *Antigone* (2: 1213; 3: 544). In honoring "Zeus alone, the dominating power over public life and social welfare," Creon represents political life or "the state, i.e. ethical life in its *spiritual* universality," while

Antigone represents the "family, that is *natural* ethical life" (2: 1213; 3: 544). Although for Hegel tragic heroes, as ethical actors, by definition—on account of their particularity (see 2: 1195–6; 3: 522–3 and 2: 1205; 535)—represent partial aspects of ethical life, he insists both that they are justified and that their claims are equal. Slavery is thereby disqualified as a topic for tragedy, since the claims of slave-owners are neither justified nor equal to the rightful claims of slaves to be free. Yet things are more complicated than this, since to say that tragic heroes are justified is only part of the story; for Hegel the deeds of tragic heroes are "legitimate" on their own terms but "blamewor-thy" in terms of the ethical order taken in its totality (2: 1198; 3: 526). The guilt of tragic heroes is bound up with their particularity and the opposition into which they are led in actualizing their pathos (2: 1196; 3: 523–4). Thus "despite all their justification" (ibid.), tragic heroes are still guilty—indeed it is their honor to be so (see 2: 1215; 3: 546). Thus, in contrast to Aristotle, for Hegel, tragic heroes "do not want to arouse sympathy or pity" (2: 1215; 3: 546).

Hegel makes a suggestion that only someone who is not oppressed by an external power, someone who was not a slave, for instance, would make: "What a man really has to fear is not an external power and oppression by it, but the might of the ethical order which is one determinant of his own free reason and is at the same time that eter-nal and inviolable something which he summons up against himself if once he turns against it" (1: 1198; 3: 525). The implication is that those, who fear things that are merely "finite and external" rather than "the power of the Absolute" (2: 1197–8; 3: 525) experience merely superficial and subjective fear. By distinguishing between gen-uine and superficial objects of fear and pity, Hegel thereby dismisses slavery as a worthy subject for tragedy. Due to its injustice, slavery is not a topic that tragedy can purify through its artistic presentation. In effect then, Hegel purifies tragic poetry of the burden of representing the ugliness that would ensue from incorporating into it conflicts based on unjustified beliefs in slavery, yet he counsels that such ugli-ness should be tolerated in life, at least when it appears to be insur-mountable. Poetry, it would seem, must be purified of the ugliness and barbarism that must be tolerated in life.

Even though there is a certain necessity that Hegel acknowledges in the actualization tragedy realizes, and in the dissonance conflict involves when the deed of one tragic hero clashes with another, the Hegelian impulse to reassert the unity that tragic conflict had dis-turbed is also evident. Above all, it is the reconciliation of conflicting individual aims in which tragedy issues, which reasserts ideality, unity, and eternal justice and which the chorus embodies in its contemplative stance.

If in one way Hegel historicizes ancient Greek tragedy by insisting on its religious significance, in another way he depoliticizes it, not only by casting it as an art that preceded the legality of the state but also by privileging a particular conception of politics as bound to the state. His understanding of tragic figures as interpretations of Greek gods exempts him from any consideration of tragedy as a site for reflecting on how to construe the political as such, and thus from seeing the contest between Antigone and Creon precisely as a contestation over the meaning of the political. Instead, Hegel takes for granted that the only representation of the political that *Antigone* offers is the one that Creon represents. In so doing he neglects to interrogate both the political significance of Antigone and the salience of any of the specific measures that were introduced during the period in which the tragedies were created.

Plenty could be said about the preconceptions Hegel brings to his understanding of *Antigone*, in terms of his evident attempt to press the play into a mold in which the claims of the protagonists can be cashed out as oppositional, as logically contradictory, and, therefore, as susceptible to a form of overcoming or reconciliation that—despite Hegel's claim that the medium of art is not that of philosophy—resembles or replicates the model of determinate negation that is the motor of his dialectical logic (see 2: 1215; 3: 547). Neither is it hard to bring into question the hierarchical and historically successive relationship Hegel sets up between art, religion, and philosophy, a relationship that tends to specify art's function as an inferior presentation of the truth that philosophy will eventually deliver as conceptual thinking.

Although art as such, considered as an independent domain, retains its own end, considered more broadly in Hegel's terms, art does not attain the self-reflective rigor of thought that is the proper sphere of philosophy. Thus, although art provides "awareness" (1: 102; 1: 141) of true spirit, it does not achieve the self-reflective capacity that thought has. As an expression of spirit, an expression, however, that has not yet advanced to the truth of thought, art does not unfold as the dialectical resolution of contradiction. Its medium is that of sensuous materiality, not that of logical reason. Yet, Hegel, the philosopher, has no reservations about using the language of *aufhebung* to account for the true meaning of art, which might escape art on its own terms but does not escape Hegel on his terms.[4] Those terms include a conception of truth and reality as an ideal that privileges ethics understood as divine and discounts the contingencies and external particularities of the finite world. Hegel includes abuses of power such as slavery in the latter.

To admit slavery as an appropriate topic for tragedy would compromise the implicit faith Hegel attaches to the resolution tragedy brings in its reassertion of the ideality and unity of eternal justice. There can be no preservation (see 1: 1215; 2: 546), raising up, overcoming, or sublation of the essentially unjustified claim that characterizes those who would uphold slavery. Apparently, then, Hegel sees a need to wait for the logical necessity of history to expunge certain glaring contradictions, a necessity for certain groups of people—slaves among them—to await the freedom promised by the eventual, inevitable working out of differences that prove unsustainable in the particularized real world.

Sculpting Antigone's Ethics from the Gods of "Nature"

Hegel's suggestion that each tragic character identifies solely with a singular aim is one that critics have disputed, as is Hegel's assumption that each tragic character can be adequately considered to fulfill a representative function. So too the mutual exclusivity of the aspects of ethical life that Antigone and Creon are said to represent has been interrogated.[5] Yet, insofar as Hegel acknowledges that the pathos of Antigone (her "interest in the family") and that of Creon (the "welfare of the community" (1: 464; 2: 60) are merely aspects of a larger, more complex whole, the ethical and communal fabric of life that the chorus represents, he would be the first to concede that things are more complex than the singular identification of either Antigone or Creon might suggest. In this sense, to insist on the mutual implication of family and state is not so much to challenge Hegel as it is to confirm one of his most important insights into tragedy, namely the one-sidedness and partiality of the tragic heroes, and thus their incompleteness.

It is certainly politically productive to ask whether, in fact, certain familial forms are not only sanctioned by but also made possible by the state, and whether in turn certain familial configurations support and legitimize the state. By doing so, the question as to whether the mutually supportive structures of family and state have naturalized heteronormative families has been foregrounded. However, neither objections about the complexity of the tragic characters nor observations that point to the mutual implication that pertains to family love and the state duty challenges the fundamental Hegelian dictum that the chief site of conflict in *Antigone* is that between family and state.

That the state legitimizes a certain representation of the family, while outlawing other representations, is undeniable, as is the fact that Hegel tends to reduce the complex and not necessarily consistent motives and aspects of the character of Antigone, in order to align her both with his reconciliatory vision of the chorus as mediating, competing, one-sided, and singular aims, and with his preconceptions about women's proper sphere of action.[6] Still to be interrogated are the purposes such an oversimplification serves, and the extent to which *Antigone* raises questions that go beyond the ways in which circumscribed representations of the family shore up the state and in turn legitimize a highly particularized and naturalized form of the family. By returning both to the question of representation and to the ways in which familial definitions accord not just with an idealized version of a particular state but also with the very emergence of the state as a state and its delineation from other states, the various strategies of purification in which Hegel's concept of tragedy is engaged can be tracked. So too, we need to consider the various ways in which the concept of the family organizes Hegel's thinking about *Antigone*, and whether the lack of a systematic conceptual genealogy of the family in relation to the historical series out of which the modern concept of the family emerges, including generation (*Geschlecht*), clan, and so forth, marks a lacunae that needs to be made good.[7] If Hegel is forthright in tracking the development of legal thinking and the state as emerging from a more communally based ethics, he is less inclined to attend systematically to the changing shape of kin relations, the modern configuration of which will find its definitive form in the nuclear, patriarchal family. One could speculate that this lack of concern is bound up with an assumption that the role of women—guardian of the familial—remains in Hegel's mind somewhat static over time.

Nor should we discount Hegel's reluctance to take up the question of what separates one generation from another—even though this distinction is precisely the one that Oedipus had confounded and is, therefore, central to Antigone's destiny—from issues of race or slavery. In this regard, it is worth emphasizing that included among the range of connotations that both the terms *Geschlecht* and γένος have is "race." Thus, discussing inherited guilt, Hegel says, "a whole generation [*Geschlecht*] suffers on account of the original criminal... he *is* what his fathers were" (1: 188–9; 1: 247). Yet he also uses the term when differentiating between the earlier and later Greek gods: the former are "a raw and savage race [*Geschlecht*], misshapen, like products of Indian or Egyptian fancy, gigantic and formless" (1: 459; 2: 53). When Creon is responding to Haemon, from whom he expects obedience, he says, "For if I am to raise my own flesh and blood [to be] unruly, then most certainly [I will raise] those outside my family [to be unruly too]."[8] The word translated as "family" is the genitive form of γένος. Of particular interest is the fact that Creon raises the question of insubordination or unruliness in relation to those inside and those outside the family/race. The borders of the family are to be established, apparently, on the basis of the obedience of its members. Given the views expressed by Aristotle, to be formulated not long after Sophocles composed the Oedipus cycle, concerning the capacity of slaves and women in relation to deliberation and authority, Creon's words take on a special significance.

The cultural requirement that male adults authorize any and every female decision, to the point where women are construed as incapable of taking any important action by or for themselves, is one that plays itself out in the political and ethical philosophies of Plato and Aristotle. *Akyron* means without a guardian.[9] Roger Just points out that, although differently configured, the rule of a free man over a slave, that of a male over female, and that of a man over a boy are all conceived as natural. Aristotle tells us that "the deliberative faculty of the psyche is not present at all in the slave; in a female it is inoperative (*akyron*), in a child, underdeveloped."[10] The difference between the ruler and the ruled is that between the rational and the non-rational.[11] In Antigone's case, Creon is both the *kurios*, the male guardian, the one who expects to give away the bride, and the father of the one who expects to receive her—a doubling of identity that echoes all the other doubled identities that structure the Oedipal myth. For Antigone to be without a guardian (*akyron*) is, then, for her to be unruly—like a slave (see Just 1991, 192–3). For Haemon to follow Antigone's lead is to show the same insubordination as she does. So too there is the contaminating influence of Polynices' corpse, which Antigone, in her disobedience, seeks to differentiate from a slave by performing burial rites. As H.S. Harris says, "To leave the dead unburied is unGreek, barbaric."[12]

Not only is there a purification of emotions at stake in Hegel's reading of tragedy, but also a narrative of racial purification. While Hegel does not take up the issue of slavery in *Antigone* directly, it is deflected in his racially purifying narrative. Antigone occupies a transitional status in which she serves at one and the same time as a vehicle for Hegel's differentiation of spirit from nature and as a mechanism that dissociates Athenians—and by implication nineteenth-century

European imperial slave owners—from those whose lineage proves to be less than pure. Admitted into the realm of spirit, Antigone nonetheless occupies its lower echelons, contaminated with nature, as prescribed by her sex. Hegel grants Antigone a marginal spirituality on the basis of his belief that tragic heroes represented gods—but not without making it clear that the particular god that Antigone represents emanates from the old order of gods and as such remains bound to nature. The gods from whom Antigone derives her spirituality are in turn distinguished from the gods of other religions, whose spirituality Hegel regards as inferior, a view he expresses in racial terms. Yet the distinction leaves a residue: Antigone is closer to these more primitive gods of nature than Creon, who represents rather the newer gods (more advanced, more rational, more masculine, more Greek, more modern, more Christian, more Hegelian).

The essence of tragedy resides, for Hegel, in a conflict between universal ethical powers, especially in the reconciliation of these opposing powers. Tragic heroes are defined by their complete identification with one such ethical power (understood as a god or a group of gods). In this respect, Hegel compares them to works of sculpture. Tragic heroes "*are* what they will and accomplish" (2: 1214; 3: 546). There is no split between the subject and what is willed. The essential pathos of tragic heroes confers on them solidity and steadfastness, which liken them to the statues of Greek gods, while the chorus, for its part, is compared to the temples that house such statues. The chorus is the architectural background against which a drama is played out, a drama constituted by the action of the heroes.

Just as the Greek theater has its external terrain, its scene, and its surroundings, so the chorus, the people, is as it were the scene of the spirit; it may be compared, in architecture, with a temple surrounding the image of the gods, for here it is an environment of the heroes in the action (2: 1211; 3: 542).

Hegel's employment of this image of a temple containing statues of gods to explain the relationship between the chorus and the tragic heroes is of more than passing interest. The chorus provides a "secure refuge" (2: 1211; 3: 541) against the "fearful collisions" that provide the stuff of tragedy, in Hegel's view. In its "equilibrium" the "ethical order appears" (2: 1211; 3: 541). If originally in Greek tragedy the relationship between the chorus and the tragic heroes was illuminated by the image of a temple containing statues of gods, the chorus disappears from modern tragedy, which concerns itself with the private, subjective aims of its characters. Hegel links the decline of ancient tragedy to the disappearance of the chorus (2: 1212; 3: 542–3).

Modern tragedy concerns itself with personal, subjective conflicts. Once the state emerged, it became the objective embodiment of ethics. The emergence and consolidation of the more formal apparatus of the state, which took on the role of rendering rationality "objective" (1: 182; 1: 240) and—supplanting the downfall of tragic heroes—the task of punishing infringements (1: 183; 2: 241), was accompanied by a transformation in the nature of tragedy. As the "actual substance of the moral life and action of the hero" (2: 1211; 3: 541), the chorus provides the security that, according to Hegel, was later to become the preserve of the state. The trouble is, as Hegel acknowledges, the state does not always uphold justice. This accounts, in part, for the fact that so many poets of the postmodern era have been obliged to break with Hegel's dictum that tragedy in the modern age has become merely subjective. *Antigone* has been taken up in so many diverse political contexts precisely because the state has failed to uphold the rights of some of its members as equal to others. Due to such failures, dramatists have turned to *Antigone* as a means of recalling the state to its proper duty, thereby enacting an appropriation that is at once political as well as ethical and also makes an intervention into the narrative of aesthetics.

The fact that Hegel construes tragic heroes as representative not merely of ethical powers but of divinities allows him to avert any confrontation both with the rampant inequalities that characterized the lives of slaves in classical Athens and with those characteristic of women's day-to-day lives. The plasticity he attributes to tragic heroes extends to actual personages of ancient Greece, suggesting that he also sees tragic heroes as representative of historical figures. Yet this inference is indirect enough to prevent Hegel from having to acknowledge the disjunctive relationship between his claim that tragic heroes are equal in their ethical justification and the fact that none of the historical examples he provides of the "actual statesmen and philosophers" or the "poets and thinkers" that populated the "beautiful days of Greece" (2: 719; 2: 374) are women. Nor is it easy to see how Hegel could have provided any such examples, given women's second class status and lack of education in the Periclean age to which Hegel refers. The "men of action" he has in mind are "Pericles himself, Phidias, Plato, Sophocles above all, Thucydides too, Xenophon, Socrates" (2: 719; 2: 374). These men are, says Hegel, in a description that unmistakably evokes the idea of Greek statues with which he associates tragic heroes, "great and free...ideal artists shaping themselves, individuals of a single cast, works of art standing there like immortal and deathless images of the gods" (2: 719; 374). Hegel's aestheticization of ancient Greece—in its beautiful days—does admit one woman as exemplary of "the same plasticity [that] is characteristic of the works of art which victors in the Olympic Games made of their bodies" (2: 720; 2: 374). Yet, it is neither her ethical actions nor her accomplishments but rather her naked beauty that gives Phryne the "appearance" (2: 720; 2: 374) of plasticity as she rises from the sea. This association of women with physical, bodily beauty, rather than political or artistic accomplishments, finds its corollary in Hegel's understanding of Sophocles' Antigone as answerable to the old order of the gods, rather than the newer order, that is, the order of gods that Hegel construes as akin to nature.[13]

As his concession to Phryne's beauty indicates, women in Hegel's version of ancient Greece are required to play a liminal role. They must be at one and the same time closer to nature and subject to male guidance, and thus capable of a limited spirituality (a view that is uncannily close to Aristotle's view that women, although possessing the faculty of deliberation, lack the authority to properly exercise it). Women are capable of being spiritual actors, of acting on behalf of a certain aspect of the ethical order, as required by Hegel's vision of tragic heroes, but only within certain limits. Their spirituality is circumscribed by their proximity to nature, a characteristic of the old gods, but one that is preserved in the new gods, albeit in a subordinated fashion (see 1: 474; 2: 73). One of the ways in which women's liminal spirituality is etched out in the contours of Hegel's thought is through his differentiation of the gods of ancient Greece from those of other countries. The ideal of beauty with which he associates Phryne or Artemis is infused with unstated assumptions about chastity and modesty. By implication the excessive, unchaste, immodest, ungovernable goddesses of the east are impure and incapable of purification, just as they are incapable of governance.[14]

The dual demand that women be closer to nature than men and yet capable of a limited display of spirituality is, indeed, exactly the situation that defines Hegel's assessment of Antigone, who represents the old order of ancient gods. In contrast, Creon (on Hegel's reading) represents Zeus, a god of the new order. The group of gods that includes Dike—on whom Antigone calls—"borders on what is inherently ideal, universal, and spiritual" but lacks "spiritual individuality," so that these gods "retain a closer bearing to what is necessary and essential in nature" (1: 462; 2: 57). In this liminal or borderline spirituality, "the categories of right and justice already obtrude" (1: 462; 2: 58), but they veer toward "abstraction" or nature. As Hegel puts it—and the formulation accords well with Antigone's devotion to

Polynices—at stake here is an "obscure right of the natural element within spiritual relationships, e.g. love of kindred and its right" (1: 462; 2: 58). In fact, as Hegel continues his thought, although this was certainly not his intention, he expresses the limitations that ancient Greece would have imposed on women's freedom to perfection: "This does not belong to the spirit which is conscious of itself in its clear freedom and therefore it does not appear as a legal right" (1: 462; 2: 58).[15] Dike is associated with "natural needs and their satisfaction" (1: 467; 2: 64); the right it represents is not "specified in laws deriving their origin from the self-conscious spirit" (1: 467; 2: 64). The distinction between the immediacy of need on the one hand and "political organization which makes its aim the spiritual realm" (1: 461; 2: 56–7) on the other hand governs Hegel's account of the gods, whom he views as becoming progressively more capable of imparting "ethics, law, property rights, freedom and community" (1: 461; 2: 57) and less bound by the immediacy of need, as they advance from nature to spirit. By associating Antigone with Dike and Creon with Zeus, Hegel thereby associates Antigone, the woman, with immediate needs, and Creon, the man, with the political realm, in which spirit has advanced to a higher level of self-consciousness. Crucially, by associating Antigone with the earlier Greek gods, rather than the later, Hegel aligns Antigone with the savagery of those gods of Eastern heritage—those misshapen, formless, gods of another race (*Geschlecht*).

It is important to point out that, far from associating Antigone with woman in general, Hegel associates Antigone with the natural, rather than the contractual, family. Specifically Hegel emphasizes Antigone's identification with her sisterly bond to her brother, a relation that Hegel distinguishes from the husband-wife relation, since he discerns in marriage the beginnings of a political bond.[16] For Hegel, therefore, Antigone's prioritizing of Polynices over her future husband is entirely consistent with her attachment to blood kindred, to the older gods, who are associated more directly with nature than are the newer ones and with the immediacy of need rather than the bonds of community. In this respect, Antigone's claim that Polynices is irreplaceable, in a passage that has proved so controversial for some commentators, poses no problem at all for Hegel. At the same time, Antigone's attachment to her natural family, rather than to her future husband or to a future son, confirms that Hegel' reading appeals to Antigone's liminal spirituality. As a tragic hero and as emblematic of ancient Greece, Antigone is inscribed within the orbit of spirit's self-progressive realization, yet her inscription, for Hegel, is such that she hovers on the edge of a world in which the ethical order is about to be submitted to legal formulae guaranteed and underwritten by the state, an ethical order no longer subsisting simply in the life of the community.

The Simplicity, Solidity, and Plasticity of Tragic Heroes in a Pre-legal Era

Hegel's attitude toward this shift is distinctly ambiguous, as we have already begun to discern. On the one hand he extols the virtues of classical Athens, in which ethics is not yet tied down to legislation but is precisely communal, but on the other hand, the informality of ethics, the fact that it is so embedded in the community, signals a lack of determinacy. In this respect, the function of tragedy is precisely to confer individuality on particular ethical commitments, a conferral that renders such claims particular, substantive, and concrete, by tying them down to actual deeds and associating them with particular characters. By the same token, it is the solidity that Hegel so admires in tragic heroes, the fact that they do not deviate or hesitate but are what they are through and through. Hegel casts this in a negative light in so far as it reflects a state of affairs prior to the emergence of a fully fledged social contract and all the legal apparatus that supports the state, while at the same time it testifies to a lack of inner complexity.[17] Yet there remains something impressive and admirable about the moral fortitude of tragic heroes. Moreover, Hegel sees in their fixity a certain necessity, as if it is precisely their refusal to be anything other than what they are that carves out the conceptual space for the religious and legal principles that will later settle in their place. It is precisely her unyielding, inflexible grasp of her position that renders Antigone so significant for contemporary dramatists.

Essential to Hegel's conception of Attic tragedy as a form of art is its historical emergence at a time during which legal and moral principles are still in the process of being formulated, when ethics have not yet been institutionalized in legal or moral precepts but remain communal. The ethical order, which the chorus articulates, is understood precisely as a communal ethics, which the poets themselves play an important part in formulating, in an age that is "pre-legal" (1: 185; 1: 244), where morality is not yet institutionalized in universal legislation and maxims. In such a situation tragic heroes confer upon the ethical force with which they coalesce a solidity that precedes any stability that could derive from the permanence of legislation or the fixity of moral imperatives. Prior to a time at which the state confers security and stability on the life of a nation, the dramatic poetry of

Athens played a decisive role in formulating ethically justified and stable characters, each of which brought to life and actualized through their pathos one of the Greek gods (see 1: 102; 1: 141). While the chorus articulated the ethical substance of the community, the tragic heroes represented partial claims of the whole fabric of the ethical order, which would later be formalized as moral and legal principles (see 1: 194; 1: 255). Hegel says "the chorus is essentially appropriate in an age where moral complications cannot yet be met by specific valid and just laws and firm religious dogmas, but where the ethical order appears only in its direct and living actuality" (2: 1211; 3: 541). In the heroic age (depicted in tragedy), "the universal ethical powers have not been explicitly fixed as either the law of the land or as moral precepts and duties" (2: 1208; 3: 539). In the absence of the fixity of such institutions, a "fixed aim" is provided by the "'pathos' and power" of the tragic hero (2: 1214; 3: 546), where there is no separation or cleavage between subject and object: "the bond between the subject and what he wills as his object remains indissoluble" (2: 1214; 3: 546). In this regard it is worth recalling that the art of sculpture, for Hegel, is "objective," whereas the art of poetry is "subjective" (1: 89; 1: 123). Sculpture—by reference to which Hegel understands tragic heroes and which are poetic interpretations of statues—constitutes the "unqualified realization of the *classical form*" of art (1: 90; 1: 123). It is in the context of this claim that Hegel's insistence upon the plasticity of tragic heroes, which he understands as interpretations of Greek statues of divinities, should be read.

Woven into Hegel's narrative of the progressive self-realization of spirit as self-consciousness is a commitment to Christianity, through the lens of which he views the religion of ancient Greece, and in distinction from which he makes pronouncements about the inadequacies of Islam. Indeed it is precisely on the grounds that Mohammaden poetry lacks a sufficiently developed sense of individual freedom vis-à-vis the individual's "subjection to the will of God" (2: 1205; 3: 535) that Hegel dismisses the possibility of it meeting his criteria for dramatic poetry. The balance is too much in favor of the "abstractly universal" and not tipped enough in the direction of particularity (2: 1205; 3: 535). If the Islamic God is too powerful, the gods of India and Egypt are not powerful enough. They are too "savage," too "raw," and thus "ungovernable" (2: 459; 2: 53). In China and India, we might say, there is too much particularity and not enough universality, for there is "no accomplishment of a free individual action" (2: 1206; 3: 535). What is given life to is merely "events and feelings," with no ethical principle or aim at stake.

Hegel is invested in positing ancient Greece as the origin of civilized Western Europe—and, therefore, as a culture based on free human individuality—yet as still undeveloped in relation to his own time. As such, the freedom he associates with ancient Greece, specifically with fifth-century BC Athens, is a freedom that is not as reflective as it will become in the modern era (see 2: 1219; 3: 551), but which already shows such potential. Thus Oedipus almost qualifies as a modern hero, in that he embodies the signs of subjectivity by developing the capacity for self-knowledge and thereby becomes a vehicle for the expression of an inner reconciliation, or of the split between subjectivity and objectivity that will not emerge fully until later (see 1: 213–4; 1: 279–90).

At the same time as identifying ancient Greece, as distinct from the East, including China and India, as the origin of dramatic art, Hegel also sees ancient tragedy as reflective of a transition from a state of nature (see 1: 466; 2: 62) to a more highly developed form of political society in which the state has established a measure of stability that was previously lacking. On the one hand, then, ancient tragedy becomes emblematic of a time that preceded the Western, Christian state, a time in which morality had not yet been fixed, either by legislation or by Christianity, while on the other hand it is celebrated for having provided a measure of fixity through its representations of tragic heroes whose passionate attachment to particular aspects of Greek ethical life brought to life their divinities. It is hard not to speculate that Hegel's conception of Greek tragic heroes as bringing to life the gods of ancient Greek religion is indebted to his Christian allegiance to spiritual incarnation.

Art Must Be Purer than Life

As we have seen, some conflicts, among them slavery, are grounded in such barbarism that they must be excluded from dramatic poetry, which would otherwise lose its beauty. In this respect, Hegel demands a higher standard of purity from art than he does from life: in life, slavery must sometimes be borne, whereas in tragedy it is impermissible to represent it thematically. On the basis of the fact that the claims of tragic heroes must be ethically justified and that slavery is an unjustified practice, Hegel excludes slavery as a proper subject for tragedy. Hegel requires that the work of art satisfy his criterion of beauty, while at the same time designating certain conflicts as unsuitable topics for tragedy on the grounds that they are based on nature (rather than spirit). It turns out, however, as Hegel himself points out, that such barbarism is not due to any conflict proceeding from nature but is rather due to the habit of attributing to nature what is, in fact, the result of convention. If, as Hegel says, some natural accident of birth is endowed by "custom or law" with the power of an insuperable barrier, so that it deprives an individual of those rights that "belong to him by the nature of man," then "that individual is from the beginning to be relegated not by his own doing, but by the accident of nature, to some class or caste irrevocably" (1: 208–9; 1: 272). In such cases, a wrong that has been inflicted through convention or legality is naturalized. It "appear[s] as a wrong that has become natural, as it were" (1: 208; 2: 272). It does not occur to Hegel that it is precisely such a process of naturalization in his own reading of Sophocles that aligns Antigone with the family and deprives her of political rights. It is conspicuous, for example, that when Hegel discusses the right of succession, a right that is linked to nature through kinship, and one that is disputed in the collision between Polynices and Eteocles and treated by Sophocles in the Theban cycle, he fails to notice that the right of succession for Antigone and Ismene is excluded from his own consideration due to an accident of birth. Antigone and Ismene are not considered to have any rights to succession, for no other reason than that, unlike their brothers, they were not born men and as such are not considered suitable political leaders.

Although Hegel acknowledges that "differences of castes, classes, privileges, etc., may have arisen from differences of nation and race," he dismisses this as of "no consequence," insisting rather that "the chief point lies only in the fact that such relationships of life, regulating the whole being of man, are supposed to derive their origin from nature and birth" (1: 209; 1: 273). Among the effects of Hegel outlawing slavery and other practices allegedly based on natural differences as legitimate subjects for tragedy is the perhaps surprising outcome that melancholy collisions are not the proper subject of tragedy. Although Hegel advocates that "true free art" should not "respect" such "melancholy and unfortunate" collisions as stemming from conflicts arising between "the position assigned to a man by his birth" and "his different measure of spiritual education and its just demands" (1: 209; 1: 273), he advises that men must "sacrifice" their interests when barriers prove to be "insuperable" (1: 211; 2: 275).

Hegel's restriction of tragedy to specific types of action that render it exclusive of slavery has a dual impact. On the one hand it preempts any attention to extant references to slavery in Greek tragedy, erasing the significance of such references, and on the other hand it operates prescriptively to discourage the exploration of such themes in the modern era. We might even read Hegel's erasure of the thematic treatment of slavery as implicated in his championing of Sophocles as having produced *Antigone*, the tragedy that (on his reading) deals with the most important conflict, and his corresponding denigration of Euripides—whose plays attend to slavery more than those of both Aeschylus and Sophocles—for falling prey to the depiction of emotions and attempting to elicit pity (see 2: 1215; 3: 546).[18] Notwithstanding Hegel, there has been a return to Greek tragedy; in particular, appropriations of *Antigone* have flourished, in which the questions that Hegel argued were not the proper content of tragedy have become thematic. Rather than following Hegel's advice to the "reasonable man" to "bear the inevitable calmly and patiently" and "at least withdraw into the *formal* independence of subjective freedom" (1: 211; 1: 275), contemporary dramatists have turned to *Antigone* as a resource for illuminating the conflicts inherent in colonialism and slavery, which arise on the basis of the type of collisions that Hegel excludes from aesthetics. They thereby offer a dual challenge to Hegel: on the one hand they hold tragedy accountable as an aesthetic form that is implicated in a history of imperialism that the discourse of Western aesthetics has justified, and on the other hand they take both the history and the ethico-political theory that has accompanied it as themes to be interrogated. At the same time these plays transform the tragic genre itself, renewing the question of what the tragic form has become.

By transgressing the formal requirements Hegel imposed upon works of art, by introducing the ugliness of slavery and colonialism into the work of art, contemporary appropriations of *Antigone* also offer resources for an alternative aesthetics, one that does not accept that the end of art is dictated by the contemplative ideal of tranquility, repose, and unity required by Hegel. Neither does it accept that art must be purified of conflicts that must be borne in life. No longer— not that it was ever only this—a vehicle for religious representation, the tragic genre has been transformed into an art that explores such human conflicts as arise from religious and racial discrimination. This aesthetic is one that confronts the ugliness of conflicts that have led to discrimination on the basis of hegemonic conceptions of gender, race, and class, inviting us to explore the implications of the fact that such ugliness is an invention of humanity, rather than passing it off as a conflict proceeding from nature.

Hegel, when considered strictly within the logic of his analysis of tragedy, aligns himself with the chorus, which accords "equal honor to all the gods" (2: 1215; 3: 547) and, in doing so, apportions equal justification and blame to both Antigone and Creon. From a broader perspective, Hegel's tendency to construe the tragic claims of Antigone and Creon as equally justified, and at the same time to see them as equally blameworthy or guilty, is fraught with difficulty because it stands in tension with the indisputable priority Hegel accords to the state over the family in his political philosophy. On the other hand it is precisely the equality Hegel accords to tragic heroes that gives his reading of *Antigone* a potentially radical edge. In this respect Hegel's reading of tragedy, of *Antigone* in particular, might be said to be ahead of its time precisely in so far as it insists in construing Antigone's and Creon's claims as ethically equal to one another. In contrast both to the mores of ancient Greece—articulated and justified by its philosophers—and to those of his day, Hegel confers on a female character—albeit a tragic female character—the capacity to be ethical. Hegel thereby joins Sophocles in treating Antigone's ethical claims as worthy of being heard. Indeed he not only gives them credibility but also confers a certain ideality and purity on the piety and holiness of Antigone's attachment to religion and her familial obligations. However, I have sought to show that this purity is attained through the racial disparagement of foreign gods, a corroboration of Antigone's assumption that slaves are not human in the same way that her royal brother is, the naturalization of her gender in relation to her attachment to family as blood kin, and in Hegel's association of her with the older, primitive order of gods who are closer to nature than the newer gods. Not coincidentally, these newer gods of ancient Greece exhibit traits that approximate more closely to a more modern, more civilized conception of ethics and the divine, one that Hegel articulates in part through racial denigration of other religions.

Antigone's liminality is severely overdetermined in Hegel's account. As a Greek mythical figure, she exemplifies the consummate hero and yet represents an ethical world that has been superseded and a religion that has given way to Christianity. As an artistic figure, she represents the pinnacle of (Greek religious) art, the true meaning of which has now, however, been revealed as (Christian) philosophy. As an ethical actor whose deed is her own, she is distinct from those whose misfortunes are brought about simply through accidents of birth, yet her fate is inseparable from that of her family. Her representational status as a tragic hero is obfuscated; she represents a god, a god who is more spiritual, more beautiful than the gods of Asia and yet more natural than the Greek gods of the newer order, whom Creon represents. She represents devotion to her natural family and piety to the gods, and yet the ethical, spiritual sensibility she embodies is considered primitive and natural in contrast to Creon's commitment to the welfare of the community, which will be supplanted by the state in the progression of history. As a mythical figure of the past, she is by definition universal, and as such shorn of particularity and yet understood as an ethical character whose fixed aim is a precursor to modern moral principles—she is determinate. In this very determinacy, she stands for a partial view that is susceptible to sublation, the terms of which are dictated by a conception of politics that privileges the authority of the modern state even while acknowledging that the state can fail to uphold justice, as when it legalizes slavery. As a female character, Antigone is made to stand for the state of nature that both precedes and threatens to disrupt the contractual obligations with which Hegel associates his masculinist account of the social contract. As sublime, Antigone is formless—like foreign gods—that is, she lacks the form of politics that Hegel attributes to Creon and his ilk.

If Antigone's liminality is overdetermined, so too is the rationale for why slavery cannot be a proper subject for tragedy for Hegel. Tragic heroes must be of a princely or royal class; otherwise their deeds will not be free or independent. Their misfortunes must not derive from contingent circumstances, which for Hegel include abuses of power such as slavery. Precisely because such abuses of power are unjustified, they cannot constitute the kind of deed characteristic of a tragic hero, whose act must be both ethically justified and on par with the contested but equally ethical claim to which Hegel opposes it, an opposition that results in a collision that leads to the reconciliation Hegel sees as the proper outcome of tragic conflicts.

Hegel's theory of tragedy, which privileges *Antigone* as exemplary, proceeds by way of intersecting discourses concerning racialized and feminized others. It is the intertwining of these motifs that, I have been concerned to demonstrate, structures Hegel's reading of *Antigone*. Even to speak of intertwining is not quite correct, since it implies an assumption about the discrete existence of race and gender, an idea that I have been at pains to resist. The point is rather that circulating within a nexus of ideas about marriage, stock, generation, and exchange are mores that we might crystallize around the concepts of race and gender, but that the language of Sophocles articulates in more mobile terms. Hegel's discrimination between the old order or race *(Geschlecht)* of the gods and the new order serves to sublimate the distinction between the familial, spiritual, unconscious, chthonic ethics incarnated by Antigone and those espoused by Creon that he couches in terms of a conscious but perilously narrow concern for welfare of the ship of state. This discrimination assumes a continuity between Hegel's racially disparaging account of eastern gods, and the gods of whom he takes Antigone to be representative, while the new gods are construed as precursors to a Christian ethics, and Creon is construed as a statesmanlike figure whose concern for the state, albeit overweening, anticipates the more rational expression of the polity that will take shape as a social contract.

Hegel's suspicion of mere feelings is coded as a rejection of the feminine. Feelings must be purified of their contingency and negativity and raised up to the level of spirit, which is thereby masculinized. The grounds on which Hegel excludes slavery as a proper theme for tragedy are bound up with the purification of spirit, from which all traces of the feminine must be expunged. Glossing slavery as the misfortune of the times, Hegel distinguishes true pity from the sympathy elicited by the accidental, human abuses of power that he characterizes in terms of external, finite circumstances, thereby distancing himself from such feminized tendencies. To put it simply, to sympathize with slaves is degrading. In defying Creon in claiming the authority to bury her brother, Antigone not only attempts to performatively distinguish the death of Polynices from that of a slave but also lays claim to her status as royalty, and in so doing she attempts to distinguish herself from a slave, from someone who has no authority to speak or do things for herself, in her own name, as a person to be accorded legal rights. She seeks to lay claim to her royal prerogative, a prerogative that her status as a woman and as a non-citizen certainly puts into question.

Just as Hegel distances himself from the sympathy elicited by the "misfortune" of the times by marking it as feminine, he specifies Antigone in racialized terms. The race *(Geschlecht)* of the eastern gods with whom Hegel associates Antigone establishes her as more savage, more akin to nature than those with whom he associates Creon. Her association with "the gods of Hades," those "inner gods of feeling, love and kinship, not the daylight gods of free self-conscious national and political life" (1: 464; 2: 60), is delineated in relation to foreign gods, whose chief content is nature. These gods come from a wilder, more primitive time and are associated with a non-Greek geographical location. They have not yet developed the more "civilized" discourse of ethics and laws that characterizes more ideal, Christian times, where an inner depth facilitates indifference to external circumstances (see 1: 191; 1: 251). Hence Hegel can counsel that when the barriers to overcoming injustice—slavery, for example—are insurmountable, the injustice must be borne. "Where battle is of no avail, a reasonable man is quit of it so that he can at least withdraw into the *formal* independence of subjective freedom" (1: 211; 1: 276). The plasticity of tragic heroes would prevent such a withdrawal to the inner recesses of subjectivity. And, in any case, since slavery might not have been brought about by the slave's own deed, and since it does not rest upon a justified ethical claim, the art of dramatic poetry cannot purify the sympathy that might be felt for slaves—whose subjection and lack of freedom would disqualify in advance any representation. Since tragedy is exemplary of a free society, only those, such as royalty, can constitute tragic heroes, so that they can be truly free and independent in their acts. That such freedom and independence are premised on the subjection of others whose labor facilitates their freedom—whether in ancient Greece or in new world slavery—is not a complication Hegel is prepared to take on.

One final note is called for. Received wisdom has it that Hegel's famous master-slave dialectic is not about slavery as such. It is about anything but that. We are taught that the master-slave dialectic is probably reflective of feudal relationships, or, as Susan Buck-Morss observes, that it has its origins in Fichte, or Aristotle, or Plato.[19] As Malcolm Bull says, in relation to Christopher Arthur's argument, commentators distance "Hegel's dialectic from classical and colonial slavery on the basis that Hegel's terms for master and slave, *Herr* and *Knecht*, are more appropriate to the feudal relation of lord and serf, or master and servant. But this is a false distinction."[20] He goes on to observe that the word Aristotle uses for slave, *doulos*, is translated both as *Sklave* and *Knecht* in an authoritative German translation of Aristotle's *Politics*, but that "where the slave is directly juxtaposed with the master—rather than discussed in general—the two are almost invariably described as *Knecht* and *Herr*."[21] Yet, Bull comments, the scholarly notes undermine any suggestion of a rigorous distinction between *Sklave* and *Knecht*. Commenting upon the diligence with which the Hegel establishment has invested itself in arguing that Hegel's master-slave dialectic has nothing to do with actual slavery, Buck-Morss maintains on the contrary that Hegel was reacting to the slave revolt that has come to be known as the Haitian Revolution. "No one has dared to suggest that the idea for the dialectic of lordship and bondage came to Hegel in Jena in the years 1803–5 from reading the press-journals and newspapers…about real slaves revolting successfully against real masters."[22]

So where does this leave us? If Bull is right that attempts to establish the rigidity of etymological distinctions between *Sklave* and *Knecht*—whether in German translations of Aristotle, or in Hegel's works—founder, and if Buck-Morss is correct in arguing that the actual case of slavery with which Hegel's master-slave dialectic is concerned was the Haitian slave revolt, of which Hegel was fully aware, then Hegel's master-slave relation has everything to do with the actual slaves. The following conclusion is incontrovertible. Although Hegel might have privileged the term *Knecht* rather than *Sklave* in his elaboration of the master-slave dialectic as a tactic of misdirection intended to deflect the true object of his consideration—new world slavery—the fact remains that whether he is discussing the famous master-slave dialectic, or slavery *(Sklaverie)* in the classical context, the same structural contours of his argument assert themselves. The death or servitude of the slave is not of any real import to Hegel. What is important is that if the slave chooses life—chooses servitude—over death (understanding that freedom is nothing without life) the dialectic can continue, premised upon the slave's subjugation. The slave resigns himself to his fate but, crucially, is also enlightened through confronting his own finitude. The slave learns to plow the land or harvest the crop and in doing so is involved in a productive negation—the story is familiar enough. The slave remains a slave until such time as the historical truth reveals itself. The historical lesson that is narrated, the truth arising from the conflict of the master-slave dialectic, in other words, is the same as the advice Hegel dispenses in the *Aesthetics*: enlightened resignation. Or, less politely, he advocates the continuation of slavery until the time is ripe for its overcoming. And when will the motor of history dictate that the time is ripe? Not yet, is Hegel's answer, in the age of new world slavery.

NOTES

1. "It was a brother, not a slave (δοῦλος), who died" Antigone says to Creon in Sophocles' *Antigone* (line 517). Elizabeth Wyckoff, trans., "Antigone," in *Sophocles 1*, ed. David Grene *The Complete Greek Tragedies*, by David Grene and Richmond Lattimore (Chicago: University of Chicago Press, 1954). F. Storr translates the line "The slain man was no villain but a brother," *Sophocles in two volumes*, vol. 1, The Loeb classical library (Cambridge, MA: Harvard University Press, 1981), 353, while Reginald Gibbons has "It was no slave—it was my brother who died," *Antigone*, trans. Reginald Gibbons and Charles Segal, *The Greek Tragedy in New Translations*, ed. Peter Burian and Alan Shapiro (Oxford: Oxford University Press, 2003), 76.

2. See, for example, Robert Bernasconi, "Hegel at the Court of the Ashanti," in *Hegel after Derrida*, ed. Stuart Barnett (London and New York: Routledge, 1998). See also Robert Bernasconi, "With What Must the Philosophy of History Begin? On the Racial Bases of

Hegel's Eurocentrism," *Nineteenth Century Contexts* 22 (2000): 171–201.

3. See G. W. F. Hegel, *Hegel's Aesthetics: Lectures on Fine Art*, trans. T.M. Knox. 2 volumes (Oxford: Clarendon Press, 1988), 1: 464. *Vorlesungen über die Ästhetik*, Suhrkamp Taschenbuch Wissenschaft, B.1, 13–15 (Frankfurt am Main: Surhkamp, 1970), B.2, 60. Hereafter volume and page numbers will be indicated in the text.

4. See, for example, Hegel, 1: 1197; 3: 524.

5. See Judith Butler, *Antigone's Claim: Kinship between Life and Death* (New York: Columbia University Press, 2000). See also Warren J. Lane and Ann M. Lane, "The Politics of Antigone," in *Greek Tragedy and Political Theory*, ed. J. Peter Euben (Berkeley and London: University of California Press, 1986). Hegel ignores the fact that Antigone appeals not only to Dike—a god Hegel associates with the old order, and thus with those gods that are closer to nature— but also to Zeus. See, for example, Hegel, 1: 188; 1: 247. Gibbons translation, op. cit., 326. University Press, 2000). See also Warren J. Lane and Ann M. Lane, "The Politics of Antigone," in *Greek Tragedy and Political Theory*, ed. J. Peter Euben (Berkeley and London: University of California Press, 1986).

6. Hegel ignores the fact that Antigone appeals not only to Dike—a god Hegel associates with the old order, and thus with those gods that are closer to nature—but also to Zeus.

7. See, for example, Hegel, 1: 188; 1: 247.

8. Gibbons translation, op. cit., 326.

9. See Roger Just, *Women in Athenian Law and Life* (New York: Routledge, 1991), 191–192. See also Hall, "Is There a *Polis* in Aristotle's *Poetics*?" in *Tragedy and the Tragic: Greek Theatre and Beyond*, ed. M.S. Silk (Oxford: Clarendon Press, 1996), 109.

10. See Aristotle, *Politics*, trans. H. Rackham. Loeb Classical Library, Aristotle, vol. 21 (Cambridge: Harvard University Press, 2005), 1260a.

11. Roger Just argues that the grounds on which Aristotle distinguishes between women and slaves are shaky, and that "consequently as a 'set of human beings' women are 'slaves by nature,'" *Women in Athenian Law and Life* (New York: Routledge, 1991), 190. See Aristotle, *Politics*, trans. H. Rackham. Loeb Classical Library, Aristotle, vol. 21 (Cambridge: Harvard University Press, 2005), 1254b.

12. Henry S. Harris, *Hegel's Ladder*, vol. 2, *The Odyssey of Spirit* (Indianapolis, IN: Hackett Publishing Co., 1997), 223.

13. As T.M. Knox's footnote clarifies, Phryne is "The famous courtesan who was the model for Apelles' picture of Aphrodite rising from the sea" (1: 720).

14. So, for example, Diana "has, as her chief content, nature in general…even in her external form, in her breasts," whereas for the Greek Artemis "this natural aspect recedes altogether into the

background in her humanly beautiful maidenly form and independence" (1: 474; 2: 72).

15. Clearly Hegel has in mind the lack of self-consciousness that he judges to be characteristic of the kind of rationality embodied in the tragic outlook (2: 1216; 3: 547).

16. For Hegel, marriage is a relationship that involves "obligations" (1: 464; 2: 59) even in the absence of love.

17. Hegel disparages the purely subjective, personal emotions he sees displayed in modern tragedy to the extent that they are not reflective of abiding, communal, ethical concerns, yet he is also suspicious of the formulaic character that the legal framework of modern morality imposes on communal ethics.

18. See also Hegel, 1: 212; 1: 276. Perhaps there is a subterranean polemic going on with Aristotle about the relative merits of Euripides versus Sophocles, and the significance of pity and fear.

19. Malcolm Bull cites as exemplary of this reading C. Arthur, "Hegel's Master-Slave Dialectic and a Myth of Marxology," *NLR* 143 (November–December 1983), 67–75, and Peter Osborne, *The Politics of Time* (London: Verso, 1995), 72. See Bull "Slavery and the Multiple Self," *New Left Review* 231 (1) 1998, 95–131. See also Susan Buck-Morss, "Hegel and Haiti," *Critical Inquiry* 26 (4) 2000, 821–865.

20. "Slavery and the Multiple Self," 103.

21. Ibid., 104.

22. "Hegel and Haiti," 843–844.

CHAPTER FIVE

Knowing Thyself: Hegel, Feminism and an Ethics of Heteronomy

Kimberly Hutchings

INTRODUCTION

Ongoing debates within feminist ethics have been preoccupied by meta-ethical questions concerning the ground and scope of feminist claims about justice and the good. This is evident in the most prominent of these debates, in which feminists have argued over whether an "ethic of justice" or an "ethic of care" is the most appropriate basis for feminist ethics. In characterizing the flaws of each others' positions, feminist philosophers have persistently returned to arguments about foundationalism and universalism in ethics. Care feminism has been argued to run the risk of essentializing women and of collapsing into ethical particularism, whereas justice feminism has been held to account for assimilating women to a masculinist construction of the human and the universal. Meanwhile, a variety of postmodernist and post-colonial feminist theorists have sought to find a way beyond the choice between justice and care.[1]

In *Hegel and Feminist Philosophy*, I described this kind of impasse between different feminist moral philosophies as following a logic closely analogous to that of Hegel's "way of despair" in the *Phenomenology of Spirit*. The main argument of the *Phenomenology*, I suggested, was to do with the unsustainability of thinking in terms of mutually exclusive oppositions and the concomitant requirement to think differently. Within the context of ethics, I interpreted this requirement in terms of a call for a fundamentally heteronomous ethics that rejected the exclusive oppositions between identity and difference, nature and culture, which have underpinned traditional accounts of moral authority, moral agency, and moral judgment.[2] This chapter is the beginning of an attempt to pursue the question of what such a heteronomous ethics would look like, and what its implications in a plural and hierarchical world might be. In order to do this, I begin by going back to Hegel's *Phenomenology* and his immanent critique of the "moral point of view," in the forms of both "the hard heart of judgment" and the "beautiful soul." In both cases, Hegel's critique rests on the unsustainability of rigid distinctions between identity and difference and between nature and culture in the accounts of moral subjectivity, agency, and judgment that underpin both versions of the "moral point of view." I then suggest that we can draw on his reading of *Antigone* to provide an alternative way of thinking about moral subjectivity, agency, and judgment. I also suggest that feminist tendencies to read the figure of Antigone in terms of either justice or care are mistaken. This in turn sets the scene for a consideration of two of the most influential (and also most Hegelian) pathways that recent work in feminist ethics has taken, both of which draw on a reading of the ethical significance of the figure of Antigone, those of Luce Irigaray and Judith Butler.[3]

It will be argued that although Irigaray and Butler both misread the significance of Hegel's *Antigone* for Hegel's own immanent critique of the moral point of view, they each develop arguments that, in addressing what they see as Hegel's mistakes, ironically contribute to what I would identify as a Hegelian project. In particular, they both offer helpful ways of working through and beyond the dichotomies between identity and difference, nature and culture that are crucial to the "moral point of view." This is not to suggest either that my argument turns out to be equivalent to those of Irigaray and Butler, or that their arguments are equivalent to each other. Neither does it mean that there are no difficulties and ambiguities in the ways in which Irigaray and Butler think through the implications of Antigone's ethical significance. Nevertheless, it is to suggest that it is helpful to conceive of Irigaray's ethics of sexual difference, which is fundamentally concerned with the impossible goal of non-appropriative relations between subjects, and Butler's version of a recognitive ethics, which sets us the difficult labor of "cultural translation" as an ethical imperative, as offering complementary rather than alternative lessons for the meaning of a feminist and Hegelian, heteronomous ethics.

Moral Reason and the Beautiful Soul

Hegel's discussion of "moral self-consciousness" in the *Phenomenology* situates it as the contemporary (his own present) culmination of the historical development of European thought.[4] This does not mean that Hegel sees ethical self-reflection as an invention of seventeenth- and eighteenth-century Europeans, he reserves the term "morality" for a particular version of ethical subjectivity and reasoning. For Hegel, *moral* consciousness is a specific form of ethical self-reflection that is born out of a distinctive social and political history within which protestant Christianity and its secularization in enlightenment ethical and political thought are crucial elements. Within this history the authorization of all different kinds of claims to truth became grounded in an assertion of self-certainty located in the individual and variously accounted for by reference to faith, reason, feeling, or will. Here, claims to truth become inseparable from claims to certainty that are located within the subject. In such a context, Hegel argues, a gulf between individual consciousness and both nature and institutionalized aspects of ethical life is confirmed, resulting in the claim to self-consciousness's difference and capacity for mastery over both nature and "objective spirit."[5] The discussion of moral consciousness follows on immediately from Hegel's account of the French revolutionary terror. And from his analysis it is clear that he sees the philosophical and cultural debates about ethical judgment and action characteristic of his time and place as a corollary of the kind of assumptions that justified Jacobin attempts to annihilate an old world and build a new one from first principles. The key presupposition of moral consciousness is the rift between the self-conscious individual understood as an autonomous moral subject (independent of God, nature, or tradition), and the realms of both nature and objective spirit.

> Self-consciousness knows duty to be the absolute essence. It is bound only by duty, and this substance is its own pure consciousness, for which duty cannot receive the form of something alien.[6]

The most significant and influential account of moral consciousness is Kant's moral philosophy, in which the rational will of the autonomous moral subject, undetermined by either natural or cultural influence, is the key to ethical judgment and action. Hegel examines Kant's account of morality and the way in which it is premised on an unbridgeable distinction between pure practical (autonomous) reason and heteronomous reason, in which judgment and action are swayed by naturally or culturally shaped desire. The former, for Kant, is universal in form, whereas the latter is irreducibly particular. The point of moral reasoning is to test out and ensure that the maxim of one's action is genuinely universalizable. Only in this way is it possible to tell whether one is really judging and acting *morally* as opposed to behaving for self-interested reasons. On this account, morality is ideally pure in the sense of being untouched by sensuous/natural motivation. But, as Hegel points out, in any actual judgment or action it is impossible to sustain the division between autonomy and heteronomy, or between universality and particularity, that grounds morality. It is always necessary for actual situations and conditions to "adulterate" morality since one must be moral within an actual world, and what can or cannot be reasonably universalized depends on the nature of that world. Moreover, morality is inherently paradoxical since what it aims at (the control of natural by rational determination) is defined in terms of a collapse of the distinction upon which the possibility of morality is grounded.[7]

One way of rescuing the purity of morality is to drive it ever further back into the recesses of subjectivity through the invocation of conscience and inner feeling or intuition. This is a move Hegel identifies in romantic reactions to Kant's rationalism and moral dualism. The romantic hero/heroine is the *beautiful soul* who exemplifies a perfection of moral subjectivity (the inner certainty of what is right). The disembodied purity of the "inner self" of the beautiful soul identifies moral authority not only with disengagement from nature, but also with the power located in an understanding of spirit in subjective terms as pure individuated self-legislation and, therefore, with a necessary disconnection from all aspects of the world, whether spiritual or natural, including other souls as well as the institutions, cultures, and practices of ethical life.[8] The claim to purity is simultaneously a claim to autonomy and difference (that is to say morality is grounded in a disconnected, uncontaminated self and in the unique power of conscience). It is Hegel's argument that this dual claim is unsustainable in any actual attempt to authorize or exercise moral agency and judgment in the world. On Hegel's account, which draws not only on Romantic literature but also on his earlier characterization of Jesus, the beautiful soul is fated to die because moral perfection (essentially ethereal) cannot realize itself within the world of sense. Not only that, but also the actions of the beautiful soul are inevitably misrecognized as selfishly motivated since there is no access for the outsider to the moral source of those actions that the beautiful soul knows instinctively.[9]

In the closing passages of the discussion of moral consciousness, Hegel sets the two exemplifications of this mode of ethical self-consciousness against each other. The Kantian moral judge, who is motivated purely by the duty to obey the moral law, confronts the beautiful soul, who knows what is right through inner intuition. The result of this confrontation, in Hegel's account, is that the moral judge identifies the beautiful soul as a hypocrite, for conflating her particular will with the universal. In the exchange between them, however, Hegel argues that the moral judge is just as vulnerable to this charge of moral particularism, since there is no way of unpacking the content of universal duty that is not itself particular.[10] In effect, Hegel's argument is that the beautiful soul, which sought to counter the self-defeat of moral reason, nevertheless replicates the logic of the Kantian moral point of view in its reinvention of unsustainable distinctions between universal and particular, autonomy (self-legislation) and heteronomy (determination by desire). In the end Hegel argues, any attempt to exercise moral authority, agency, and judgment on the part of the Kantian moral judge and the Romantic beautiful soul threatens to undermine what have been claimed to be its necessarily pure conditions of possibility.

There are strong parallels between Hegel's critique of moral consciousness and his discussion of law and love in his early essay "The Spirit of Christianity and Its Fate." The standpoint of legalism and judgment is exemplified in the earlier text by the pharisee who cannot see beyond the letter of the law and in the *Phenomenology* by the Kantian moralist, who has internalized duty to the moral law as a categorical imperative.[11] The standpoint of love is exemplified in the earlier essay by the historical character of Jesus and by Goethe's fictional character in the *Phenomenology*.[12] But across both texts similar arguments are being made. In both cases the beautiful soul counters the tyranny of pure legalism with the power of love and purity of heart. In both cases also, Hegel suggests that both the slave of law and the beautiful soul become trapped and ineffective because they are caught within exclusive oppositions. The two standpoints not only are unsustainable in their own terms but also have nothing to say to one another, degenerating in their confrontation into mutual incomprehension and accusation. There is, however, one significant difference between the discussions in the earlier essay and those of the *Phenomenology*. In the former work a third figure contrasts with that of both slave of law and beautiful soul, that of the Greek tragic hero who makes his own fate. In the *Phenomenology* no such contrast is drawn. Nevertheless, there is a discussion of Greek tragedy within the text; in the next section I will suggest that we can still find in Hegel's interpretation of the significance of the Greek tragedy of *Antigone* a possible alternative to ethical self-reflections that evades the traps of self-defeat into which, Hegel has argued, contemporary moral consciousness falls.[13]

Antigone: Toward an Ethics of Contamination

The account of *Antigone*, and of the other Sophoclean plays about Oedipus and his descendants, takes place at the beginning of Hegel's exploration of the historical development of Western ethical life in the *Phenomenology*, providing a counterpoint to the end of the story in modern moral consciousness.[14] Hegel argues that these plays express the hidden tensions within the apparently harmonious ethical life of the Greek city states in the era before its overcoming in Macedonian and Roman imperial rule.[15] The source of these tensions, according to Hegel, is an ongoing duality in Greek ethical life between "old gods" and "new gods," the pre-Olympian gods identified with the life cycle of birth, decay, and death and the personalized gods of Olympia, with their specific powers and attachments to particular rulers and cities. In Hegel's account, this tension is accommodated through a distinction between private and public spheres, with the private sphere of kinship and family serving the needs of the life cycle and the public sphere serving the requirements of the polity. He refers to the norms governing the private spheres as "divine law" and associates these with the ethical life specific to women as guardians of kinship. He refers to the norms governing the public sphere as "human law" and associates these with the ethical life specific to men as the guardians of the city.[16] For Hegel, Greek tragedy in general gains its power from its reflection of the tensions between divine and human law and how they are lived by the central characters. But it is the Oedipal dramas in particular that capture this tension and the moment at which it reaches a breaking point that indicates a significant shift in terms of ethical life from city to empire. As is well known, within this play the drama centers around Antigone's refusal to obey her uncle's (Creon, the ruler of the city) edict that she should not bury her brother, Polyneices, who died killing his (and her) brother in an attempt to usurp his rule of Thebes.

Commentators generally interpret Hegel's treatment of *Antigone* as confirming a clear and hierarchical distinction between the realms of divine and human law. For Hegel, it is argued, the tragedy of Antigone the character is to represent the feminine force of natural connection that is to be overcome by the second (superior) nature of masculine political community, spirit in its fullest sense. In my interpretation, however, the ethical significance of both character and play in Hegel's work is rather different. This reading centers on Hegel's insistence that both Creon and Antigone are fundamentally mistaken in their understanding of their own ethical domains and authorities.[17] Creon and Antigone both see their action as legitimated by mutually exclusive authorities. They act as if uncontaminated by each other's law, but in Greek ethical life these are, in fact, mutually dependent and derived from common identities and obligations.[18] The insistence on seeing the clash between the two laws in terms of an absolute, hierarchical difference is what ultimately undermines the ethical authority of both stances and precipitates the collapse of Greek ethical life.[19] Let us look more closely at what is signified by the idea of mutual dependence of the two laws, what is Hegel pointing to in his insistence that one cannot survive without the other? There are, I believe two aspects to this: the first relates to the conceptualizing of natural and spiritual being and how they should be thought in relation to each other; the second relates to the link between subjective and objective spirit and the ways in which individual members of Greek ethical life are commonly implicated in divine and human law.

One of Antigone's and Creon's mistakes is to understand spirit in the form of either human or divine law in immortal terms, that is to say terms that transcend both natural and spiritual (in Hegel's sense) existence. Rather than understanding spirit as mediated by nature and vice versa, in which view the two are mutually determining and fundamentally inseparable, Antigone and Creon both present their ethical existence as essentially without limit. They are, therefore, closed to the acknowledgment of their dependence on each other for survival, either as the representatives of two ethical domains or as embodied human beings. Antigone and Creon are nature *and* spirit but they speak as participants in an authority that transcends both of these categories. When Hegel distinguishes the realm of animal nature from that of spirit he does so in terms of a distinction between determinate and self-determining being. Self-determination involves a self-conscious recognition of limitation, fundamentally an awareness of death that is not available to animal species. Without this recognition of the mutual dependence of nature and spirit, spirit paradoxically becomes reduced to nature by treating itself as a natural kind that transcends the death of its members. As such, Hegel is cutting the ground from under the feet of any moral authority that, as with the Kantian moral judge or the beautiful soul, takes itself to be grounded in a unique, self-legislating, self-legitimating force that somehow transcends either nature or ethical life.

The second dimension of Hegel's argument asserts the common implication of both Creon and Antigone in both divine and human law. Hegel presents the fact that Creon treats the human law as entirely self-legitimating without regard to its dependence on and entwinement with the ties of blood and kinship as at the heart of his crime. Similarly, for Hegel, Antigone's crime is not that she contravenes human law as such but that in doing so she fails to recognize the dependence of divine on human law—the identity of Polyneices as citizen depends on his birth; his identities as brother and citizen are inextricably related to one another. What we can extrapolate from this is again a fundamentally ontological point about the being of Greek ethical life. Not only is what it means to be any given individual bound up with both divine and human law in ways that are difficult to disentangle, but individual being is also mediated through practices and institutions that shape, constrain, and enable modes of being and acting within and outside of the polis. Antigone and Creon do not confront each other as two separate, unique individuals in the sense that they present themselves, but as individuals who share the identities and values that they are involved in rejecting. Once again this contrasts with the proclaimed purity of moral consciousness and her independence not only from nature but also from ethical life. This is an independence that can be sustained only by a fundamental misrecognition of the meaning of ethical identity as absolute, self-identical difference. Furthermore, the stories of Antigone and Creon not only show us that it is false to see ethical identity in terms of the moral point of view, they also demonstrate that it is false to see ethical identity as secured through identification with a particular cultural ground. Instead, it is the incapacity to know the grounds of ethical subjectivity and judgment and the ways in which these necessarily exceed the compass of the ethical agent that establishes the pathos of these characters for the audience.

If we read Hegel's account of *Antigone* along the lines suggested above then we must also read both Antigone's and Creon's ethical significance differently. In essence the positive lesson to be learned from both relates to what we (according to Hegel, the audience of the play as well as his own readers) know as opposed to the terms in which they represent themselves. What we learn from the play is the degree to which both Creon and Antigone are ignorant of the meaning of their own ethical subjectivity. They do not know themselves and the sources of their capacity for judgment and action, even though they are certain of themselves and what authorizes what they do. For most readers, of course, Creon's self-presentation has always been contrary to the ethical significance of his part in the story. It has been repeatedly noted by commentators that Creon is not only tyrannical and murderous but also fundamentally hypocritical in his denial of his dependence on the ties of blood. In contrast, Antigone has been celebrated, in particular by feminist critics, for her heroic crossing of the borders between private and public realms and her bold representation of the devalued feminine realm of blood ties and kinship. Uses of the figure of Antigone as a feminist heroine reflect the debate internal to feminist ethics between an "ethic of justice" and an "ethic of care." From the point of view of the former, Antigone's moral authority derives from her capacity to identify and speak for universal justice in principle in a way that challenges the exclusion of women from the masculine public sphere. From the point of view of an ethic of care, Antigone's voice is the particular, "different" voice that gains its authority from an alternative perspective to that of masculine justice—a perspective in which the notion of moral responsibility is tied to obligations of care embedded in her own being. The two (justice/ care) positions correspond closely to the contrast between, on the one hand, the moral points of view of the Kantian moral judge, whose autonomous reason enables the grasp of universal principles of right, and, on the other, the beautiful soul, whose particular inner being enables a direct intuition of what is right.

In both of these interpretations, I argue that the ethical significance of Antigone is misunderstood precisely in so far as she becomes seen as a representative of the moral point of view either in terms of the Kantian moral agent or in terms of the beautiful soul. In contrast to this the implication of my reading of Hegel's *Antigone* is that neither the "justice" nor "care" accounts of her moral authority can be accepted, since they both necessitate a choice that Hegel's reading of the play demonstrates to be impossible at all levels. This is so in terms not simply of the action and speech of the characters but in terms of their identities. At the same time, it is also clear that the ethical significance of Antigone (and other characters in the play) is not reducible to her representation of a particular, self-identical cultural identity. As with Creon, Antigone's identity is not closed and coherent but open and contradictory and continually exceeds her own self-certainties about what gives her voice ethical authority and renders her ethical claims intelligible. In my view, the ethical significance of the character of Antigone is twofold. First, she constantly reminds us of the impossibility of understanding the

meaning of justice as in any way relying on a ground above or beyond that of heteronomies inherent in ethical life. From this perspective Antigone's moral authority (her capacity to move and persuade us, the readers and audience) is inherent in the fundamentally
adulterated nature of her being, acting, and speaking rather than in
her mistaken identification with a pure, self-identical domain of
divine law. Second, Antigone's ethical significance lies in the way
that she reminds us not only that self-certainty is not knowledge but
also that there are limits on the extent to which any of us are transparent to ourselves in any capacity, including that of ethical judge
and actor. The two points are connected, since it is because of our
"contamination" by a range of factors that transcend our individual
being that we are never fully able to grasp who we are. In Butler's
words, there is "no uncontaminated voice with which Antigone
speaks," but there is also no uncontaminated voice with which any
ethical subject speaks or that any ethical subject would be able to
hear.[20]

Beyond Antigone: Toward a Feminist Ethics of Heteronomy

If we take Antigone's moral authority to be immanent to the insepa-
rability of the categories of identity and difference, nature and culture
within ethical life, then this suggests a very different orientation for
feminist ethics than the search to locate the ground of feminist moral
authority within either human (justice) or divine (care) law. I want
now to turn to Irigaray and Butler, who both draw on the interpretation of Antigone in developing an ethics and politics based on the
denial of the binary oppositions on which the moral point of view
relies. I will argue that even though these thinkers appear to be dia-
metrically opposed on the question of sexual difference, they end up
articulating a surprisingly similar account of the ethical implications
of the Antigone story.

Irigaray's interpretation of Hegel's treatment of *Antigone* in
Speculum of the Other Women is well known. In this text she reads
Hegel's treatment of *Antigone* as confirming the patriarchal symbolic
order and blocking the subversive potential of the dependence of
human law on divine law by his reading of that relation in terms of a
hierarchical overcoming.[21] In contrast to this, in her reading of the
story of Antigone, Irigaray points to the way in which Antigone is
trapped by both the masculinist order that excludes her *and* subversive of that order. Antigone is trapped by the masculinist order in so
far as she is read in relation to male as norm, so that her difference is

captured only in terms of not-man or like-man rather than in terms that take her being as their starting point. She subverts the masculinist order to the extent that she eludes definition in its terms and suggests that a new vocabulary is needed in order to define her. Although I disagree with Irigaray's interpretation of Hegel, there is clearly considerable common ground in how we both come to read the ethical significance of Antigone. In both cases her defiance of the categorizations that are fundamental to traditional ways of understanding moral authority, agency, and judgment is key.

In Irigaray's case, Antigone's ethical significance points toward the simultaneous impossibility and necessity of an ethics of sexual difference.[22] The point here is that although Antigone provokes a thinking of sexual difference in terms different from those premised on familiar hierarchical binary divisions—in which woman can only be thought as not, other to, same as, or less than, man—the only way to respond to the challenge is through recognizing the impossibility of that response in a world premised on male-as-norm. This impossibility can be explored through readings of the philosophical tradition, but it can also be explored through the positing of sexuate rights that highlight the absurdities of thinking in terms of an ethical relation to others that does not depend on their being defined in terms of same or other-to-man in the world as it is.[23] Irigaray suggests the path of an ethics of sexual difference in which the feminine subject position opens up new ways of thinking the interrelation of identity and difference, nature and culture, in fundamentally non-appropriative terms, that is to say terms in which neither pole of the binary oppositions is subsumed under the other.

Masculinist ethics, Irigaray argues, follows the logic of assimilation and/or hierarchy between subjects, because it is incapable of grasping what it means to recognize the other as different, without reference to an existing matrix of interpretation through which the other's difference is again erased. The possibility of a non-appropriative relation to the other is always blocked by the appropriative languages available to us.[24] This in turn means that we need to create a new language not just to express but also to enact the meaning of a genuinely ethical relation to oneself and to others, a kind of relation that is currently unobtainable. In *The Way of Love*, in a critical engagement with Hegel as well as Heidegger, Irigaray calls for a move from dialectic to dialogue, language to speech:

The interval between the other and me can never be overcome. It has to be cleared of *a prioris*, freed from prescribed or solipsistic certitudes, arranged as a reserve of silence appropriate neither simply to me nor simply to the other, space between us where we are going our way toward one another through the gesture (of) speaking.[25]

In extrapolating what this means, Irigaray explicitly argues that this new kind of ethical relation requires a reaching toward the other and a questioning of the self in which categorical distinctions between identity and difference as well as nature and spirit are undermined. In this ethical relation, neither subject is subsumable by the other, but at the same time the difference between the two is internalized within each subject and externalized in the intersubjective relation that is constituted by them. Difference is subjectively *internalized* not only in the self's recognition that neither self nor other is self-generating, but also because it is only in relation to the other that the self is able to approach the question of what its difference means, a question that does not admit of a definitive answer.[26] Difference is *externalized* in the open, creative unity that is constituted in the relation between self and other, an ethical life that is always, in principle, open and unfinished.[27] Both internal and external difference in identity, or identity in difference, are embedded in an account of human "becoming" that is "corporeal and spiritual, material and conscious."[28] One of the metaphors through which Irigaray expresses the "new" kind of communication she is looking for, beyond masculinist language, is that of the placental economy, and the way in which mother and fetus are joined, materially, by a bond that both unites and separates, enabling the flourishing of both.[29] The ethical significance of this relation inheres not only in the way in which it captures the self and other as both mutually dependent and differentiated, but also in the fact that the mutual toleration of the difference of the physical systems of mother and fetus is vital to the survival of both. Should either assert their autonomy as self-identical, bounded systems, then the consequence is death.[30]

Irigaray's attempts to articulate a new kind of ethical relation are a response to the impossibility of a culture of sexual difference in the contemporary world. But her focus on *sexual difference* as the locus of her thinking about a different way of understanding moral subjectivity and moral agency has been seen by some critics as courting a heterosexist essentialism, in which Antigone and her moral authority assume the form of the beautiful soul defending divine law.[31] To hold onto the impossibility of a culture of sexual difference is to refuse a world constructed in terms of hierarchical binary oppositions between identity and difference, nature and culture. It is, therefore, a refusal to conceive of moral subjects as self-legislating and self-certain. But it can be argued that this refusal ceases to be thought when the implication of "two" in heterosexual woman's subject position itself becomes identified with an ethical privilege that claims a unique legitimacy and legitimating function.[32]

> It [sexual difference] presents the double advantage of being globally shared and of being able to join together the most elemental aspect of the natural with the most spiritual aspect of the cultural.[33]

Irigaray's argument for the ethical primacy of sexual difference in *Between East and West* is reminiscent of the "moral point of view," insofar as it locates moral authority in a particular kind of sexed being.[34] The consequence of this, as Deutscher has pointed out, is that the moral authority of sexual difference trumps the ethical significance of the impossibility of other cultures of difference that are equally ruled out in the contemporary world, differences related to sexuality, class, and race amongst others.[35] To ask Christine de Pisan's question "what would it mean to speak as a woman and be heard?" is crucial for feminist ethics, but to suggest that it might be answered in relation to woman as one of a primary duality is to suggest a degree of self-certainty about the meaning of sexed identity that is challenged in much of Irigaray's own argument. In this respect, Irigaray's work demonstrates how difficult it is to hold to a positive notion of difference in a world in which the temptation is always to privilege some particular difference and thereby re-inaugurate the negative logic of a master identity. It is all too easy to lose hold of the ethical significance of Antigone's contamination and the necessary impurity of all moral voices.

In *Antigone's Claim*, Butler reads Irigaray's interpretation of the figure of Antigone as a "beautiful soul" account, one in which Antigone acts "as a principle of feminine defiance of statism and an example of anti-authoritarianism."[36] Nevertheless, Butler's discussion of Hegel's version of *Antigone* shares much common ground with Irigaray's. Like Irigaray, Butler concludes that Hegel's reading essentially effaces recognition of Antigone as a character in her own right and uses her to confirm the banishment of "womankind" from the public sphere to their proper place as the guardians of kinship. As with Irigaray too, Butler finds a very different ethical significance in Antigone's character, one that subverts the terms of the patriarchal symbolic and social order. In Butler's case, however, this subversion is not understood, in Irigaray's terms, as a currently unthinkable idea of a culture of sexual difference, but instead as an exemplification of the scandalous performative disruption of the patriarchal order. Antigone represents a mode of being that cannot survive in terms of the hegemonic orders of kinship and state, and yet she acts to disrupt and change those orders. Butler finds a genuine alternative to patriarchal ethics and politics, in contrast to Irigaray, in the possibility of challenge *from within* the play between social and symbolic orders.

According to my interpretation of the readings of Antigone in Hegel, Irigaray and Butler are alike in drawing out the impossibility of adequately expressing her ethical significance within the binary terms of divine and human law. We need to ask what it would mean to express this ethical significance in other kinds of terms that do not in turn slip back into the hierarchical binaries they are intended to displace. For Butler the ethical significance of Antigone's inexpressibility in terms of both kinship and state implies the need for a highly contextualized ethics and politics in which the terms of survivability of subjects are negotiated and renegotiated in ways that are maximally inclusive. If Irigaray's work invokes the question "what it means to speak as a woman and be heard?" then Butler's raises another question that is equally provoked by Hegel's reading of Antigone: what would it mean to speak in terms that were not gendered and be heard? I suggest that Butler's work demonstrates and uses productively the impossibility of transcending gender in a way that offers an interesting parallel to Irigaray's demonstration and productive use of the impossibility of a culture of sexual difference.

For Butler, the character of Antigone is ethically significant because of the way in which she subverts the terms of the patriarchal symbolic and social order, not by transcending them but by rearticulating them through using and at the same time challenging the vocabularies that they place at her disposal. Antigone inspires us because of the ways in which she draws attention to the fact that her fate (death) follows from the fact that she cannot be accommodated in terms of the supposed universals of either divine or human law. To the extent that we are moved by her death, we put the accepted terms of the universal into question and, like her, look for modes of articulating it that would render her life livable.[37] Antigone, therefore, provides a ground for ethics not in the sense of being a model for moral authority, but because her attempts to articulate her own moral agency pose the question that Butler sees as foundational to ethics: which lives are allowed to be livable?

In her writings since *Antigone's Claim*, Butler has become increasingly preoccupied with the "livability" question.[38] The problem for her is that the ways in which this question has traditionally been answered in moral theory has required *either* the establishment norms of recognition that somehow transcend the nature of the human condition (the moral point of view) *or* the acceptance of the contextually dominant norms of recognition as authoritative (cultural relativism). Butler is unhappy with both of these responses. With the first because, following Hegel's critique of the moral point of view, she regards all sources of moral authority as necessarily contaminated by natural and spiritual determinations that the agent is incapable of either wholly recognizing or controlling. With the second, again following Hegel, because culture is not a self-identical whole that can be known and there are, therefore, no grounds on which to dismiss alternatives to dominant articulations of the norms governing livability in any given case that don't also require moral transcendence, because they require some account of why dominant norms should be privileged as such.

Butler argues that any adequate account of ethics needs to recognize the contaminated and "given over" position of the ethical subject and that the ethical meaning of the universal is always capable of re-signification. At the same time, however, any such re-signification is always conditioned and, therefore, fails to keep the promise of the idea of universality, even as it keeps that promise in place. For Butler, this does not mean the abandonment of universality as a meaningful category in ethics.[39] Part of her argument is that the universal is an ineradicable category, whether we like it or not, when we make ethical claims, even when those are the claims of culture, we always invoke the universal. The challenge is to articulate an ethics that simultaneously recognizes the universal's both contamination and promise. For Butler this means an ethics that is grounded in a process of cultural translation.

> Clearly there is an establishing rhetoric for the assertion of universality and a set of norms that are invoked in recognition of such claims. Moreover, there is no cultural consensus on an international level about what ought and ought not to be a claim to universality, who may make it, and what form it ought to take. Thus, for the claim to work, for it to compel consensus, and for the claim, performatively to enact the very universality it enunciates, it must undergo a set of translations into the various rhetorical and cultural contexts in which the meaning and force of universal claims are made.[40]

As Butler points out, translation may be understood in two different ways. It can operate as a process in which competing meanings are adjudicated in relation to an authoritative meta-language. Or, it can be understood as a process of trial and error in which the understanding and endorsement of ethical claims depends crucially on the scope for recognition and negotiation between the authors, audiences, and referents of the claims in question. The former understanding is the one implied by the moral point of view, whether in the form of the Kantian moral judge or of the beautiful soul. But Butler's analysis of the moral point of view, following Hegel, demonstrates that there is no such fixed, authoritative ground for moral judgment. Cultural translation, therefore, cannot be a matter of subsuming all languages under a meta-language. Neither, however, is cultural translation a straightforward impossibility as would be implied by certain versions of cultural relativism. Instead it should be understood as the ongoing attempt to forge common ground across different languages, whilst acknowledging not only that there may be limits to mutual intelligibility but also that, as with Antigone, no one is actually "master" of the language and, therefore, the sources of moral authority that they understand as their own. This is a process, according to Butler, that allows for (even if it cannot guarantee) the possibility of mutual transformation and the articulation of more inclusive moral vocabularies. At the heart of this possibility is a "letting go" that is foreign to the ways of thinking about moral judgment that, as Hegel pointed out in his critique of the moral point of view, are embedded in the predominant ethical traditions of the post-reformation, post-enlightenment West. Within that context, the mark of moral authority is moral conviction and the heroic stance of "here I stand, I can do no other." In contrast, Butler argues that the ethical promise of universality depends on willingness to recognize its (the universal's) essential contingency and, therefore, the limitations of any given moral stance.

> To acknowledge one's own opacity or that of another does not transform opacity into transparency. To know the limits of acknowledgement is to know even this fact in a limited way; as a result, it is to experience the very limits of knowing. This can, by the way, constitute a disposition of humility and generosity alike.[41]

Butler's rejection of the self-certainties inherent in the moral point of view are interestingly reminiscent of Irigaray's critique of dialectic and appropriative language, in favor of an ideal of dialogue and speech. In her account of the dialogic ethical relation between self and other, Irigaray is insistent that there is no "metalanguage" that governs the meaning of that communicative exchange. And, as with Butler's ethical imperative of cultural translation, the creation of new meanings is seen as vital to ethics in the contemporary world, and the abandonment of self-certainty is a prerequisite of that creation.

> How will we respond, or correspond, to the challenges of globalization, if not through the invention of another language? Through making our way toward finding a language that is more communicative and less subjected to information? Through cultivating the relation between two subjects in the respect for difference(s)? Which allows creating little by little a language of exchange between cultures, traditions, sexes, generations.[42]

CONCLUSION

I have argued that the implications of Hegel's reading of Antigone for feminist ethics cannot be realized in ethical theories that remain attached to the moral point of view, either in the form of the "hard heart of judgment" or of the "beautiful soul." However, the abandonment of the moral point of view is not easy, as we can see both in the ongoing disputes between ethics of justice and ethics of care, and in the critical debates over the significance of Irigaray's ethics of sexual difference. The readings of the character of Antigone offered by Hegel, Irigaray, and Butler all point to the need for careful examination of the complex conditions of possibility that underpin the ethical resonance of her claims to justice. In all cases, their arguments imply an ethics that is extremely cautious about moral claims that transcend time and place, and one for which there are no shortcuts, through moral self-certainty, to avoid the politics of actual feminist contestation. Rather ethics becomes a painful and incremental process in which reckoning with our own incapacity to know ourselves is intrinsically linked to our potential capacity to communicate with others in ways that are non-assimilative and may make it possible to forge intersubjective links in the construction of new forms of ethical life.

NOTES

1. Carol Gilligan first formulated the "ethic of care"/"ethic of justice" distinction in her groundbreaking book, *In a Different Voice: Psychological Theory and Women's Development* (Cambridge, MA: Harvard University Press, 1982). In summary: "justice" approaches to feminist ethics are premised on universal principles that apply to the values and conduct of all human beings; "care" approaches to feminist ethics are closer to virtue ethics, in that they premise feminist morality

on virtues and values associated with the practice of care. For further discussion of the ethics of care and its critics, see: Nell Noddings, *Caring: A Feminine Approach to Ethic and Moral Education* (Berkeley: University of California Press, 1984); Seyla Benhabib, "The Debate over Women and Moral Theory Revisited," in *Situating the Self: Gender, Community and Postmodernism in Contemporary Ethics* (Cambridge: Polity Press, 1992); Virginia Held, *Feminist Morality: Transforming Culture, Society and Politics* (Chicago: University of Chicago Press, 1993) and *The Ethics of Care: Personal, Political and Global* (Oxford: Oxford University Press, 2006); Rosalyn Diprose, *The Bodies of Women* (London: Routledge, 1994); G. Clement *Care, Autonomy and Justice: Feminism and the Ethic of Care* (Boulder, CO: Westview Press, 1996); Martha Nussbaum, *Women and Human Development: The Capabilities Approach* (Cambridge: Cambridge University Press, 2000), 264–270.

2. Kimberly Hutchings, *Hegel and Feminist Philosophy* (Cambridge: Polity Press, 2003), 8, 130–132.

3. In *Hegel and Feminist Philosophy* I drew a sharp contrast between my interpretation of the implications of the section on *Antigone* in Hegel's text and, amongst others, the interpretations offered by Irigaray and Butler. I suggested, in brief, that both Irigaray's and Butler's readings, though radically different to each other, threatened to collapse back into the oppositions and exclusions that both thinkers identify as crucial to Hegel's masculinist philosophy. At the heart of my critique was the claim that in their very different ways Irigaray and Butler both provide an account of Antigone's ethical authority that links that authority to a claim to absolute difference. This claim, I argued undermined the feminist project to escape the binary terms of patriarchal thought (Hutchings, *Hegel and Feminist Philosophy*, 80–111). In reconsidering these arguments, I remain convinced of my central claim as to the key message of Hegel's text. However, I have also come to see that the constructive implications of Irigaray's and Butler's readings of Hegel for feminist ethical and political thought may be less antithetical either to the reading I want to offer or in relation to each other, than I had initially argued.

4. Hegel, *Phenomenology of Spirit*, trans. A. V. Miller (Oxford: Oxford University Press, 1977), 364–409. Hegel is discussing moral self-consciousness as a specific aspect of his own present, but it is striking how relevant his discussion remains to debates in contemporary ethical philosophy, from mainstream arguments between utilitarians, contractarians and Kantians to feminist disputes over justice versus care.

5. Ethical life (*Sittlichkeit*) refers in Hegel's work not simply to the prevalent ethical values within any particular society, but to the ways in which these are concretely institutionalized, collectively in formal and informal social, political, economic and religious laws, language, customs and practices, and at the level of the individual's lived identification or lack of identification with these mores. Ethical life is always complex and frequently contradictory on Hegel's account. In many

respects, the concept of "ethical life" in Hegel overlaps with his concepts of objective and subjective "spirit" (*Geist*). For Hegel, "spirit" does not signify anything other-worldly. It refers essentially to self-determining being as it is instantiated in both individual and collective life. Spirit is contrasted with nature (the realm of determinate being) and thought (the abstract conceptualization of the movement or logic of both nature and spirit). Objective spirit encompasses collective life in its outward manifestations, from buildings and clothes to laws and institutions. Subjective spirit refers to self-conscious individuals and their self-understandings.

6. Hegel, *Phenomenology*, 365.

7. Ibid., 381; 382–383; see also Hutchings, *Hegel and Feminist Philosophy*, 122–127.

8. Hegel, *Phenomenology*, 400.

9. Hegel, "The Spirit of Christianity and Its Fate," in *Early Theological Writings*, trans. M. Knox, fragments trans. R. Kroner (Chicago: University of Chicago Press, 1948); *Phenomenology*, 400; 404; 407.

10. Ibid., 403.

11. Hegel himself makes this parallel explicit in the earlier text, when he draws a direct connection between legalism in Judaism and the autonomous (self-legislating) Kantian judge (Hegel, 1948, 211)

12. Hegel's account of the "beautiful soul" draws on a character in Goethe's *Wilhelm Meister's Apprenticeship and Travels*, see Gillian Rose, *The Broken Middle: Out of Our Ancient Society* (Oxford: Blackwell, 1992), 188–192.

13. To draw on Hegel's discussion of *Antigone* in this way could be claimed to be wholly inappropriate in Hegelian terms, given that Antigone belongs to an entirely different, and superseded, form of spirit than the modern figures of the "beautiful soul" and the "hard heart of judgment." However, Hegel's own attitude to the character of Antigone, as with his views on women in general, is hardly consistent in this respect, his discussions of her in the *Phenomenology*, in his *Aesthetics* (see Chapter Three in this volume) and in *Elements of the Philosophy of Right* suggest that he did not confine her ethical significance to her own era, see *Elements of the Philosophy of Right*, ed. A. Wood and trans. H. B. Nisbet (Cambridge: Cambridge University Press, 1991), 189, 206.

14. The section in the *Phenomenology of Spirit* entitled "Spirit" begins with Ancient Greece and the ethical life embodied in Greek tragedy and ends with the defeat of modern moral consciousness. At each stage in his historical journey through Western thought and history, Hegel explores the forms of ethical self-reflection specific to different forms of spirit and traces their different faultlines.

15. Hegel, *Phenomenology*, 266–289.

16. Ibid., 267–276.

17. Ibid., 280.

18. Ibid., 278.
19. Ibid., 285.
20. Judith Butler, *Antigone's Claim: Kinship between Life and Death* (New York: Columbia University Press, 2000), 88.
21. Luce Irigaray, *Speculum of the Other Woman*, trans. G. C. Gill (Ithaca: Cornell University Press, 1985): 214–226.
22. Irigaray, *An Ethics of Sexual Difference*, trans. C. Burke and G. C. Gill (London: Athlone Press, 1993), 108; *Thinking the Difference: For a Peaceful Revolution*, trans. K. Montin (London: Athlone Press, 1994), 16.
23. *Ethics of Sexual Difference*: 86–90; *Thinking the Difference*, 67–87.
24. Ibid., 57; *The Way of Love*, trans. H. Bostic and S. Pluhàček (London: Continuum, 2002), 47.
25. Ibid., 66.
26. Ibid., 72; 81–82.
27. Ibid., 78–79.
28. Ibid., 129.
29. Irigaray, *Je, Tu, Nous: Towards a Culture of Sexual Difference*, trans. A. Martin (New York: Routledge, 1993), 40–41. .
30. See Deborah Berghoffen, "Irigaray's Couples," in *Returning to Irigaray: Feminist Philosophy, Politics and the Questions of Unity*, ed. Maria C. Cimitile and Elaine P. Miller (Albany: State University of New York Press, 2007), 157.
31. Irigaray, *Thinking the Difference*, 16.
32. See Penelope Deutscher, *A Politics of Impossible Difference: The Later Work of Luce Irigaray* (Ithaca: Cornell University Press, 2002); and also Deutscher, "Between East and West and the Politics of 'Cultural Ingénuité': Irigaray on cultural difference"; Ann V. Murphy, "Beyond Performativity and against Identification: Gender and Technology in Irigaray"; and Berghoffen "Irigaray's Couples," all in *Returning to Irigaray*, op. cit.
33. Irigaray, *Between East and West: From Singularity to Community*, trans. S. Pluhàček (New York: Columbia University Press, 2002), 129.
34. *Between East and West*, op. cit.
35. Deutscher, "Between East and West," 142–143.
36. Butler, *Antigone's Claim*: 1.
37. Ibid., 78–82.
38. See Butler, "Restaging the Universal: Hegemony and the Limits of Formalism" and "Competing Universalities," in *Contingency, Hegemony and Universality: Contemporary Dialogues of the Left*, by J. Butler, E. Laclau and S. Žižek (London: Verso, 2000); *Undoing Gender* (New York: Routledge, 2004); *Precarious Life: The Powers of Mourning and Violence* (London: Verso, 2004); *Giving an Account*

of Oneself (New York: Fordham University Press, 2005); *Frames of War: When Is Life Grievable?* (London: Verso, 2009).

39. Butler, "Restaging the Universal," 24–25.
40. Ibid., 35.
41. Butler, *Giving an Account*, 42.
42. Irigaray, *The Way of Love*, 42.

CHAPTER SIX

Longing for Recognition

Judith Butler

Jessica Benjamin's recent work seeks to establish the possibility for intersubjective recognition, thereby setting a philosophical norm for a therapeutic discourse. Her work has always been distinctively defined by its groundedness in critical social theory and clinical practice.[1] Whereas the Frankfurt School maintained a strong theoretical interest in psychoanalysis and spawned the important work of Alexander and Margarete Mitscherlich, *The Inability to Mourn*,[2] among other texts, it has been rare since that time to find a critical theorist trained in that venue who actively practices psychoanalysis, and whose theoretical contributions combine critical reflection and clinical insight in the way that Benjamin's does. Central to her philosophical inheritance is the notion of recognition itself, a key concept that was developed in Hegel's *Phenomenology of Spirit* and which has assumed new meanings in the work of Jürgen Habermas and Axel Honneth.[3] In some ways, Benjamin's work relies on the presumption that recognition is possible, and that it is the condition under which the human subject achieves psychic self-understanding and acceptance.

There are several passages in almost any text of hers that give a sense of what recognition is. It is not the simple presentation of a subject for another that facilitates the recognition of that self-presenting subject by the Other. It is, rather, a process that is engaged when subject and this reflection does not result in a collapse of the one into the Other (through an incorporative identification, for instance) or a projection that annihilates the alterity of the Other. In Benjamin's appropriation of the Hegelian notion of recognition, recognition is a normative ideal, an aspiration that guides clinical practice. Recognition implies that we see the Other as separate, but as structured psychically in ways that are shared. Of utmost importance for Benjamin, following Habermas in some ways, is the notion that communication itself becomes both the vehicle and the example of recognition. Recognition is neither an act that one performs, nor is it literalized as the event in which we each "see" one another and are "seen." It takes place through communication, primarily but not exclusively verbal, in which subjects are transformed by virtue of the communicative practice in which they are engaged. One can see how this model supplies a norm for both social theory and therapeutic practice. It is to Benjamin's credit that she has elaborated a theory that spans both domains as productively as it does.

One of the distinctive contributions of her theory is to insist that intersubjectivity is not the same as object relations, and that "intersubjectivity" adds to object relations the notion of an external Other, one who exceeds the psychic construction of the object in complementary terms. What this means is that whatever the psychic and fantasmatic relation to the object may be, it ought to be understood in terms of the larger dynamic of recognition. The relation to the object is not the same as the relation to the Other, but the relation to the Other provides a framework for understanding the relation to the object. The subject not only forms certain psychic relations to objects, but the subject is formed by and through those psychic relations. Moreover, these various forms are implicitly structured by a struggle for recognition in which the Other does and does not become dissociable from the object by which it is psychically represented. This struggle is one that is characterized by a desire to enter into a communicative practice with the Other in which recognition takes place neither as an event nor a set of events, but as an ongoing process, one that also poses the psychic risk of destruction. Whereas Hegel refers to "negation" as the risk that recognition always runs, Benjamin retains this term to describe the differentiated aspect of relationality: the Other is not me, and from this distinction, certain psychic consequences follow. There are problematic ways of handling the fact of negation, and these are, of course, explained in part through Freud's conception of aggression and Kleinian conceptions of destruction. For Benjamin, humans form psychic relations with Others on the basis of a necessary negation, but not all of those relations must be destructive. Whereas the psychic response that seeks to master and dispel that negation is destructive, that destruction is precisely what needs to be worked through in the process of recognition. Because human psychic life is characterized by desires both for omnipotence and for contact, it vacillates between "relating to the object and recognizing the outside [O]ther."[4]

In a sense, Benjamin tells us that this vacillation or tension is what constitutes human psychic life fundamentally or inevitably. And yet, it seems that we are also to operate under a norm that postulates the transformation of object-relations into modes of recognition, whereby our relations to objects are subsumed, as it were, under our relation to the Other. To the extent that we are successful in effecting this transformation, we seem to put this tension into play in the context of a more fluid notion of communicative practice mentioned above. Benjamin is insistent upon the "inherently problematic and conflictual make-up in the psyche,"⁵ and she does not go back on her word. But what becomes difficult to understand is what meaning recognition can and must assume, given the conflictual character of the psyche. Recognition is at once the norm toward which we invariably strive, the norm that ought to govern therapeutic practice, and the ideal form that communication takes when it becomes a transformative process. Recognition is, however, also the name given to the process that constantly risks destruction and which, I would submit, could not be recognition without a defining or constitutive risk of destruction. Although Benjamin clearly makes the point that recognition risks falling into destruction, it seems to me that she still holds out for an ideal of recognition in which destruction is an occasional and lamentable occurrence, one that is reversed and overcome in the therapeutic situation, and which does not turn out to constitute recognition essentially.

My understanding of her project is that whereas the tension between omnipotence and contact, as she puts it, is necessary in psychic life, there are ways of living and handling that tension that do not involve "splitting," but which keep the tension both alive and productive. In her view, we must be prepared to overcome modes of splitting that entail disavowal where we either disparage the object to shore ourselves up, or project our own aggression onto the object to avoid the psychically unlivable consequences that follow when that aggression is recognized as our own. Aggression forms a break in the process of recognition, and we should expect such "break-downs," to use her words, but the task will be to work against them and to strive for the triumph of recognition over aggression. Even in this hopeful formulation, however, we get the sense that recognition is something other than aggression or that, minimally, recognition can do without aggression. What this means is that there will be times when the relation to the Other relapses into the relation to the object, but that the relation to the Other can and must be restored. It also means that misrecognition is occasional, but not a constitutive or insurpassable feature of psychic reality, as Lacan has argued, and that recognition, conceived as free of misrecognition, not only ought to triumph, but can.

In what follows, I hope to lay out what I take to be some of the consequences of this view and its component parts. For if it is the case that destructiveness can turn into recognition, then it follows that recognition can leave destructiveness behind. Is this true? Further, is the relationship assumed by recognition dyadic, given the qualification that the process of recognition now constitutes "the third" itself based upon a disavowal of others forms of triangulation? And is there a way to think triangulation apart from oedipalization? Does the dyadic model for recognition, moreover, help us to understand the particular convergences of straight, bisexual, and gay desire that invariably refer desire outside the dyad in which it only apparently occurs? Do we want to remain within the complementarity of gender as we seek to understand, for instance, the particular interplay of gender and desire in transgender? Finally, I'll return to Hegel to see the way in which he offers us another version of the self than the one emphasized by Benjamin in order to understand whether a certain division in the subject can become the occasion and impetus for another version of recognition.

From Complementary to Postoedipal Triangularity

Over time, Benjamin's work has moved from an emphasis on complementarity, which assumes a dyadic relation, to one that accommodates a triadic relation. What is the third term in relation to which the dyad is constituted? As one might expect from her earlier contributions, the triad will not be reducible to oedipalization. It will not be the case that the dyad is tacitly and finally structured in relation to a third, the tabooed parental object of love. The third emerges, however, in a different way for Benjamin, indeed, in a way that focuses not on prohibition and its consequences but on "both partners [in a] pattern of excitement." This pattern is the third, and it is "co-created": "outside the mental control of either partner we find a site of mediation, the music of the third to which both attune."[6] Indeed, the third constitutes an ideal of transcendence for Benjamin, a reference point for reciprocal desire that exceeds representation. The third is not the concrete Other who solicits desire, but the Other of the Other who (or which) engages, motivates, and exceeds a relation of desire at the same time that it constitutes it essentially.

Benjamin is careful in *The Shadow of the Other* to distinguish her position from that of Drucilla Cornell or any position inspired by the Levinasian notion that the Other is transcendent or ineffable (93). But in her most recent writing, she admits this Other is external to the psychic object, nearing the Levinasian position and so perhaps enacting for us the expansive possibilities of the critic who makes an identification with formerly repudiated possibilities.

This way of approaching the triadic relation is a very happy one, and I'll confess that I am not sure it is finally credible or, indeed, desirable. It is indisputably impressive, though, as an act of faith in relationships and, specifically, in the therapeutic relationship itself. But as an act of faith, it is difficult to "argue" with. So what I hope to do in what follows is less to counter this exemplar of happiness than to offer a few rejoinders from the ranks of ambivalence where some of us continue to dwell. Further, I think that some less jubilant reflections on triangulation and the triadic relation (to be distinguished from one another) may be possible and will not return us to the prison house of Oedipus with its heterosexist implications for gender. Finally, I'd like to suggest that a triadic structure for thinking about desire has implications for thinking gender beyond complementarity and reducing the risk of heterosexist bias implied by the doctrine of complementarity.

I'm no great fan of the phallus, and have made my own views known on this subject before,[7] so I do not propose a return to a notion of the phallus as the third term in any and all relations of desire. Nor do I accept the view that would posit the phallus as the primary or originary moment of desire, such that all desire either extends through identification or mimetic reflection of the paternal signifier. I understand that progressive Lacanians are quick to distinguish between the phallus and the penis and claim that the "paternal" is a metaphor only. What they do not explain is the way the very distinction that is said to make "phallus" and "paternal" safe for use continues to rely upon and reinstitute the correspondences, penis/phallus and paternal/maternal that the distinctions are said to overcome. I believe in the power of subversive re-signification to an extent and applaud efforts to disseminate the phallus and to cultivate, for instance, dyke dads and the like. But it would be a mistake, I believe, to privilege either the penis or paternity as the terms to be most widely and radically re-signified. Why those terms rather than some others? The "other" to these terms is, of course, the question interrogated here, and Benjamin has helped us to imagine, theoretically, a psychic landscape in which the phallus does not control the circuit of psychic effects. But are we equipped to rethink the problem of triangulation now that we understand the risks of phallic reduction?

The turn to the pre-oedipal has been, of course, to rethink desire in relation to the maternal, but such a turn engages us, unwittingly, in the resurrection of the dyad: not the phallus, but the maternal, for the two options available are "dad" and "mom." But are there other kinds of descriptions that might complicate what happens at the level of desire and, indeed, at the level of gender and kinship? Benjamin clearly asks these questions, and her critique of the Lacanian feminist insistence on the primacy of the phallus is, in large part, a critique of both its presumptive heterosexuality and the mutually exclusive logic through which gender is thought. Benjamin's use of the notion of "over-inclusiveness" implies that there can be, and ought to be, a post-oedipal recuperation of over-inclusive identifications characteristic of the pre-oedipal phase, where identifications with one gender do not entail repudiations of another.[8] Benjamin is careful in this context to allow for several coexisting identifications and even to promote as an ideal for therapeutic practice the notion that we might live such apparently inconsistent identifications in a state of creative tension. She shows as well how the oedipal framework cannot account for the apparent paradox of a feminine man loving a woman, a masculine man loving a man. To the extent that gender identification is always considered to be at the expense of desire, coherent genders might be said to correspond without fail to heterosexual orientations.

I am in great sympathy with these moves, especially as they are argued in Chapter 2, "Constructions of Uncertain Content," in *Shadow of the Other*. Although I continue to have some questions about the doctrine of "over-inclusiveness," in spite of liking its consequences, I believe that Benjamin is working toward a non-heterosexist psychoanalysis in this book (45–49). I do think, however, that (a) triangulation might be profitably rethought beyond oedipalization or, indeed, as part of the very post-oedipal displacement of the oedipal; (b) certain assumptions about the primacy of gender dimorphism limit the radicalism of Benjamin's critique; and (c) that the model of over-inclusiveness cannot quite become the condition for recognizing difference that Benjamin maintains because it resists the notion of a self that is ek-statically[9] involved in the Other, de-centered through its identifications which neither excludes nor includes the Other in question.

Let us first consider the possibilities of post-oedipal triangulation. I suggest we take as a point of departure the Lacanian formulation that suggests that desire is never merely dyadic in its structure. I would like to see not only whether this formulation can be read apart from any reference to the phallus, but whether it might also lead in directions that would exceed the Lacanian purview. When Jean Hyppolite introduces the notion of "the desire of desire" in his commentary on Hegel's *Phenomenology of Spirit*, he means to suggest not only that desire seeks its own renewal (a Spinozistic claim), but that it also seeks to be the object of desire for the Other.[10] When Lacan rephrases this formulation of Hyppolite, he enters the genitive in order to produce an equivocation: "desire is the desire *of* the Other" (my emphasis).[11] What does desire desire? It clearly still continues to desire itself; indeed, it is not clear that the desire which desires is different from the desire that is desired. They are homonymically linked, at a minimum, but what this means is that desire redoubles itself; it seeks its own renewal, but in order to achieve its own renewal, it must reduplicate itself and so become something other to what it has been. It does not stay in place as a single desire, but becomes other to itself, taking a form that is outside of itself. Moreover, what desire wants is the Other, where the Other is understood as its generalized object. What desire also wants is the Other's desire, where the Other is conceived as a subject of desire. This last formulation involves the grammar of the genitive, and it suggests that the Other's desire becomes the model for the subject's desire.[12] It is not that I want the Other to want me, but I want to the extent that I have taken on the desire of the Other and modeled my desire after the Other's desire. This is, of course, only one perspective within what is arguably a kaleidoscope of perspectives. Indeed, there are other readings of this formulation, including the oedipal one: I desire what the Other desires (a third object), but that object belongs to the Other, and not to me; this lack, instituted through prohibition, is the foundation of my desire. Another oedipal reading is the following: I want the Other to want me rather than the sanctioned object of its desire; I want no longer to be the prohibited object of desire. The inverse of the latter formulation is: I want to be free to desire the one who is prohibited to me and, so, to take the Other away from the Other and, in this sense, *have* the Other's desire.

Lacan's way of formulating this position is, of course, derived in part from Lévi-Strauss's theory of the exchange of women. Male clan members exchange women in order to establish a symbolic relation with other male clan members. The women are "wanted" precisely because they are wanted by the Other. Their value is thus constituted as an exchange value, though one that is not reducible to Marx's understanding of that term. Queer theorist Eve Sedgwick came along in *Between Men* and asked who was, in fact, desiring whom in such a scene.[13] Her point was to show that which first appears to be a relation of a man who desires a woman turns out to be implicitly a homosocial bond between two men. Her argument was not to claim, in line with the "phallus" affiliates, that the homosocial bond comes at the expense of the heterosexual, but that the homosocial (distinct from the homosexual) is articulated precisely through the heterosexual. This argument has far-reaching consequences for the thinking of both heterosexuality and homosexuality, as well as for thinking the symbolic nature of the homosocial bond (and, hence, by implication, all of the Lacanian symbolic). The point is not that the phallus is had by one and not by another, but that it is circulated along a heterosexual and homosexual circuit at once, thus confounding the identificatory positions for every "actor" in the scene. The man who seeks to send the woman to another man sends some aspect of himself, and the man who receives her, receives him as well. She circuits, but is she finally wanted, or does she merely exemplify a value by becoming the representative of both men's desire, the place where those desires meet, and where they fail to meet, a place where that potentially homosexual encounter is relayed, suspended, and contained?

I raise this issue because it seems to me that it is not possible to read the profound and perhaps inescapable ways that heterosexuality and homosexuality are defined through one another. For instance, to what extent is heterosexual jealousy often compounded by an inability to avow same-sex desire?[14] A man's woman lover wants another man, and even "has" him, which is experienced by the first man at his own expense. What is the price that the first man has to pay? When, in this scene, he desires the desire of the Other, is it his lover's desire (let us imagine that it is)? Or is it also the prerogative that his lover has to take another *man* as her lover (let us imagine that it also is)? When he rages against her for her infidelity, does he rage because she refuses to make the sacrifice that he has already made? And even though such a reading might suggest that he identifies with her in the scene, it is unclear how he identifies, or whether it is, finally, a "feminine" identification. He may want her imagined position in the scene, but what does he imagine her position to be? It cannot be presumed that he takes her position to be feminine, even if he imagines her in a receptive response to the other man. If that is his receptivity that he finds relocated there at the heart of his own jealous fantasy, then perhaps it is more appropriate to claim that he imagines her in a position of passive male homosexuality. Is it, finally, really possible to distinguish in such a case between a heterosexual and a homosexual passion? After all, he has lost her, and that enrages him, and she has acted the aim he cannot or will not act, and that enrages him.

Benjamin's insistence that we do not have to understand desire and identification in a relation of mutual exclusion clearly makes room for such simultaneous passions. But does she give us a way to describe how heterosexuality becomes a venue for homosexual passion or how homosexuality becomes the conduit for heterosexual passion? It seems that the dyadic structure, when it is imposed upon gender, comes to assume a gender complimentarity that fails to see rigors at work to keep the "dyadic" relation reassuringly just between those two. To claim, as Benjamin does, that the third comes in as the intersubjective process itself, as the "surviving" of destruction as a more livable and creative "negation," is already to make the scene definitionally happier than it can be. Of course, she lets us know that incorporation and destruction are risks that every relation runs, but these are to be worked through in order to reach the possibility of a recognition in which the "two" selves in relation are transformed by virtue of their dynamic relation with one another.

But what are they to do with the other third? Note here that the queer theoretical redescription of the "exchange of woman" does not return to the Lacanian feminist insistence on the primacy of the phallus. It is not that one wants the desire of the Other, because that desire will mimetically reflect one's own position as having the phallus. Nor does one want what other men want in order more fully to identify as a man. Indeed, as the triangulation begins in which heterosexuality is transmuted into homosociality, the identifications proliferate with precisely the complexity that the usual Lacanian positions either rule out or describe as pathology. Where desire and identification are played out as mutually exclusive possibilities against the inescapable background of a (presumptively heterosexual) sexual difference, the actors in the scene I describe can be understood only as trying to occupy positions in vain, warring with a symbolic that has already arranged in advance for their defeat. Thus, the man is trying to "refuse" sexual difference in imagining himself in his lover's position with another man, and so the moralizing relegation of desire to pathology takes place once again within the pre-orchestrated drama of sexual difference. I believe that both Benjamin and I agree on the untenability of such an approach.

But where precisely do we differ? In the first place, as I've suggested above, the relationship cannot be understood apart from its reference to the third, and the third cannot be easily described as the "process" of the relationship itself. I do not mean to suggest either that the third is "excluded" from the dyad or that the dyad must exclude the third for the dyad to take place. No the third is both inside the relationship, as a constituting passion, and "outside" as the partially unrealized and prohibited object of desire.

So let's complicate the scene again by rethinking it from the woman's point of view. Let's imagine that she is bisexual and has sought to have a relationship with "man number 1," putting off for a while her desires for women, which tend to be desires to be a bottom. But instead of finding a woman as the "third," she finds a man (man number 2), and "tops" him. Let's say, for argument's sake, that man number 1 would rather die than be "topped" by his girlfriend, since that would be too "queer" for him. So he knows that she is topping another man, possibly penetrating him anally, and he is furious for several reasons. But what is she after? If she is bisexual, she is a bisexual who happens to be "doing" a few men right now. But perhaps she is also staging a scene in which the outbreak of jealousy puts the relation at risk. Perhaps she does this in order to break from the relationship in order to be free to pursue "none of the above." Would it be possible to see her intensification of heterosexual activity at this moment as a way of (a) seeing her first lover's jealousy and goading him toward greater possessiveness; (b) topping her second lover and gratifying the desire that is off limits to her with the first; (c) setting the two men against one another in order to make room for the possibility of a lesbian relationship in which she is not a top at all; and (d) intensifying her heterosexuality in order to ward off the psychic dangers she associates with being a lesbian bottom? Note that it may be that the one desire is not in the service of another, such that we might be able to say which one is the real and authentic one, and which is simply a camouflage or deflection. Indeed, it may be that this particular character can't find a "real" desire that supersedes the sequence that she undergoes, and that what is real is the sequence itself. But it may be that the affair with man number 2 becomes, indirectly, the venue for the convergence of these passions, their momentary constellation, and that to understand her one must accept something of their simultaneous and dissonant claims on truth. Surely, the pattern in which a man and woman heterosexually involved both amicably break their relationship in order to pursue homosexual desires is not uncommon in urban centers. I don't claim to know what happens here, or what happens when a gay male and a lesbian who are friends start to sleep with one another. But it seems fair to assume that a certain crossing of homosexual and heterosexual passions takes place such that these are not two distinct strands of a braid, but simultaneous vehicles for one another.

I think that this comes out most distinctly in discussions of transgender. It becomes difficult to say whether the sexuality of the transgendered person is homosexual or heterosexual. The term "queer" gained currency precisely to address such moments of productive undecidability, but we have not yet seen a psychoanalytic attempt to take account of these cultural formations in which certain vacillating notions of sexual orientations are constitutive. This becomes most clear when we think about transsexuals who are in transition, where identity is in the process of being achieved, but is not yet there. Or, most emphatically, for those transsexuals who understand transition to be a permanent process. If we cannot refer unambiguously to gender in such cases, do we have the point of reference for making claims about sexuality? In the case of transgender, where transsexualism does not come into play, there are various ways of crossing that cannot be understood as stable achievements, where the gender crossing constitutes, in part, the condition of eroticization itself. In the film *Boys Don't Cry*,[15] it seems that transgender is both about identifying as a boy and wanting a girl, so it is a crossing over from being a girl to being a heterosexual boy. Brandon Teena identifies as a heterosexual boy, but we see several moments of dis-identification as well, where the fantasy breaks down and a tampon has to be located, used, and then discarded with no trace. His identification thus recommences, has to be re-orchestrated in a daily way as a credible fantasy, one that compels belief. The girl lover seems not to know, but this is the not-knowing of fetishism, an uncertain ground of eroticization. It remains unclear whether the girlfriend does not know, even when she claims she does not, and it is unclear whether she knows even when she claims to know. Indeed, one of the most thrilling moments of the film is when the girlfriend, knowing, fully reengages the fantasy. And one of the most brittle moments takes place when the girlfriend, knowing, seems no longer to be able to enter the fantasy fully. The disavowal not only makes the fantasy possible, but strengthens it, and on occasion strengthens it to the point of being able to survive avowal.

Similarly, it would not be possible to say that Brandon's body stays out of the picture, and that this occlusion makes the fantasy possible, since it does enter the picture but only through the terms that the fantasy instates. This is not a simple "denial" of anatomy, but the erotic deployment of the body, its covering, its prosthetic extension for the purposes of a reciprocal erotic fantasy. There are lips and hands and eyes, the strength of Brandon's body on and in

Lana, his/her girlfriend, arms, weight, and thrust. So it is hardly a simple picture of "disembodiment," and hardly "sad." When s/he desires his/her girlfriend's desire, what is it that s/he wants? Brandon occupies the place of the subject of desire, but s/he does not roll on his/her back in the light and ask his/her girl to suck off his/her dildo. Perhaps that would be too "queer," but perhaps as well it would kill the very conditions that make the fantasy possible for both of them. S/he works the dildo in the dark so that the fantasy can emerge in full force, so that its condition of disavowel is fulfilled. S/he occupies that place, to be sure, and suffers the persecution and the rape from the boys in the film precisely because s/he has occupied it too well. Is Brandon a lesbian or a boy? Surely, the question itself defines Brandon's predicament in some way, even as Brandon consistently answers the predicament by doing himself as a boy. It will not work to say that because Brandon must do himself as a boy that this is a sign that Brandon is lesbian. For boys surely do themselves as boys, and no anatomy enters gender without being "done" in some way.

Would it be any easier for us if we were to ask whether the lesbian who only makes love using her dildo to penetrate her girlfriend, whose sexuality is so fully scripted by apparent heterosexuality that no other relation is possible, is a boy or a "boy"? If she says that she can only make love as a "boy," she is, we might say, transgendered in bed, if not in the street. Brandon's crossing involves a constant dare posed to the public norms of the culture, and so occupies a more public site on the continuum of transgender. It is not simply about being able to have sex a certain way, but also about appearing as a masculine gender. So, in this sense, Brandon is no lesbian, despite the fact that the film, caving in, wants to return him to that status after the rape, implying that the return to (achievement of?) lesbianism is somehow facilitated by that rape, returning Brandon, as the rapists sought to do, to a "true" feminine identity that "comes to terms" with anatomy. This "coming to terms" means only that anatomy is instrumentalized according to acceptable cultural norms, producing a "woman" as the effect of that instrumentalization and normalizing gender even as it allows for desire to be queer. One could conjecture that Brandon only wants to be a public boy in order to gain the legitimate right to have sexual relations as he does, but such an explanation assumes that gender is merely instrumental to sexuality. But gender has its own pleasures for Brandon, and serves its own purposes. These pleasures of identification exceed those of desire, and, in that sense, Brandon is not only or easily a lesbian.

Recognition and the Limits of Complementarity

Can gender complementarity help us here? Benjamin writes, "the critique of gender complementarity results in a necessary paradox: It at once upsets the oppositional categories of femininity and masculinity while recognizing that these positions inescapably organize experience."[16] And right before this statement, she asks, "if we do not begin with the opposition between woman and man, with woman's negative position in that binary, we seem to dissolve the very basis for our having questioned gender categories in the first place." But what were those questions, and were they really posed in the right way? Were we right to presume the binary of man and woman when so many gendered lives cannot assume that binary? Were we right to see the relation as a binary when the reference to the tertiary is what permitted us to see the homosexual aims that run through heterosexual relationality? Should we have asked these questions of gender instead? At what psychic price does normative gender become established? How is it that presuming complementarity presumes a self-referential heterosexual that is not definitionally crossed by homosexual aims? If we could not ask these questions in the past, do they not now form part of the theoretical challenge for a psychoanalysis concerned with the politics of gender and sexuality, at once feminist and queer?

It is important to ask these questions in this way if what we want to do is offer recognition, if we believe that recognition is a reciprocal process that moves selves beyond their incorporative and destructive dispositions toward an understanding of another self whose difference from us is ethically imperative to mark. As I hope is clear, I do not have a problem with the norm of recognition as it functions in Benjamin's work, and think, in fact, that it is an appropriate norm for psychoanalysis. But I do wonder whether an untenable hopefulness has entered into her descriptions of what is possible under the rubric of recognition. Moreover, as I indicated above, I question specifically whether over-inclusiveness as she describes it can become the condition for the recognition of a separate Other, neither repudiated nor incorporated.

Let us turn first to the question of whether negation can be clearly separated from destruction, as Benjamin suggests. And then let us reconsider the Hegelian notion of recognition, emphasizing its ek-static structure and ask whether that is compatible with the model of over-inclusiveness. How do such different models fare regarding the ethical question of whether they facilitate recognition, and in what form? Finally, what are the implications of these different notions of recognition for thinking about the self in relation to identity.

Benjamin clearly states that it has been her position since the publication of *The Bonds of Love* that "negation is an equally vital moment in the movement of recognition. Nor can any appeal to the acceptance of otherness afford to leave out the inevitable breakdown of recognition into domination."[17] This represents her position published in 1998. And yet, since then she has moved away from this "inevitable breakdown." Whereas the earlier position seemed to claim that recognition presupposes negativity, her present one seems to imply that negativity is an occasional and contingent event that befalls recognition, but which in no sense defines it. She writes, for instance, that "we should expect breakdowns in recognition," but that "destruction" can be surmounted: "destruction continues until survival becomes possible at a more authentic level." Recognition is the name given to this authentic level, defined as the transcendence of the destructive itself. It is subsequently described as a "Dialogic" process" in which externality is recognized. The analyst in such a situation is not an idealization, for that is still a failure to release the analyst from internality. It is the Other as he or she breaks through either the ideal or the persecutory image that marks the "authentic" emergence of a dialogic encounter and the creation of what Benjamin refers to as "intersubjective space."[18]

My question is whether inter-subjective space, in its "authentic" mode, is really ever free of destruction? And if it is free of destruction, utterly, is it also beyond the psyche in a way that is no longer of use for psychoanalysis? If the "third" is redefined as the music or harmony of dialogic encounter, what happens to the other "thirds"? The child who interrupts the encounter, the former lover at the door or on the phone, the past that cannot be reversed, the future that cannot be contained, the unconscious itself as it rides the emergence of unanticipated circumstance? Surely, these are all negativities, even sources of "destruction" that cannot be fully overcome, sublated, resolved in the harmonious music of dialogue. What discord does that music drown out? What does it disavow in order to be? What if the music turns out to be Mahler? If we accept that the problem in relationship is not just a function of complementarity, of projecting onto another what belongs to the self, of incorporating another who ought properly to be regarded as separate, it will be hard to sustain the model of recognition that remains finally dyadic in structure. But if we accept that desire for the Other might be desire for the Other's desire, and accept as well the myriad equivocal formulations of that position, then it seems to me that recognizing the Other requires assuming that the dyad is rarely, if ever, what it seems. If relations are primarily dyadic, then I remain at the center of the Other's desire, and narcissism is, by definition, satisfied. But if desire works through relays that are not always easy to trace, then who I am for the Other will be, by definition, at risk of displacement. Can one find the Other whom one loves apart from all the Others who have come to lodge at the site of that Other? Can one free the Other, as it were, from the entire history of psychic condensation and displacement or, indeed, from the precipitate of abandoned object-relations that form the ego itself? Or is part of what it means to "recognize" the Other to recognize that he or she comes, of necessity, with a history which does not have oneself as its center? Is this not part of the humility necessary in all recognition, and part of the recognition that is involved in love?

I believe that Benjamin might say that when one recognizes that one is not at the center of the Other's history, one is recognizing difference. And if one does not respond to that recognition with aggression, with omnipotent destruction, then one is in a position to recognize difference as such and to understand this distinguishing feature of the Other as a relation of "negation" (not-me) that does not resolve into destruction. Negation is destruction that is survived. But if this is her response, it seems to me to entail a further recognition of the necessary breakdown of the dyadic into something that cannot be contained or suppressed within that limited structure. The dyad is an achievement, not a presupposition. Part of the difficulty of making it work is precisely caused by the fact that it is achieved within a psychic horizon that is fundamentally indifferent to it. If negation is destruction that is survived, in what does "survival" consist? Certainly, the formulation implies that "destruction" is somehow overcome, even overcome once and for all. But is this ever really possible—for humans, that is? And would we trust those who claimed to have overcome destructiveness for the harmonious dyad once and for all? I, for one, would be wary.

We do not need to accept a drive theory that claims that aggression is there for all times, constitutive of who we are, in order to accept that destructiveness poses itself continually as a risk. That risk is a perennial and irresolvable aspect of human psychic life. As a result, any therapeutic norm that seeks to overcome destructiveness seems to be basing itself on an impossible premise. Now, it may be that the ethical imperative that Benjamin wishes to derive from her distinction between destruction and negation is that the former must continually be survived as negation, that this is an incessant task. But the temporal dynamism she invokes is not that of a struggle that repeats itself, a laboring with destructiveness that must continually be restaged, a relationship where forms of breakdown are expected and inevitable; it is, rather, a dialogue that sustains tension as "goal in itself," a teleological movement, in other words, where the overcoming of destruction is the final end.

When Hegel introduces the notion of recognition in the section on lordship and bondage in *The Phenomenology of Spirit*, he narrates the primary encounter with the Other in terms of self-loss. "Self-consciousness…has *come out of itself*…it has lost itself, for it finds itself as an *other* being (111)." One might understand Hegel to be describing merely a pathological state in which a fantasy of absorption by the Other constitutes an early or primitive experience. But he is saying something more. He is suggesting that whatever consciousness is, whatever the self is, will find itself only through a reflection of itself in another. To be itself, it must pass through self-loss, and when it passes through, it will never be "returned" to what it was. To be reflected in or as another will have a double significance for consciousness, however, since consciousness will, through the reflection, regain itself in some way. But it will, by virtue of the external status of reflection, regain itself as external to itself and, hence, continue to lose itself. Thus, the relationship to the Other will be, invariably, ambivalent. The price of self-knowledge will be self-loss, and the Other poses the possibility of both securing and undermining self-knowledge. What becomes clear, though, is that the self never returns to itself free of the Other, that its "relationality" becomes constitutive of who the self is.

On this last point Benjamin and I agree. Where we differ, I believe, is how we understand this relationality. In my view, Hegel has given us an ek-static notion of the self, one which is, of necessity, outside itself, not self-identical, differentiated from the start. It is the self over here who considers its refection over there, but it is equally over there, reflected, and reflecting. Its ontology is precisely to be divided and spanned in irrecoverable ways. Indeed, whatever self emerges in the course of the *Phenomenology of the Spirit* is always at a temporal remove from its former appearance; it is transformed through its encounter with alterity, not in order to return to itself, but to become a self it never was. Difference casts it forth into an irreversible future. To be a self is, on these terms, to be at a distance from who one is, not to enjoy the prerogative of self-identity (what Hegel calls self-certainty), but to be cast, always, outside oneself, Other to oneself. I believe that this conception of the self emphasizes a different Hegel from the one found in Benjamin's work. It is surely one for which the metaphor of "inclusion," as in "the inclusive self" would not quite work. I'll try to explain why.

In the chapter titled "The Shadow of the Other Subject,"[19] Benjamin offers a sustained discussion, possibly the most important published discussion that exists, on the volume *Feminist Contentions*, which I co-wrote with four other feminist philosophers. She worries that I subscribe to a notion of the self that requires exclusion (102), and that I lack a complementary term for "inclusion." She suggests that if I object to certain ways in which the subject is formed through exclusion, it would make sense that I embrace a normative ideal in which exclusion would be overcome: "only inclusion, the avowal of what was disavowed, in short *owning*, could allow that otherness a place outside the self in the realm of externality, could grant it recognition separate from self" (103). A metaphorical problem emerges, of course, insofar as "inclusion" names the process by which the "external" is recognized. But is this more than a metaphorical difficulty or, rather, does the metaphorical difficulty trace the outlines for us of a more problematic theoretical question at hand? Benjamin offers "inclusion" as the complementary opposite to the negative form of exclusion or abjection that I discuss in *Bodies that Matter*, but she also reserves the term "external" for the aspect of the Other that appears under conditions of authentic dialogue. So, exclusion, in the sense of expulsion or abjection or disavowal, remains within the orbit of a complementary form of splitting, in her view, one that fully eclipses the Other with a disavowed projection. The Other emerges as "external," then, only when it is no longer "excluded." But is the Other "owned" at such a moment, or is there a certain dispossession that takes place that allows the Other to appear to begin with? This would be Laplanche's point, and it would certainly be that of Levinas and Drucilla Cornell as well.[20] It is precisely the movement beyond the logic of owning and disowning that takes the Other out of the narcissistic circuit of the subject. Indeed, for Laplanche, alterity emerges, one might say, beyond any question of owning.[21]

I would suggest that the ek-static notion of the self in Hegel resonates in some ways with this notion of the self that invariably loses itself in the Other who secures that self's existence. The "self" here is not the same as the subject, which is a conceit of autonomous self-determination. The self in Hegel is marked by a primary enthrallment with the Other, one in which that self is put at risk. The moment in "Lordship and Bondage" when the two self-consciousness come to recognize one another is, accordingly, in the "life and death struggle," the moment in which they each see the shared power they have to annihilate the Other and, thereby, destroy the condition of their own self-reflection. Thus, it is at a moment of fundamental vulnerability that recognition becomes possible, and need becomes self-conscious. What recognition does at such a moment is, to be sure, to hold destruction in check. But what it also means is that the self is not its own, that it is given over to the Other in advance of any further relation, but in such a way that the Other does not own it either. And the ethical content of its relationship to the Other is to be found in this fundamental and reciprocal state of being "given over." In Hegel, it would only be partially true to say that the self comes to "include" the Other. (Benjamin would distinguish here between "inclusion" and "incorporation" and, indeed, poses them as opposites.) For the self is always other to itself, and so not a "container" or unity that might "include" Others within its scope. On the contrary, the self is always finding itself as the Other, becoming Other to itself, and this is another way of marking the opposite of "incorporation." It does not take the Other in; it finds itself transported outside of itself in an irreversible relation of alterity. In a sense, the self "is" this relation to alterity.

Although Benjamin sometimes refers to "postmodern" conceptions of the self that presume its "split" and "decentered" character, we do not come to know what precisely is meant by these terms. It will not do to say that there is first a self and then it engages in splitting, since the self as I am outlining it here is beyond itself from the start, and defined by this ontological ek-stasis, this fundamental relation to the Other in which it finds itself ambiguously installed outside itself. This model is, I would suggest, one way of disputing any claim concerning the self-sufficiency of the subject or, indeed, the incorporative character of all identification. And in this sense, it is not so far from Benjamin's position. This may not be "splitting" in the precise psychoanalytic sense, but it may be an ontological dividedness that the psychoanalytic notion of splitting relies upon and elaborates. If we assume that the self exists and then it splits, we assume that the ontological status of the self is self-sufficient before it undergoes its splitting (an Aristophanic myth, we might say, resurrected within the metapsychology of ego psychology). But this is not to understand the ontological primacy of relationality itself and its consequences for thinking the self in its necessary (and ethically consequential) disunity.

Once we think the self this way, one can begin to see how verb forms come closest to expressing this fundamental relationality.

Although common sense would have us ask: Is there not a self who identifies? A self who mourns? Don't we all know that such a self exists? But here it seems that the conventional and pre-critical needs of grammar trump the demands of critical reflection. For it makes good sense to talk about a self, but are we sure it is intact prior to the act of splitting, and what does it mean to insist upon a subject who "performs" its splitting? Is there nothing from which a subject is split off at the outset that occasions the formation of the subject itself? Is there no production of the unconscious that happens concomitantly with the formation of the subject, understood as a self-determining activity? And if it is a self who is already at a distance who splits itself, how are we to understand what splitting means for such a self? Yes, it is possible and necessary to say that the subject splits, but it does not follow from that formulation that the subject was a single whole or autonomous. For if the subject is both split and splitting, it will be necessary to know what kind of split was inaugurative, what kind is undergone as a contingent psychic event, and how those different levels of splitting relate to one another, if at all.

It is, then, one perspective on relationality derived from Hegel which claims that the self seeks and offers recognition to another, but it is another which claims that the very process of recognition reveals that the self is always already positioned outside itself. This is not a particularly "postmodern" insight, since it is derived from German Idealism and earlier medieval ecstatic traditions. It simply avows that that "we" who are relational do not stand apart from those relations and cannot think of ourselves outside of the decentering effects that that relationality entails. Moreover, when we consider that the relations by which we are defined are not dyadic, but always refer to a historical legacy and futural horizon that is not contained by the Other, but which constitutes something like the Other of the Other, then it seems to follow that who we "are" fundamentally is a subject in a temporal chain of desire that only occasionally and provisionally assumes the form of the dyad. I want to reiterate that displacing the binary model for thinking about relationality will also help us appreciate the triangulating echoes in heterosexual, homosexual, and bisexual desire, and complicate our understanding of the relation between sexuality and gender.

We have Jessica Benjamin to thank for beginning the most important dialogue on gender and sexuality that we have at the interstices of philosophy and psychoanalysis. Let us now begin to think again on what it might mean to recognize one another when it is a question of so much more than the two of us.

Notes

1. Jessica Benjamin, *The Bonds of Love: Psychoanalysis, Feminism, and the Problem of Domination* (New York: Pantheon Books, 1988); *Like Subjects, Love Objects: Essays on Recognition and Sexual Difference* (New Haven, CT: Yale University Press, 1995); *The Shadow of the Other: Intersubjectivity and Gender in Psychoanalysis* (New York: Routledge, 1998); "How Was It for You? How Intersubjective Is Sex?" Keynote Presentation. Division 39, American Psychological Association, Boston, April 1998. On file with the author; Afterword to "Recognition and Destruction" [1990] in *Relational Psychoanalysis: The Emergence of a Tradition*, ed. S. A. Mitchell and L. Aron (Hillside, NJ: Atlantic Press, 1999), 201–210.

2. Alexander and Margaret Mitscherlich, *The Inability to Mourn: Principles of Collective Behaviour*, trans. B. Placzek (New York: Grove Press, 1975).

3. G. W. F. Hegel, *Phenomenology of Spirit*, trans. A. V. Miller (Oxford: Oxford University Press, 1977), 111–119; Axel Honneth, *The Struggle for Recognition: The Moral Grammar of Social Conflicts*, trans. Joel Anderson (Cambridge, MA: Polity Press, 1995); Jürgen Habermas, *The Theory of Communicative Action*, 2 vols., trans. Thomas McCarthy (Boston: Beacon Press, 1982).

4. Jessica Benjamin, Afterword to "Recognition and Destruction."

5. Benjamin, *The Shadow of the Other*, 2–3.

6. Benjamin, "'How Was It for You?'" 28.

7. Judith Butler, "The Lesbian Phallus," in *Bodies that Matter: On the Discursive Limits of "Sex"* (New York: Routledge, 1998), 57–92.

8. Benjamin, *Like Subjects, Love Objects*, 54.

9. I offer the etymological version of ecstasy as *ek-stasis* to point out, as Heidegger has done, the original meaning of the term as it implies a standing outside of oneself.

10. Jean Hyppolite, *Genesis and Structure of Hegel's "Phenomenology of Spirit*," trans. Samuel Cherniak and John Heckman (Evanston, IL: Northwestern University Press, 1974), 66.

11. Jacques Lacan, *Écrits: A Selection*, trans. Alan Sheridan (New York: Norton, 1977), 58.

12. For a critique and radicalization of the Lacanian formulation of this account of the mimetic formation of desire, see Mikkel Borsch-Jacobsen, *The Freudian Subject* (Stanford: Stanford University Press, 1988).

13. Eve Sedgwick, *Between Men: English Literature and Male Homosocial Desire* (New York: Columbia University Press, 1985).

14. On Jealousy and the displacement of homosexual desire, see Freud's "Certain Neurotic Mechanisms in Jealousy, Paranoia and Homosexuality," *The Standard Edition of the Complete works of*

Sigmund Freud, vol.18, ed. James Strachey et al. (London: Hogarth Press and the Institute of Psychoanalysis, 1953–1974).

15. *Boys Don't Cry* (Twentieth Century Fox, Director, Kimberly Peirce, 1999).

16. Benjamin, *The Shadow of the Other*, 37.

17. Ibid., 83–84.

18. Afterword to "Recognition and Destruction," 203.

19. *Shadow of the Other*, 79–108.

20. See Drucilla Cornell, *The Philosophy of the Limit* (New York: Routledge, 1992); Emanuel Levinas, *Otherwise than Being*, trans. Alphonso Lingis (Boston: M. Nijhoff, 1981).

21. See Jean Laplanche, *Essays on Otherness*, trans. John Fletcher (London: Routledge, 1999).

PART TWO

Re-Reading Hegel's Method

Beyond Tragedy: Tracing the Aristophanian Subtext of Hegel's *Phenomenology of Spirit*[1]

Karin de Boer

INTRODUCTION

Hegel's account of the Greek ethical world in the *Phenomenology of Spirit* seems to have inspired more feminist philosophers than any other classical text. This is hardly surprising, given Hegel's explicit reflection on the issue of gender in the sections devoted to the ethical world. Since he seems to maintain, moreover, that men and women should comply with the roles assigned to them by nature, it is no more surprising that feminist readings of this text have generally assumed the form of criticism. There is no doubt that these criticisms have played an important part in the development of feminist philosophy. It seems to me, however, that the time has come to assess critically these criticisms of Hegel themselves. In order to contribute to such a critical assessment I will, in this chapter, try to extricate Hegel's text from some of the preconceptions that have guided feminist readings of Hegel. As I see it, these readings generally presuppose, first, that the sections of the *Phenomenology* devoted to Greek ethical life purport to offer an interpretation of Sophocles' *Antigone* and, second, that Hegel uses the *Antigone* to express his own view on the issue of gender.[2] In order to challenge these claims I will reconsider the texts at stake in light of the peculiar method that Hegel deploys throughout the *Phenomenology*. In doing so, I will largely focus on the section entitled *Ethical Action* and dwell in particular on its final pages. I thus hope to reconstruct the hidden subtext of these pages and, hence, to illuminate some of its most abstruse sections.

Hegel's Phenomenological Method

Hegel's *Phenomenology of Spirit*, to put it briefly, seeks to comprehend the modes of thought that have defined human culture. In order to achieve this aim, Hegel cannot relate to his object in the same way as, for instance, sense-certainty does. Whereas sense-certainty comprehends its content—the "this"—as a fixed entity, the *Phenomenology* treats each mode of thought as enacting a particular movement.[3] According to the first moment of this movement, a particular mode of thought grasps its proper principle in a defective way. According to the second moment, it is impelled to recognize the content it took for its very principle as merely one moment of this principle. Thus, the *Phenomenology* considers any particular mode of thought in such a way that its initial self-comprehension turns out to be untenable. Since this mode of thought is defined by this very self-comprehension, however, it cannot survive the recognition of its one-sidedness and must give way to a less one-sided mode of thought. In order to expose this movement, Hegel does not describe the mode of thought at issue from an external point of view. He rather goes along with it so as to let it discover the inadequacy of its initial presupposition by itself. With regard to sense-certainty, Hegel explains this aspect of his method as follows:

> To this end, we do not have to reflect on [the object] and consider what it might truly be, but all we have to do is to examine the way in which sense-certainty relates to this object. (*Phen*, 83/59)

> We must therefore enter the same point...[as sense-certainty], let the truth be shown to us, that is, let ourselves be transformed into the very "I" that knows [its object] with certainty. (*Phen*, 87/63)

It might be argued, accordingly, that the *Phenomenology* consists in a series of undercover operations, each of which lets a particular mode of thought become aware of the contradiction between its actual relation to its object and its ultimate principle. This awareness urges it to incorporate the content it had initially posited over against itself into itself.

Whereas the first chapters of the *Phenomenology* consider modes of thought constitutive of scientific knowledge and basic forms of self-knowledge, the subsequent chapters are concerned with modes of thought Hegel took to be constitutive of Western culture. Since particular cultures are implicitly or explicitly aware of their basic principles and values, Hegel can treat them as particular modes of self-consciousness. He refers to these modes of thought as "spirit" because they do not relate to their contents as objects external to thought, but as products of thought itself (*Phen,* 324/263–64). This does not mean, however, that a finite mode of spirit is able to resolve the opposition between its initial content and its ultimate principle in all respects. Because each finite mode of spirit is defined by this opposition in some way, each of them has to surrender to the methodological principle at work in the *Phenomenology* as a whole. Since this method roughly concords with the way in which particular historical epochs emerged, flourished, and perished, it seems less far-fetched to apply this method to the realm of world history than to the modes of thought constitutive of scientific knowledge. Yet, even when Hegel considers historical modes of spirit he deliberately abstracts from the external side of their development in order to comprehend the logical sequence of their inherent moments.

GREEK ETHICAL LIFE

Let me now turn to the mode of thought that Hegel calls Greek ethical life. Hegel conceives of this mode of thought as a mode of spirit proper because it comprehends its contents—that is, ethical principles—as its own product. The *Phenomenology* defines spirit as the ethical life of a nation that must go through a number of stages to comprehend itself (*Phen,* 325/265). In order to reconstruct the movement that is marked by these stages, Hegel identifies, as it were, with the self-comprehension of classical Greek culture. This should allow him to let Greek culture recognize the one-sidedness of its initial understanding of the principles of ethical life. But how can a nineteenth-century philosopher gain access to the actual self-comprehension of Greek culture? Hegel offers an unambiguous answer to this question in the *Lectures on the Philosophy of History* delivered in Berlin from 1822 onward:

> If we wish to gain the general idea and conception of what the Greeks were, we find it in Sophocles and Aristophanes, in Thucydides and Plato. In these individuals the Greek spirit conceived and thought itself. This is the profounder kind of satisfaction which the spirit of a people attains; but it is "ideal," and distinct from its "real" activity.[4]
>
> It was before this people [of Athens] that the dramas of Aeschylus and Sophocles were performed. ...[This people] originated a group of

men...to which belong, besides those already named, Thucydides, Socrates, Plato, and Aristophanes—the last of whom preserved the entire political seriousness of his people at the time of its corruption and who, imbued with this seriousness, wrote for the sake of his country's weal.[5]

These passages confirm that Hegel's account of Greek ethical life in the *Phenomenology* takes its bearings from classical poets and philosophers. Unlike them, however, Hegel seeks to achieve insight into the *logic* of the process that pushed Greek culture toward its downfall. Since the classical texts on which he draws are exclusively selected in this light, Hegel nowhere purports to offer an interpretation of particular plays. I would like to recall, moreover, that the second part of Hegel's account of Greek ethical life, which concerns the ethical act, does not draw on the *Antigone* alone. The sections devoted to the issue of guilt (*Phen*, 345–46/282–84) are so abstruse that they pertain as much to such tragedies as the *Oresteia* and *Oedipus Rex*. At one point, Hegel refers to Oedipus as someone who acted against the paradigm of divine law by treating his parents as mere citizens (*Phen*, 346/283). Before turning to the last stage of Greek culture, he clearly evokes Aeschylus' *Seven against Thebes*, which is concerned with the conflict between Oedipus's sons Polynices and Eteocles (*Phen*, 349/285).

Instead of defining Greek spirit from an external point of view, Hegel draws on these texts to consider how Greek spirit itself conceived of its ethical principles, the unity of which he terms the ethical substance (*Phen*, 327–28/267). He does this, moreover, by identifying with the prevailing mode of Greek culture, that is, with the paradigm of human law represented by the government. This new paradigm, he suggests, tended to oppose the archaic paradigm of justice that preceded the emergence of democratic city-states, that is, divine law. Greek culture thus threatened to annul one of its vital elements. This is, in my view, the gist of the following passages:

> In this determination, therefore, the ethical substance is actual substance, [is] absolute spirit realized in the manifold of existing consciousness; this spirit is the community, which...here has become manifest for itself in its truth as conscious ethical being and [has become manifest] as the essence *for the consciousness which here is our object*. (*Phen*, 328/267, my emphasis)

> This spirit can be called the human law, because it is essentially in the form of a reality that is conscious of itself. In the form of universality this spirit is the *known* law and the prevailing custom; in the form of

individuality it is the actual certainty of itself in the individual as such, and the certainty of itself as a simple individuality is that spirit as government. (*Phen,* 328/267–68)

Yet this ethical power and public life is confronted with another power, namely, with divine law. For the ethical power of the state, being the movement of self-conscious action, finds its opposite in the simple and immediate essence of the ethical sphere;…as actuality in general it finds in that inner essence something other than it is itself. (*Phen,* 329/268)

In my view, Hegel here identifies with the prevailing paradigm of human law in order to consider how divine law first and foremost presented itself *to it*. Since only the paradigm of human law is clearly articulated in the classical texts that have been preserved, Hegel's choice is not unreasonable (cf. *Phen,* 335/274). I would like to note, however, that Hegel identifies with the prevailing mode of Greek culture only to show that its one-sided determination of ethical life contradicts the very principle of Greek culture as such, that is, the unity of divine law and human law.[6] As we will see, Hegel comprehends this unity as an instance of the unity of individuality and universality at stake in human culture as such.

Evidently, Hegel primarily draws on Sophocles' *Antigone* to comprehend the clash between human law and divine law that he considers to have determined the first stage of classical Greek culture. Yet this does not entail that Hegel's perspective on this clash coincide with that of Sophocles in all respects. Whereas the latter presented the various perspectives on the central conflict without identifying with any of them, Hegel implicitly sets out from the way in which this conflict became present "for" human law. Yet he proceeds in this way to comprehend this tragic conflict—and hence the inherent limit of Greek culture as such—not only as it appeared to it, but also as it is "in and for itself." Since Greek culture itself was unable to adopt this perspective, Hegel must, in his analysis, move back and forth between the actual self-comprehension of Greek culture and the speculative comprehension of its tragic history that is only "for us." The difficulty of the text is partly due to the fact that Hegel generally does not mark the transition between these two perspectives.

The Tragic Clash between Human and Divine Law

As regards the content of the clash that Hegel considered to define the first phase of Greek culture, I will limit myself to a few remarks. As I see it, the conflict between divine law and human law pertained primarily to the conflict between, on the one hand, the archaic paradigm of justice from which fifth-century Greek culture emerged and, on the other, the new paradigm of justice deliberately established by city-states such as Athens. Whereas the former paradigm, relying on such values as kinship, revenge, and pollution, had suited the self-organization of relatively small clans, it could no longer serve as the paradigm of large-scale, urban communities such as Athens. As this new, enlightened paradigm came to hold sway over public life, however, it tended to repress elements of the ancient paradigm that many—and not just women—continued to regard as vitally important. Thus unfolded the clash between divine law and human law that is addressed in many classical tragedies.

Just as in these tragedies, Hegel relates the realm of divine law to the sphere of kinship and women, and human law to the sphere of public life, the government, and men (cf. *Phen*, 340/278). Many tragedies, including the *Antigone*, set out from these neat divisions in order to show that both sides are mutually dependent and destroy themselves if they fail to acknowledge their one-sidedness. Contrary to these tragedies, the *Phenomenology* does not dwell on the way in which individual heroes are impelled to relinquish their initial position. Hegel does not mention, for instance, that Antigone, completely identifying with her duties as a sister, can defend the divine right to bury her brother only in terms proper to the realm of human law. Neither does he discuss how Creon, for his part, gradually develops from a moderate ruler into a tyrant and finally, after the death of his son, completely identifies with his fatherhood. Whereas tragedies reflect the basic clash between divine law and human law by representing the tragic fate of individual heroes, Hegel goes along with this reflection but abstracts from this concrete representation so as to comprehend this clash as a necessary moment in the tragic downfall of Greek culture as such. Greek culture realized that it had a problem, so to speak, but it could neither interpret this problem as the "germ of [its] corruption" (*Phen*, 353/289) nor comprehend its true cause. According to Hegel, Greek culture had to perish because its ethical determinations remained dependent on the element of natural immediacy. Since Greek culture organized the various aspects of its ethical life in accordance with the natural distinction between the male and female sex, it could not grasp the unity of its contrary moments:

> This ruin of the ethical substance...is thus determined by the fact that ethical consciousness is directed on to the law in a way that is

essentially *immediate*. This determination of immediacy implies that nature as such enters into the ethical act. (*Phen*, 353/289, cf. 337/276).

An ethical act of this kind

> contains the moment of crime, because it does not sublate the *natural* allocation of the two laws to the two sexes, but rather...remains within the sphere of natural immediacy. Such an act turns this one-sidedness into guilt, a guilt that consists in seizing only one side of the essence, while adopting a negative attitude toward the other, that is, violating it.[7]

Due to this dependence on the realm of nature, Hegel suggests, both paradigms could perceive their contrary only as a hostile force.[8] He emphasizes that the true resolution of their conflict cannot consist in the subordination of the one by the other:

> The victory of one power and its character, and the defeat of the other side, would thus be only the part and the incomplete work, a work that advances relentlessly toward the equilibrium of both. Only in the sub-jugation (*Unterwerfung*) of both sides alike is absolute right accomplished and has the ethical substance manifested itself as the negative power that absorbs (*verschlingt*) both sides.[9]

Hegel seems to hold that Greek culture actually survived the clash between divine law and human law by incorporating elements of the former into the latter, *but that it thereby did not accomplish the work of spirit in an adequate way*. It did not succeed, that is, in resolving the opposition between individuality and universality that, within Greek culture, initially manifested itself merely in the form of an opposition between divine law and human law. In Hegel's view, the mode of human law that resulted from the incorporation of divine law had, at some point, to emerge as a one-sided paradigm as well. This happened when it became confronted with a new mode of the principle of individuality. The conflict that emerged from this new opposition actually took place during the last decades of the fifth century, when Athens was entangled in an endless war and was losing its command over the rest of Greece. As I will argue in the remainder of this chapter, Hegel primarily draws on Aristophanian comedy to comprehend the fatal implications of this conflict.

THE SELF-DESTRUCTION OF GREEK CULTURE AND ITS REFLECTION IN ARISTOPHANIAN COMEDY

Toward the end of the section it emerges that Hegel seeks to comprehend the whole of Greek culture in light of the one basic conflict between individuality and universality. For this reason, he regards divine law as the first and poorest manifestation of the principle of individuality (cf. *Phen*, 330/269). The sphere of human law that Hegel implicitly considers to define the bloom of Greek culture is no longer opposed to this archaic mode of individuality but contains the principle of individuality as one of its vital moments:

> As a moment of the public community, its activity is not confined merely to the underworld,...but, within the actual nation, it gains an equally public existence and movement. *Taken in this form*, what was represented as a simple movement of the individualized "pathos" now acquires a different appearance, and the crime and the ensuing destruction of the community acquire a form that is proper to their existence. (*Phen*, 351/287, my emphasis)

Whereas Hegel continues to conceive of the public sphere as a particular determination of human law, this sphere no longer opposes itself to divine law, but to the sphere of the family:

> Human law, of which the community constitutes the universal existence, manhood the general activity, and the government the actual enactment, is, moves, and maintains itself by...absorbing into itself...the separation into independent families presided over by womankind, and by keeping them dissolved in the fluid continuity of its own nature. (*Phen*, 351/287–88)

Now it would seem to me that Hegel here refers to the reflection on Greek culture elaborated in Plato's *Republic*. Hegel repeatedly refers to Plato as someone who attempted to ward off the dangers entailed by the principle of individuality.[10] One of the ways in which Plato proposed to do this was, of course, by completely absorbing the sphere of the family into the sphere of the state so as to let women, if talented, share in such activities as hunting and warfare. According to Hegel, however, the sphere of human law cannot annul the sphere of the family and the spirit of individuality it harbors, since its very existence depends on it:

> At the same time, however, the family is [the] element [of human law] as such, individual consciousness [is] the general principle of execution.

Since the community can only maintain itself...by dissolving self-consciousness into universal [consciousness], it creates that which it suppresses and what is at the same time essential to it, that is, womanhood as such, as its internal enemy. (*Phen*, 351/288)

Hegel, I would contend, does not characterize womanhood as "enemy" from an external point of view but seeks to explain how the community, presided over by the government, threatened to oppose itself to one of its inherent moments. In agreement with the thrust of his account of Greek culture as a whole, Hegel describes this process from the perspective of human law. If Hegel here criticizes Plato's position at all, then I do not think that he does so in his own voice.

In the passage from the *Lectures on the Philosophy of History* quoted at the beginning of this chapter, Hegel mentions Sophocles, Aristophanes, Thucydides, and Plato as individuals in which "Greek spirit conceived and thought itself." In various other later texts, he relates both Plato and Aristophanes to the period of decay of Greek culture.[11] Yet whereas Plato responded to the emerging principle of individuality by repressing it, Aristophanes both affirmed and criticized the principle of individuality. In such times of war as Athens was going through, comedy was perhaps the only form in which such criticisms could be voiced. It is, at any rate, the only form that Hegel could employ to explicate—in philosophical terms—the way in which Greek culture itself understood the cause of its imminent downfall. In what follows I will argue that Aristophanian comedies form indeed the hidden subtext of the last section of Hegel's account of Greek ethical life.

Given the emphasis on womanhood in this section, Hegel seems to assume that Athenian culture interpreted the conflict between individuality and universality with which it was faced primarily in terms of the relation between female and male values. This is the case in three of the eleven plays by Aristophanes that have been preserved. In the *Lysistrata*, produced in 411, an Athenian woman called by that name incites women from Athens and other Greek cities to begin a sex strike in order to persuade their husbands to make peace. *The Poet and the Women*, also produced in 411, stages women who set up a lawsuit to condemn Euripides for his negative account of women in his plays. *The Assemblywomen*, produced in 391, is the only one of these comedies to which Hegel explicitly refers in his *Lectures on Aesthetics*.[12] In this play, women, dressed up as men, infiltrate a meeting of the Assembly and persuade the male attendants to hand over all political and juridical power to the women (AW, 238). Their leader,

Praxagora, decrees that all private property must be converted into common property. Another of her laws stipulates that men wishing to make love to a young girl must satisfy an elder woman first (AW, 254). This law completely disregards the principle of wedlock.[13] In each of these plays, both women and men are portrayed as transgressing the roles traditionally assigned to their gender.[14] Just as Antigone, Aristophanes' women leave their homes in order to take part in the public life of the *polis* and to defend their rights. With this in mind, I would like to consider Hegel's infamous remarks on womanhood, which I have divided into five parts.

After Hegel has noted that the community creates womanhood as its internal enemy, he refers to womanhood as "the eternal irony of the community" (*Phen*, 351/288). This remark cannot bear on the *Antigone*, in my view, because at this point in the text Hegel is no longer concerned with the sphere of divine law.[15] In Aristophanes' plays, moreover, women never oppose men in a direct way but imitate their way of life in order to undermine the realm of male values as such. This procedure might well be called ironical. Hegel continues,[16]

(1) Womanhood...changes by intrigue the universal end of the government into a private end.

It seems improbable that Greek women actually ever plotted against the government. They do so, however, in two of the three Aristophanian comedies at issue. In the *Assemblywomen*, women disguise themselves as men to seize power by democratic means. Their leader, Praxagora, practicing her public speech in front of the disguised women, states, "Gentlemen, my interest in the welfare of this state is no less than yours, but I deeply deplore the way in which its affairs are being handled,...you think of nothing but your individual pockets" (AW, 229, cf. 232–33). Yet whereas Praxagora claims that she wishes to save the city, she raises such "family" values as food, sex, and shared property into the ultimate principles of the city as such. Insofar as she intends to convert the city into a large-scale home, Praxagora is not pursuing her private ends. She precisely repudiates politicians, citizens, and army leaders for employing public means for private purposes. Insofar as she annuls the very distinction between the public and the private, however, she might indeed be held to subvert the public realm.

In the *Lysistrata*, Lysistrata defends the sex strike by proclaiming that "we women have the salvation of all Greece in our hands" (Lys, 142). Yet the elderly magistrate who tries to stop the women from barricading the Acropolis claims that they want to keep their husbands and sons at home only so as to secure the interests of the household (Lys, 156). Thus, in both plays women purport to act for the sake of the city, whereas male characters suggest that their actions are driven by private ends. Hegel apparently identifies with the perspective of such male characters as the elderly magistrate in the *Lysistrata*.

(2) Womanhood...transforms [the] universal activity [of the government] into a work of some particular individual.

In the *Assemblywomen*, Praxagora is democratically elected as the leader of the city. Once she has become "Chief of State" (AW, 246, cf. 230), however, she issues decrees without seeking the consent of the citizens. Not unlike Creon, she reigns the city as a tyrant, thus reflecting, perhaps, the deep fear of tyranny felt by most Athenian citizens at the time. This fear—now with regard to the women who occupy the Acropolis—is explicitly voiced by the male chorus in the *Lysistrata*.[17]

(3) Womanhood...perverts the universal property of the state into a property and ornament of the family.

At first sight, this passage can hardly refer to the *Assemblywomen*, where all private property is precisely converted into common property (AW, 242–46) and where the nuclear family is largely dismantled. Yet since Praxagora uses the means of the state to organize huge public diner parties (cf. AW, 251), it might be argued that she deals with public means as she is supposed to deal with private means.[18] This passage might also refer to the view, expressed in the *Lysistrata* by such characters as the magistrate and the male chorus, that women wish to keep their husbands and sons at home for their own good instead of letting them defend the city.

(4) Womanhood...thus turns the earnest wisdom of mature age, which...only thinks of and cares for the universal, into the object of the willful mockery and enthusiastic contempt characteristic of immature youngsters.

Seen from the feminine perspective on male values presented by *Aristophanes*, politicians, magistrates, and generals are concerned not so much with the well-being of the city as with becoming rich and famous. In the *Lysistrata*, women ridicule the elderly magistrate by adorning him with female attributes (Lys, 162–165). *The Poet and the Women* features an elderly man who, dressed up as a woman, equally becomes the object of feminine derision. In the *Assemblywomen*, Praxagora's husband subjects himself to the power of his wife, thus adopting a female role as well. None of these plays, however, attributes the mockery of elderly men to young men. In the *Clouds*, by contrast, the young Pheidippides mocks his father Strepsiades. I can make sense of this passage, therefore, only by assuming that Hegel here combines elements that Aristophanes himself treated separately. This allows Hegel to suggest that women would always side with young men against the elderly men in charge of the city. Here again, Hegel seems to give voice to the perspective of the adult, male citizen, a perspective that Aristophanes' plays always present as challenged by its contraries.

(5) Generally, [womanhood] raises the force of youth into an ultimate value, and this with regard to the son which the mother will come to consider her master, to the brother whom the sister regards as her equal, and to the young man by dint of which the daughter, gaining independence, achieves the enjoyment and respect granted to womankind.

Hegel here seems to express the adult male's frustration about his subordinate role in the private sphere. Women are held to value their sons above their husbands, their brothers above their fathers, and to value their marriage primarily because it grants them independence from their parents. Neither case presents women as subordinated to their husbands. This view, in line with the spirit of Aristophanian comedy, is made particularly clear by Lysistrata. When the magistrate blames women for contributing nothing to the war, she replies,

We've contributed to it twice over and more. For one thing, we've given you sons, and then had to send them off to fight....For another, we're in the prime of our lives, and how can we enjoy it, with our husbands always away on campaign and us left at home like widows? And...what about the unmarried ones who are slowly turning into old maids? (Lys, 164)

In this passage, Lysistrata clearly presents women as motivated by private interests. However, she discusses the significance of sons merely in general terms and does not mention the relation between brothers and sisters. As regards this latter case, Hegel clearly recalls his earlier treatment of the relation between Antigone and Polyneikes. At any rate, Lysistrata's perspective on men clearly evokes the war in which Athens was involved at the time.

Before Hegel, in his turn, addresses the war, he notes that the feminine perspective on young men described in the foregoing passage testifies to the "spirit of individuality." Once again, he notes that the community can maintain itself only by repressing this spirit and yet in so doing converts the latter into a hostile principle.[19] According to this second passage, the community opposes itself no longer to the sphere of womanhood, but to the principle of individuality such as it manifested itself in its angry young men. Whereas the community depended on these men to defend the city, the egoism displayed by politicians and warriors undermined the well-being of the community as a whole.[20] According to Hegel, this mode of the principle of individuality constituted the "germ of corruption" that gradually developed in the natural soil of Greek culture (*Phen* 353/289). Because Greek culture continued to organize its ethical life according to quasi-natural distinctions, it could not incorporate this final manifestation of the principle of individuality and had, in the end, to meet its tragic fate.

CONCLUSION

Hegel's *Phenomenology*, I have argued, comprehends the conflict to which the principle of individuality gave rise by going along the way it was perceived by Greek culture itself. Yet whereas the community dominated by elderly men could perceive the principle of individuality only as a threat, Hegel shows that it thereby deprived itself of elements vital to its own being. Since this latter insight did not become "for itself" in Greek culture, Hegel goes along with the only critical perspective on late Greek culture available to him, that of Aristophanes' comedies. It is not easy to recognize the thrust of these comedies in Hegel's abstruse references, however, because he, first, always adopts the position of the adult male citizen and, second, identifies the sphere of womanhood with the sphere of self-centered individuality. This identification, assumed by some of the male characters, allows Hegel to emphasize the unity of the three modes of individuality he is concerned with. Unlike Hegel, however, Aristophanes does not go along with the tendency of male citizens to assign this principle to the sphere of women alone. Overturning the quasi-natural distinction between female and male values, he rather deploys female voices to criticize the male egoism that he considered to corrupt Athenian public life. However, he ridicules women for completely annulling the distinction between the private and the public, a distinction he apparently considered pivotal to a large-scale community such as Athens.

As I see it, Hegel implicitly draws on the insights achieved in Greek comedy to argue that Greek culture, organizing its ethical life in accordance with the natural distinction between the male and female sex, contradicts the principle of individuality it harbors. I believe, therefore, that contemporary reflections on gender might profit from the insights achieved in the *Phenomenology of Spirit* in unexpected ways. Yet in order to let these insights speak to us we need not identify, like Hegel, with the perspective on womanhood adopted by male adult citizens. We might as well go along with those scarce moments where Aristophanes apparently allows women to speak for themselves. Thus, the female leader of a chorus, impersonated, of course, by a male actor, addresses the audience as follows:

> It's time we women stood up for ourselves,
> and glorified the name
> of a sex that nobody praises much,
> and everyone seems to blame.
> . . .
> Just mention a man: think as hard as you can,
> We'll surpass him, whatever his fame;
> We'll produce, I repeat, a woman to beat
> Any man that you're willing to name.[21]

This passage is taken from *The Poet and the Women*, the comedy that stages women who take to task a famous poet—Euripides—for his distorted representation of female characters in his plays.[22] This reversal of subject and object, comical and liberating, seems to announce not just the corruption of Greek culture, but also the beginning of an age where men and women may identify with particular values in a way that is no longer defined by their sex.[23] As such, this scene might serve as a model for philosophers, male and female, who today seek to confront the prevailing paradigm of modernity with its one-sidedness.

NOTES

1. A different version of the article was published under the title "The Eternal Irony of the Community," *Inquiry* Vol. 52 No. 4 (2009): 311–334.
2. Among those who have criticized Hegel's account of Sophocles' *Antigone* from a feminist perspective are Patricia Mills and Judith Butler. They rightly argue that Hegel does not do justice to the intricacies of Sophocles' play. On their reading, Antigone's position is much more complicated than Hegel recognizes, in that she transcends the sphere of the family, among other ways, by taking part in a *political* debate to defend the principle of the family. See Patricia J. Mills, "Hegel's *Antigone*," in *Feminist Interpretations of G.W.F. Hegel*, ed.

Patricia J. Mills (University Park, PA: Pennsylvania State University Press, 1996), esp. 68–69, 74. In search of a "politics of kinship" that affirms the mutual dependence of the domains of state and kinship, Butler argues that Antigone's speech and action challenge the oppositions between nature and culture, female and male, kinship and state, oppositions that the play as a whole seem to endorse. See Judith Butler, *Antigone's Claim: Kinship between Life and Death* (New York: Columbia University Press, 2000), 5, 29. If, however, Hegel draws on Sophocles' play and other Greek sources to offer an account of the prevailing self-understanding of Greek culture in order to lay bare its one-sidedness, then he cannot be blamed for this reason. I take it that many feminist criticisms of Hegel's *Antigone* are, at least in part, motivated by his conservative account of gender in his later *Philosophy of Right* (esp. §§ 165–166). This text, which falls outside the scope of this essay, is problematic indeed because Hegel here seems to abstract from the crucial difference between ancient and modern forms of ethical life. Kimberly Hutchings, offering a clear account of feminist readings of Hegel's *Antigone*, takes this to imply that Hegel's account of women in the *Phenomenology* transcends the specific context of Greek tragedy as well, thereby losing its validity. See Kimberly Hutchings, *Hegel and Feminist Philosophy* (Cambridge: Polity Press, 2003), 84, 108. As I will argue below, however, it is hard to decide where exactly, if at all, Hegel transcends the context of Greek culture. I am not sure, moreover, that the question concerning Hegel's own view on women necessarily enhances our understanding of his account of Greek culture in the *Phenomenology*.

3. Cf. G. W. F. Hegel, *Phänomenologie des Geistes*, translated as *Phenomenology of Spirit*, by A.V. Miller (Oxford: Oxford University Press, 1977), 89/64 (henceforth "*Phen*"). All references to Hegel's texts are to the Suhrkamp edition. The cited page numbers refer to the German and English pagination respectively. I have sometimes modified the translations.

4. Hegel, *Vorlesungen über die Philosophie der Geschichte*, translated as *The Philosophy of History*, by J. Sibree (Buffalo: Prometheus Books, 1991), 102/76 (henceforth "*LPH*").

5. *LPH*, 318/261. Cf.: "Aristophanes presents to us the absolute contradiction between the true essence of the gods, political and ethical existence, and the subjective attitude of citizens and individuals who should actualize these contents. But this very triumph of the subjective attitude, whatever its insight, constitutes one of the greatest symptoms of the corruption of Greece." Hegel, *Vorlesungen über die Ästhetik 3*, translated as *Aesthetics: Lectures on Fine Art, Vol. 2*, by T. M. Knox (Oxford: Oxford University Press, 1975), 555/1222 (henceforth "*Aesth* 3").

6. By acting, self-consciousness discovers "the contradiction of those powers into which the substance divided itself and their mutual

destruction, as well as the contradiction between, on the one hand, its *knowledge* of the ethical nature of its own action and, on the other, that which is ethical in and for itself, thus finding its own downfall" (*Phen*, 327/266, my emphasis).

7. *Phen*, 345/282. Cf.: "The original essence of tragedy consists in the fact that within such a conflict each of the opposed sides, if taken by itself, has *justification*; while each can establish the true and positive content of its own aim and character only by denying and infringing the equally justified power of the other. For this reason both sides, insofar as they constitute the sides of moral life, become involved in *guilt*" (*Aesth* 3, 523/1196). Cf.: "On account of this natural aspect, this ethical nation is...an individuality determined by nature and, therefore, limited, and thus meets its downfall at the hands of another" (*Phen*, 353/289). See Mills, "Hegel's *Antigone*," who ascribes to Hegel the view that "nature...assigns woman to divine law and man to human law" (61) without mentioning his remarks about the necessity to overcome this natural allocation. The same is true of Seyla Benhabib, "On Hegel, Women, and Irony," in *Feminist Interpretations of G.W.F. Hegel*, 29.

8. "The law which is manifest [to ethical self-consciousness] is in the essence tied to (*verknüpft mit*) its opposite; the essence is the unity of both; but the deed has only carried out one law in contrast to the other. Being in the essence tied to the other [law], however, the accomplishment of the one calls forth the other, which, due to the action performed against it, now manifests itself as a violated and hostile being demanding revenge" (*Phen*, 346/283).

9. *Phen*, 348/285. Cf.: "[B]oth sides suffer the same destruction. For neither power has any advantage over the other that would make it a more essential moment of the substance" (*Phen*, 310–11/285).

10. Hegel notes in the Preface to the *Philosophy of Right* that Plato's *Republic* was precisely intended to ward off the allegedly destructive effects of the principle of individuality: "Plato, aware that the ethics of his time were being penetrated by a deeper principle, which, within this context, could appear...only as a destructive force,...imagined he could counter [this] destructive force, and he thereby inflicted the gravest damage on the deeper drive behind it, namely, free infinite personality." Hegel, *Grundlinien der Philosophie des Rechts*, translated as *Elements of the Philosophy of Right*, by H.B. Nisbet (Cambridge: Cambridge University Press, 1991), 24/20, cf. § 46, rem, § 185, rem. Cf. Hegel, *Vorlesungen über die Geschichte der Philosophie*, translated as *Lectures on the History of Philosophy*, vol.2, by E. S. Haldane and H. Simson (Lincoln and London: University of Nebraska Press, 1995), 114/99. See Allegra de Laurentiis, *Subjects in the Ancient and Modern World: On Hegel's Theory of Subjectivity* (Basingstoke, UK: Palgrave Macmillan, 2005), 131–148, for a detailed discussion of Hegel's account of subjectivity in Greek culture.

Hegel, she argues, "sees the *Politeia* as a work that, far from pitching a lofty ideal against a supposedly monolithic reality, rather gives voice to...[the] contradiction between 'substantial' and increasingly 'subjective' experiences of the good...Plato aims at resolving the fundamental antagonism between knowing substance and self-knowing subjectivity by depriving the latter of any validity" (147).

11. In the *Lectures on the Philosophy of History*, Hegel notes that what lacks in Greek ethical life is "the infinite form,...the liberation from the natural moment, from the sensuous,...as well as from the immediateness characteristic of natural ethical life; what lacks is the infinity of self-consciousness." Insofar as the element of subjectivity actually did emerge, it "was the source of the further progress and corruption" (*LPH*, 323/264–265). Cf.: "In Athens, the higher principle which proved the ruin of the substantial existence of the Athenian state, developed ever more....Amiable and cheerful even in the midst of tragedy is the light-heartedness and nonchalance with which the Athenians accompany their ethical life to its grave. We recognize the higher interest of the new culture in the fact that the people made themselves merry over their own follies, and found great entertainment in the comedies of Aristophanes, which have the severest satire for their contents, while they bear the stamp of the most unbridled mirth" (*LPH*, 330/270–271).

12. I refer to the following edition of Aristophanes' comedies: "Lysistrata," in *Lysistrata and Other Plays*, trans. Allan H. Sommerstein (London: Penguin Books, 2002), henceforth "Lys"; "The Poet and the Women," in *The Birds and Other Plays*, trans. David Barrett and Allan H. Sommerstein (London: Penguin Books, 1978), henceforth "PW"; "Assemblywomen," in *The Frogs and Other Plays*, trans. David Barrett (London: Penguin Books, 1964), henceforth "AW." In one of the forms comedy can adopt, Hegel notes, the individual character and the aim to be achieved become entangled in a contradiction. "An example of this kind is *The Assemblywomen* of Aristophanes. There the women wish to decide on and to found a new political constitution, but they still retain all the whims and passions of women" (*Aesth* 3, 529/1201). The following remark seems to refer to *The Poet and the Women*: "But what Aristophanes especially loves is to expose...the follies of the masses,...and above all, most mercilessly, the new direction that Euripides had taken in tragedy" (ibid., 554/1221).

13. Cf.: "First I declare all private possessions to be common property" (AW, 242); "I am making girls common property too" (243). "Home life shall be communal as well."(245); "There will be enough of everything for everybody" (246). Some of her measures, such as communal diners and a non-democratic government, correspond to actual practices in Sparta. In "The 'Female Intruder' Reconsidered: Women in Aristophanes' Lysistrata and Ecclesiazusae," *Classical Philology* 77, no.1 (1982), 15, Helene Foley points out that this com-

edy was probably produced a few decades before Plato's *Republic*, which was written around 360.

14. For a few decades, various classical scholars have treated the issue of gender in Greek tragedy and comedy from a feminist perspective. Among them is Froma Zeitlin, who offers a detailed interpretation of the *Poet and the Women* in "Travesties of Gender and Genre in Aristophanes' Thesmophoriazousae," in *Reflections of Women in Antiquity*, ed. Helene P. Foley (New York: Gordon and Breach, 1981), 169–217. Focusing on Aristophanes' ironical references to Euripides' plays, she shows how the play explores, destabilizes, and reinstates the hierarchical relations between such oppositions as male and female, tragedy and comedy, theater and ritual. In "The 'Female Intruder' Reconsidered" Helene Foley brings out the complicated role of the "female intruder" in the *Lysistrata* and *The Assemblywomen*. See Laura McClure, *Spoken like a Woman: Speech and Gender in Athenian Drama* (Princeton: Princeton University Press, 1999), 205–264, for an analysis of Aristophanes' *The Poet and the Women* and *The Assemblywomen*, in which she focuses on the role of gender in the deployment of obscene comical language. With regard to Athenian drama as a whole she contends that the "disturbance of social and political hierarchy entailed by woman's appropriation of men's speech functioned not simply as a morality tale intended to teach the male spectators to be more vigilant about their wives....Women, traditionally viewed as political outsiders,...provided the dramatic poets with a vehicle for illustrating the disastrous consequences of political power placed in the wrong hands" (264).

15. The term is mentioned for the last time in *Phen*, 351/287, but even here retrospectively. According to Hutchings, Hegel's examination of "Antigone's specific crime" is, in this passage, transformed into "a generalized transhistorical claim about the role of women in relation to the community," thus providing feminist critiques of Hegel with an important focal point. See Hutchings, *Hegel and Feminist Philosophy*, 99. As I argue in the remainder of this section, however, these claims concerning womanhood in general, voiced by Hegel, are no less bound to the context of Greek culture than his references to Sophocles' *Antigone*.

16. Extracts 1–5 below are all taken from *Phen*, 288/351.

17. "I smell the odor very strong of Hippias' tyranny!" (Lys 165). "If once we let these women get the semblance of a start, before we know, they'll be adept at every manly art" (Lys, 166).

18. See Foley, "The 'Female Intruder' Reconsidered," 15–20.

19. "The community, however, can only maintain itself by repressing this spirit of individualism, and, because this spirit is an essential moment, it at once creates this spirit; due to its repressive attitude toward it, it creates this spirit as a hostile principle" (*Phen* 352/288).

20. *Phen,* 352/289. See Helene P. Foley, "The Conception of Women in Athenian Drama," in *Reflections of Women in Antiquity,* 127–168. Foley stresses that "the democratic polis made extraordinary demands on the male citizen to subordinate private interests to public, while simultaneously encouraging ambition and competition." Female characters, she maintains, often expose and challenge the failure of the male to comply with these demands (162). The playwright, she argues elsewhere, uses such female intrusions into the male political sphere "to deliver a stinging and constructive critique of the contemporary polis" as a whole. See Foley, "The 'Female Intruder' Reconsidered," 6, cf. 20.

21. PW, 126–127.

22. This is the current English translation of *Thesmophoriazusae,* which means "the women celebrating the Thesmophoria," a three-day religious festival for women only.

23. See on this Karin de Boer, "Hegel's Antigone and the Dialectics of Sexual Difference," *Philosophy Today,* SPEP Supplement 47, no.5 (2003), 140–146.

CHAPTER EIGHT

Reading the Same Twice Over: The Place of the Feminine in the Time of Hegelian Spirit

Rakefet Efrat-Levkovich

It is well known that within the *Phenomenology of Spirit*[1] Hegel explicitly refers to the notion of the feminine only in a single chapter—the one that deals with the ancient Greek ethical order. This fact apparently renders the feminine marginal to the historical constitution of the Hegelian subject/Spirit. However, in this chapter I shall claim that the notion of the feminine is entrenched in the entirety of this work, as it signifies the point of origin from which the Hegelian subject departs on his historical journey and to which, as Hegel famously claims, he aspires to return. More explicitly, I shall locate the place of the feminine both formally, in Hegel's dialectical procedure, and thematically within the historical journey of the Hegelian self-consciousness. On the basis of this I shall claim that the feminine is allotted a much more fundamental place in Hegel's *PS* than is commonly appreciated. In order to do this I shall put forward in sequence two different lines of interpretation that will thereafter be integrated into a concluding discussion: the first will briefly examine the explicit conception of the feminine as it appears in Hegel's discussion of the ancient Greek Spirit while the second will include a concise interpretation of Hegel's argument in the first four chapters of his work. In my concluding discussion I shall, first, analyze the nature and function of Hegel's notion of the feminine within his system, mostly in epistemological and temporal terms and, second, contest the stability of sexual difference in this system. Before turning to do this, however,

I will explain the methodological grounds and theoretical presuppositions that underpin this undertaking.

A Methodological Note

My working assumption is that the notion of the feminine is intelligible within the *PS* philosophical system owing to the fact that it is constituted in terms of the Hegelian subject's/Spirit's self-signification, as it is historically constructed. Hence, I take Hegel's explicit signification of the feminine as a manifest (symbolic) edifice that is constructed upon hidden foundations that can be disclosed in the historical narrative that Hegel put forward. In order to identify these foundations I take advantage of the distinctive character of the *PS*, namely, the fact that Hegel's philosophical ideas are organized and represented in it via a systematic and especially conspicuous method, that is, the dialectical procedure. This characteristic offers, in my account, an "analytical" key by which it is possible to analyze and categorize the various forms of consciousness that Hegel presents in each historical phase of his narrative, in general, and the feminine consciousness, in particular.

The dialectical procedure consists in a recurring three-phased movement that is generated by the "I's 'work of negation'" and proceeds throughout time. In this movement, (1) an original unity or identity that is comprised of undistinguishable opposites ("I" and other) is (2) "negated" by a conceptual distinction between these opposites, whereas difference is then (3) "negated" for a second time, so as to dialectically reunite or re-identify the opposites. Following Charles Taylor I shall name the three dialectical phases: "Immediacy," the "Understanding," and "Reason."

Within the *PS* Hegel utilizes the dialectical procedure in various ways. For the purposes of my argument, two principal, distinct uses are of particular importance: first, the protagonist of the *PS* practices the dialectical procedure in a *formal* way, that is, as a thinking procedure. This procedure is the fundamental spiritual tool that the protagonist employs in his ongoing self-constitution, as it is the modus operandi of supersession. Second, depending on the actual relation between the "I" and the other, and on the presence or absence of a mediating universal, each historical form of consciousness that the protagonist stages is structured by, and so "materializes" one of the three phases of the dialectical procedure identified above. This is so regardless of the fact that throughout his historical development, the protagonist is assumed to *think* through the threefold dialectical procedure in the first, *formal* way. Thus, for example, in "Sense-Certainty" consciousness is shown to carry out this thought procedure although, as I shall claim, it is structured upon the "Immediate" phase. My analysis in what follows employs the second usage of the dialectical procedure as an "analytical key" by which I identify the specific structure of Hegel's explicit notion of the feminine consciousness and, based on this, locate among the various forms of consciousness that Hegel examines in the first four chapters of his work the ones that are similar to it in this regard.

My claim that the origin of woman's signification is to be found in the four opening chapters of the *PS* depends on the particular status of these chapters within the whole work. Since the publication of the *PS* many of Hegel's commentators have pointed out the problematic nature of these opening chapters, as a textual unit, within Hegel's book. As Robert Pippin[2] explicates, the narrative that is conveyed in these chapters seems to defy the main philosophical contention that Hegel aims to defend in this book which is to show that knowledge is necessarily both social and historical. Whereas most of Hegel's narrative is in tune with this goal, its opening chapters examine how a solitary consciousness practices knowledge. However, I will show that this apparent inconsistency can be resolved, at least in part, once we take this section of the text to represent the *prehistorical* and pre-social phase of Hegelian knowing and the sociohistorical subject, while at the same time making evident the *conditions for the possibility* of the sociohistorical subject (hence, of Spirit).

The *PS'* protagonist is evidently masculine, as follows from the fact that woman is represented in it as his (dichotomous) other. However, the protagonist's masculinity, I will suggest, is only instituted in a signifiable manner in the event depicted in the fifth chapter wherein self-consciousness is simultaneously recognized by another self-consciousness and constitutes a preliminary *social* order (the master-slave dialectic). Implicitly, however, gender difference can be claimed to be determined in the stage that *precedes* this event wherein, once the protagonist becomes *self-determining*, he implicitly signifies himself as masculine. In this event the protagonist already constitutes his *possibility* to realize an inter-subjective form of life, that is, Spirit (as Hegel explicitly claims in section 177), which he next realizes in actual relation to a *similar* other. As a result the two constitute a mutual-recognition pact that can be seen as the origin of patriarchy. Significantly, both self-determination and this pact are attained via the repression and overcoming of the *natural other*.

My suggestion is that this event can be identified as the point in Hegel's historical narrative where *sexual difference* is initially (yet implicitly) determined. This exegetical point underlies my claim that the origin of the feminine's signification (hence, its notional "model") can be found in the early stages of the *PS* historical narrative that precede this event.

My interpretation of these chapters builds on the established tradition that reads the *PS* as a *Bildungsroman*. In general, this literary genre tends to describe the happenings of a young protagonist who goes through a process of maturation, while the author typically focuses on the inner and outer forces and events that contribute to the protagonist's growth and shape his or her developing personality. As some of Hegel's commentators have already demonstrated, a reading of the *PS* along the line of this genre offers an effective tool for intensifying the understanding of this work and, particularly, as I hope to show in what follows, for clarifying some of its textual conundrums. Together with this, a feminist starting point makes it impossible to ignore the facts that the *PS*' sociohistorical protagonist is masculine and that the book's general outlook is thoroughly androcentric. Because my aim is to reconstruct *her* story out of his, my focal point will shift to the *antagonist* of Hegel's narrative with the effect of decentering the protagonist's viewpoint. More particularly, my interest in sexual difference leads to a reading that is attentive to the hidden, the implied, and the repressed in Hegel's story and, as a result, shows that Hegel's *bildungsroman* is better read as a *dual* narrative in more than one respect. Particularly, my reading will show that the dominant, explicitly articulated narrative of the protagonist's constitution is conditioned on an unspoken narrative that is that of the *other*.

My reading is based on an ambivalent stance toward Hegel's system where alongside my stated critical approach I shall provisionally accept Hegel's own fundamental philosophical principles and presuppositions. This strategy reflects my belief that an effort to *de*construct Hegel's notion of the feminine should begin with reconstructing the latter's meaning and function within his system as faithfully as possible to its underlying terms. By this means, the ways in which the feminine is interwoven into the system in a manner that renders the system *dependent* on what the feminine signifies in it can be disclosed and eventually turned against itself.

SECTION ONE

Hegel's explicit consideration of women or the feminine appears in the chapter on the ancient Greek ethical order that is the first concrete historical social order examined in his book. Noticeably, Hegel assumes that this form of Spirit is, to a large degree, determined by natural laws that are inexplicable for the ancient Greek community. Hegel's construal of this order put emphasis on the underlying social institutions that constitute it, namely, the family and the community, which are defined by him in mutually exclusive terms: the community is conceived as the realization of "human law" that is a local, collective, and self-consciously constituted scheme of knowledge, rules, and norms while the family is seen to realize the "divine law" that consists in eternal and unintelligible natural laws. It is determined by nature, Hegel claims, that men realize in this form of Spirit the first law and women the second. Accordingly, men are able to surpass their familial origin and to enter into the community where they become citizens of the Polis, whereas women are determined to remain confined to the family. This implies that woman is solely constituted by familial, natural relations, whereas man is constituted both by these and by communal, self-conscious relations, while defining himself in terms of the latter. It follows that in this chapter woman's constitution should be analyzed in terms of familial relations. Hence, while the category of "family members" includes both men and women, I shall refer in the following to family members mainly as feminine.

Hegel specifies two types of relations that constitute family members, both of which, I claim, can be identified as "immediate" and "sensible": the first is the interpersonal relationship between individual family members, and the second is the relation between each individual member of the family and the family as a whole. The interpersonal relationship is driven by sexual desire and love and constitutes kinship. It is an "immediate" relation in the sense of being constituted without the shared, self-conscious knowledge scheme of the community. Hence, it is unreflective and unethical in character. In Hegelian terms, in this relationship woman is "determined by the other" while the category of the "other" should be understood as signifying here both woman's intrinsic needs and bodily desires and other family members. Because of this, woman is unable to distinguish between herself and these "others": the intentional principle that guides her "thought" and action is "the desire of the other" in which *her desire* of the other and the *other* that she desires cannot be separated by her.

This noncognitive, sensible, and affective relationship constitutes woman both as "universal" and as "particular." Her universality is determined by the fact that all women (or family members) are subjected to the same desires that equally arise in each and every natural organism and that can be expressed by each one of them only in a similar, non-individualized manner. However, family members are considered to be sensuous particular beings determined by natural, bodily inclinations. This means that women are determined to act without being able to articulate and explain the reasons for their actions. It follows that the dyadic relationship of kinship constitutes woman as a particular, sensuous, and ineffable being that is expressible only in a practical and universal manner.

The second kind of familial relation holds between woman and her family as a whole. As a whole, the family is a "universal" that sets for its members particular goals and interests that they all share in common. Notably, these "goals" and "interests" originate in nature and hence are not self-consciously determined; thus, Hegel claims that they mainly involve "the acquisition and maintenance of power and wealth" and are "concerned only with needs and belon[g] to the sphere of appetite."[3] Women are "immediately unified" with this universal as they are unable to distinguish between the goals that it sets and their own personal goals. It follows that the familial "universal" determines the deeds of family members, in general, and of women, in particular, in an unreflective manner. Thus, it must be distinguished from the self-conscious communal universal: only the latter is, according to Hegel, "what is truly universal."[4] In effect, Hegel claims that familial "universals" are held by the community as "individuals" that are at odds with it and hence constitute its "antithesis."

Accordingly, Hegel clarifies that the universal of the family is "ethical" only in the restricted sense that it is general and abstract, as it is shared by family members in common. The exception to this rule that grants the family (and, particularly, women) recognizable ethical significance within the community emerges from the role that it plays in fulfilling the community's self-determined ends. This role, as Hegel famously claims, consists of women's "last duty" to bestow the dead (of their families) with a proper burial. The crucial significance of this ethical duty emanated from the fact that, specifically in the ancient Greek ethical order, men were unable to reconcile *in life* between their mutually excluding senses of self, namely, their familial-constituted particularity and their community-constituted universality. Such reconciliation, Hegel claims, was achieved only through the burial ceremony that women, as realizers of the "natural law," executed in the service of communal ends.

SECTION TWO

The first four chapters of the *PS* are generally understood to be about "the relation to the object." In these chapters, Hegel describes how consciousness constituted itself in relation first to inanimate being and second to the living object (nature), primarily through knowledge relations and thereafter through carnal interaction with it, in respect. The relation to the object necessarily conditions the development of the ethical subject and yet this relation must ultimately be superseded in order for the ethical, sociohistorical subject to emerge in a recognizable form. In the same event where the protagonist overcomes its relation to the object it also overcomes its natural determination. This event marks its self-supersession as object-like and, simultaneously, its acquisition of the possibility to express itself, and to be recognized as a subject in relation to another, similar subject.

It follows that the forms of consciousness that are structured by the relation to the object stand merely on the *threshold* of subjecthood. This is just another way of saying what I have begun to claim earlier, namely, that through examining the relation to the object Hegel put forward the constitution[5] of what he regards as the *conditions for the possibility* of the kind of self-consciousness that can *realize* itself as an ethical subject in relation to another self-consciousness and be conferred with recognition of being just that. In this regard, the relation to the object constitutes necessary yet insufficient conditions for the becoming of the ethical subject, whereas the sufficient condition is the relation with another subject. In rough terms, Hegel presents two different yet interdependent conditions that are constituted in relation to the object: the first is constituted through a theorizing approach to the object and produces self-consciousness' possibility to be a self-reflexive knowing being; the second is constituted through a practical approach to the world and produces self-consciousness' ability to create and act on its own self-determined ends. In accordance with the above, both possibilities become viable and effective tools for historical self-constitution only as a result of the "master-slave dialectic" that is in relation to another subject. Yet, the very possibility of self-consciousness being able to enter into such a relation is dependent on its *practical* supersession of the object, as it were, "in person," that is carried out in the act in which it supersedes *itself as "natural desire."* In this act, it can be suggested, self-consciousness implicitly traverses the threshold of subjecthood.

It is impossible in this framework to suggest even a concise explication of the ideas that Hegel put forward in the first four chapters of the *PS* in their order of appearance.[6] Hence, my analysis will be organized by a categorization of the various forms of consciousness that Hegel examines in these chapters, in line with what I have suggested at the outset, according to the dialectical phase that they materialized.

I suggest these forms of consciousness be categorized into two fundamental types: the first includes both the one that appears at the opening of Hegel's narrative that is "sense-certainty" and the one that embarks on the fourth chapter, that is, "desire." The second includes the other forms of consciousness that Hegel considers in these chapters, namely, "Perception" and the "Understanding." According to this suggestion, the first type realizes the "Immediate" phase, as it is unmediated by a self-constituted universal. Particularly, as I shall shortly justify and explain in more detail, it introduces twice over an *immediate and sensible* type of consciousness. The second realizes the phase of the "Understanding" as it is mediated by what can be called a "subjective" or "imaginary" universal (to distinguish from an objective and shared universal that constitutes "Reason"). In passing, it can be noted that this means that the protagonist takes up the form (or phase) of "Reason" only following his experience of "lordship and bondage" in the fifth chapter.[6] The justification of this categorization makes up the heart of my reading and I shall clarify it throughout the rest of this part.

"Sense-Certainty" explicitly introduces at its outset an immediate and sensible form of consciousness that is positioned within the sensuous world. Hegel assumes that this consciousness resides outside any imaginary or linguistic universal scheme but is intentional and, specifically, invested with the desire to create knowledge of the world. Thus in this chapter Hegel examines consciousness' effort to create knowledge of the sensuous particulars it apprehends. He claims that consciousness must carry this out by the use of words in which the particular's meaning (or consciousness' "internal" reference to them, that is, *meinen*) is determined. Hegel contends that by so doing, consciousness brings *mediating* universals into the (its) world; consequently, it obliterates the criterion of immediacy and transgresses its original constitution. Furthermore, by employing language, the world, that originally appeared to this immediate and sensible consciousness as furnished with material and singular particulars, is abstracted and generalized; by the same token, consciousness itself is turned into an abstract universal. Thus, the sensuousness of the world and of consciousness itself is also obliterated. According to the latter, Hegel contends in this chapter what later on Lacan will avow, namely, that language "kills" the materiality of things.

In addition, Hegel stresses that because the words that consciousness utters are not entrenched within a linguistic scheme, their meaning is indeterminable. Thus, consciousness' attempt to signify a particular thing ends up signifying it in the most general and uninformative way that makes it impossible to distinguish it from other things. In fact, any word turns out to signify the entirety of being ("being in general"). This particularly implies that consciousness is unable to tell the difference between itself and the other and can only know itself to be unified and identical to the whole of being. Nevertheless, at the end of this chapter Hegel describes, through an explicit dialectical argument, how consciousness comes to be able to determine the meaning of words. Subsequent to this, "Sense-Certainty" is transformed into "Perception," that is, a mediated being that is able to utilize universal concepts for creating more meticulous knowledge of the world.

More generally, throughout the first to the third chapters Hegel examines consciousness' attempts to create knowledge of the world through employing a purely theoretical approach to it. In the third chapter Hegel shows that when followed consistently in its pure form, this kind of approach leads to the constitution of consciousness, now in the form of the "Understanding," as a self-reflexive "self-consciousness" that can only know itself, while stressing that this end point marks, at one and the same time, an important achievement and an utter failure. It is an achievement in the sense that self-consciousness arrives at self-knowledge in the form of "truth." Specifically, it becomes able to know how it is constituted and that this constitution is the product of its own making. Moreover, it comes to know the process and means by which it has accomplished its present self-identity. However, this result marks a failure in considering that consciousness' original goal was to create knowledge of the world/object, but then it ended up in knowing only itself. Even more so, the world/object is known to this form of self-consciousness in two incongruous ways, which it is able neither to decide between nor to reconcile into a coherent understanding; owing to self-consciousness' present unity with this object, its own self-knowledge is thereby obstructed. This predicament follows from self-consciousness' reflection on its process of becoming in which it has recollected its past forms (since "sense-certainty"). Self-consciousness recalls that the world first appeared to it, when it was "consciousness," as a sensuous and independent being. This understanding, however, clashes with self-consciousness' present understanding of the world as a universal of its own making: a "theory" or a scheme of representations that, as such, is both abstract and dependent on its own thought. The impossibility of deciding between these incongruous understandings emanates from the fact that self-consciousness' persistent practice of representation has led it to create a subjective "curtain of appearances" that is, at one and the same time, a *mediating* universal scheme through which it constitutes knowledge; a product of its knowing activity that reflects and so is identical to self-consciousness itself (as "I"); and something that the object is reduced to, or determined in/ as, and so also something that is identical to the object. This means that nothing is present to self-consciousness independent of itself. But without any independent, objective other, self-consciousness lacks an arbiter to which it could appeal in order to resolve the dilemma in which it is caught.

Thus, self-consciousness arrives at a blind alley. Via this discussion, I suggest Hegel claims that as long as self-consciousness continues to employ the same form of activity that it has been employing thus far, knowledge cannot be press forward since theorization only repositions once again the same blind of appearances. Self-consciousness thus finds itself incarcerated in its constituted all-inclusive subjective conceptual space whereas, by means of representation, it can only endlessly reiterate itself while (re)producing nothing but "more of the Same."

More generally, one of Hegel's significant philosophical contentions conveyed in the *PS* is that an inclusive explanation of the human subject, in particular, and of the human form of life, in general, cannot be suggested (as some of his predecessors did) through considering only the epistemological, conceptualizing, and theorizing way in which subjects approach the world. Rather, such an explanation must additionally take account of the subjects' *practical* activities in which they physically interact with the material world and work on it.[7] In Hegel's view, these two modes of actions (that make up the two necessary conditions that I have specified earlier) are both, interdependently, indispensible for the constitution of the distinctive *historical* form of life that humans realize, seeing that they complement each other: theory without practical action is impotent[8] while practical action without theory is pure animality. Thus Hegel takes upon himself to methodically examine the constitution and implementation of both forms of action. He does so through positioning a protagonist that practices and thereby demonstrates both.

Significantly, however, Hegel's discussion implies that the employment of a pure theoretical approach to the sensuous world, if it is to be examined in a consistent manner, *excludes* the very possibility of (examining) the practical interaction with it. As I have shown above, the claim that Hegel makes throughout the first three chapters is that signification eliminates the sensuous world as well as the physical, effectual body that conditions the possibility of work. The third chapter draws out this idea ad absurdum by stressing that this practice can only yield reflective self-knowledge, while producing self-consciousness in the form of mere *res cognitans*, on the verge of solipsism. It follows that if Hegel wants to provide a complementary explanation of the *preliminary* constitution of the subject through employing a practical mode of action—particularly if it is to be represented by a protagonist of a *bildungsroman*—he must represent this explanation *apart* from the first, epistemological one. For this reason, I claim, Hegel doubles his narrative: he repositions his protagonist in its original point of departure through reintroducing the immediate and sensible form of consciousness. Now, however, consciousness steps on the previously untaken road by beginning with the (ineffable) *deed* rather than with the *word*; hence, it becomes desire.

It appears that this countermovement of the protagonist goes against the main guideline of the *bildungsroman* that stipulates its systematic forward movement. However, by returning his protagonist back to its point of departure, I suggest, Hegel assumes a *synchronic* constitution of his protagonist and, hence, this return does not defy the general notion of consistent historical progression. In other words, this countermovement should be seen only as theoretical or, rather, methodological and not as temporal or "historical." This claim is based on the following: in reality, the protagonist's advance through theorization alone (that is, from "Sense-Certainty" to the truth of self-consciousness, which is the stage that precedes "desire") could not affect any actual difference in the world and hence could not transfer the protagonist to a subsequent historical stage. Thus its development through the constitution of knowledge must be seen to be carried out, as it were, only "in its head." As Hegel claims, it was all a matter of "reflection-into-itself" in which self-consciousness' "self-sundering" and "becoming self-identical" were performed without experiencing difference and opposition as more than mere abstractions.[9] However, consciousness' progressive transformation into a reflexive self-consciousness can be seen to mark a *notional* or epistemological progression and, in this respect, self-consciousness' becoming into "desire" can be seen as a backward movement.

The excluding relation between language and practical action is assumed by Hegel to be mutual, at least methodologically. That is, Hegel assumes that the practical approach to the word must first be considered in the absence of thought and knowledge. The reason for this is his premise that the becoming-subject must be assumed to *experience* his incarnation through an intimate and intense (that is, immediate) relation to his body since only in this way can he come to know the deep meaning of being embodied, in the first instance, so as to overcome the enslaving aspects of embodiment, in the second. This discussion, in which self-consciousness *is* a naturally determined organism, is, therefore, vital to Hegel's ambition of offering a philosophical account of the human subject/form of life in its living and lavish, as it were, three-dimension shape.

Self-consciousness' transformation into desire marks what Robert Pippin[10] calls a "transitional point." In this moment, self-consciousness transfigures itself into its sheer opposite, that is, *being*. Through this radical move it goes behind the "curtain of appearances." Doing so, it commits what Slavoj Žižek[11] calls a "suicidal act," that is, an act in which it frees itself from everything it knows (thus, *is*) only to find itself annulled, having to recreate itself all over again.

Consciousness-as-desire acts corporally, its body (that now endures instead of being immediately abstracted) is put in service of consuming the object/other for the sake of self-preservation. Thus, desire's senses become means of carnal satisfaction rather than a source of knowledge. Hence, this immediate and sensuous consciousness is *"begierde,"* that is, animal appetite or, a natural organism. In accordance, Hegel makes clear at the opening of this discussion that the sensuous object in which desire dwells is no longer the inanimate being that it has been for the knowing consciousness. Rather it is correspondingly transformed into a *living* and dynamic object, that is, nature. Desire is a sensuous particular that is immediately unified with the natural object in a twofold sense, seeing that the latter both signifies the universal whole in which desire is submerged and the particular body to which it is, as consciousness, closely attached. Yet, at this initial moment, desire is ignorant of this distinction. This is so because without conceptual thought it necessarily *experiences* the natural object as unified. Desire's overall goal is thus to overcome natural determination; the satisfaction of this goal is conditioned by its ability to obliterate its immediate relation with the particular and universal natural object. Hegel's key point is that by superseding its body, consciousness instantly surmounts the entire universal of nature, in its abstract form, and becomes independent of its determining power.

It appears, however, that as desire, consciousness is also dependent on its body. The latter constitutes its living and vigorous aspect while facilitating its practical action in the world through which it nourishes itself and sustains its life. Evidently, then, desire's overriding goal to become independent of the natural object cannot be achieved through completely destroying it. In effect, desire finds itself, already in this early stage, in a blind alley, since by continuing to employ its present ("natural") form of action it will only reproduce "more of the same": the consumption of the other only sustains desire in its current form or, put otherwise, the satisfaction of desire instantly reinstates desire. Hegel thus claims that desire's ability to overcome its current predicament is necessarily dependent on recovering the knowledge skills that it has constituted earlier but then misplaced. Thus, in the second stage desire invokes its knowledge skills and signifies the universal of nature in opposite terms to itself. Thereby it breaks its unity with the object in an implicit way. Now desire takes itself to be the determining being (as signification is a form of determination). Yet, since this determination occurs only in and by *thought*, desire nevertheless still remains *actually* unified with, determined, and threatened by the living object. Hence, a third stage is needed.

In the third stage, desire acts upon its newly gained knowledge with the aim to make it explicit, that is, to objectify its *denial* of the object's determining power over itself. It does so through *suppressing* its natural, bodily desire to consume the *outside* other for the sake of carnal satisfaction. This means that its destructive power is directed *inward*; and in this sense, it negates itself as desire. Moreover, desire *substitutes* the wanton, bodily desire that is of natural origin with another kind of "desire" that it self-consciously created and so is better described as a *self-determined End*. Through enacting this End, desire externalizes its ability to defy the authority of natural laws over its body (or, itself) and to self-consciously subject itself to an alternative law that is its own self-legislated law. Noticeably, by becoming able to objectively express its particular and self-determined subjective space (that was, generally, up to this point, abstract, internal, and, therefore, imperceptible to others) through inscribing it on its own body, the protagonist accomplishes a necessary condition for being recognized by another as a subject. More generally, in this act it actually supersedes itself as natural desire while simultaneously becoming an implicit and preliminary form of *Spirit*: a particular that epitomizes the entire human "genus."

In the next, inter-subjective trial self-consciousness will establish the law-like, that is, universal and objective applicability of its self-determined end by compelling another self-consciousness to conform to it. Accomplishing this, it will form, together with the other self-consciousness (the slave), a primordial social order wherein the latter will seal the fate of nature (in a primordial but decisive sense) by realizing the possibility to determine its *universal material* form through working on it and shaping it according to his own ideas. In this moment history will become a viable possibility for the Hegelian subject.

SECTION THREE

Drawing together the two lines of interpretation suggested above, the primary outcome that stands out is that the feminine consciousness is constituted (symbolically and metaphysically) in Hegel's narrative, through the same immediate and sensible relation to the object/other that constitutes the forms of consciousness dubbed "sense-certainty" and "desire." This outcome established a linkage between Hegel's notion of the feminine and the immediate and sensible form of consciousness in general, and as described in the "historical" stages that are represented at the *outset* of the first and fourth chapters of the *PS*, in particular. The first, more general sense of this linkage discloses the intrinsic rationale on which Hegel founds his discussion of the feminine or women in the chapters on the ancient Greek ethical order and deepens our understanding of its particular nature. The second, more particular sense enables the locating of the place of the feminine within Hegel's overall narrative both "historically" and philosophically. In this limited framework I can elaborate only briefly on some of these implications. I will focus on the epistemological implications of this linkage using temporal terms of analysis.

It would not be a hyperbole to say that the connection between woman and immediate sensibility, particularly in the form of *natural* "desire" (as distinct from "desire" as an "ethical end"), yields a conception that satisfies almost every conventional stereotype of woman, as summed up in Beauvoir's account of "the myth of the feminine."[12] Just as Beauvoir notes, the contents of the notion of woman are revealed to be diverse and inconsistent with each other yet can be shown to commonly assume shared themes such as: the association of woman with nature and, particularly, with the basic natural inclination to sustain and reproduce life; her exclusion from subjectivity; her failure to reach the standard of ethicality with which (and in terms of which) man identifies himself; and her tendency to (or, the expectation that she will) sacrifice herself for the sake of her significant other in the name of love.

Furthermore, in light of the suggested connection, Hegel's explicit characterization of woman in the chapter on the ancient Greek culture is seen to rest on grounds that emerge out of, and cohere with the rest of his system. In general, this linkage implies that, according to Hegel, woman exhibits a "developmental failure" that hinders her ability to form and practice abstract, universal thought and, hence, to transcend and enhance her self-identity in an historical manner. That is, woman is assumed to be eternally wedged in the first dialectical phase and to materialize a form of consciousness that is unified with her body in a way that makes her susceptible to natural determination: both to unreflective, carnal inclinations, necessities, and desires, and to undying cyclical "natural" regulations that specifically involve the procreation and that preservation of life. This characteristic is, according to Hegel, exactly what makes woman ideal for the constitution of the family—but only for this.

Moreover, according to Hegel, in its bare preliminary state, natural desire is incapable of overthrowing the independence of the other with which it is unified, neither by totally consuming it nor, evidently, by conceptually determining it. Hence, as Judith Butler[13] explicates, desire experiences incompetence and limitation on its "self." Constantly unsatisfied, it oscillates to and fro between two mutual excluding experiences, each of which is characterized by a sense of lack or loss: desire of the other/object leads the "I," on the one hand, to passionately focus on, thus, to be engrossed in the other to the point of "self loss" or, on the other hand, to withdraw into itself and to lose the outer object/world.[14]

This description is in accord with Hegel's explicit representation of woman as analyzed above where, on the one hand, woman is driven by desire and love to completely identify with her familial others to the point of lacking any distinctive sense of self;[15] and, on the other hand, as Hegel suggests happens in the case of conflicts between the family and the community, woman exhibits a self-indulgent conduct while being indifferent or antagonistic both to non-familial individuals and to the universal of the community at large.

On account of this, the intrinsic reason for Hegel's advocacy of woman's exclusion from the community[16] also becomes visible: seeing that woman is a sensuous particular that is incapable of abstract thought, she can be occupied only with particular things and practical matters, without the ability either to generate or follow normative, general and objective rules that constitute the practices of the public sphere and concern the common good. Together with this, it becomes transparent why, as Terry Pinkard[17] critically comments, Hegel believes that in the rational ethical order not only men but also women accomplish their highest possible self-fulfillment or, "ethical vocation."[18]

Immediate sensibility is positioned twice within what I have identified as the *prehistorical* phase of the subject/Spirit: in its beginning and in its ending. Through the practical supersession of immediate sensibility, the protagonist crosses the threshold of subjecthood in an implicit manner, and becomes able to enter the inter-subjective realm in which history becomes a realizable possibility. Thus in this event, I suggest, the "fate" of the immediate and sensible form of consciousness is determined to permanently reside in prehistory. Moreover, Hegel's claim that the protagonist's possibility to become a "subject of history" is *dependent* on practically suppressing and substituting immediate sensibility (as "desire") particularly rests on its essentially *ahistorical* nature. Because natural desire can only sustain, reproduce, and reiterate its original form, it cannot but constantly remain in its point of departure or, in its original place. It follows from this that the one who is constituted exclusively by immediate sensibility must fail to exceed its original form (to utilize Hannah Arendt's terms)[19] as *"animal laborans"* and to become *"homo faber"* whereas only the latter, according to Hegel, sets in motion the wheels of history.

In this regard, the constitution of the feminine in the *PS* exemplifies what Julia Kristeva calls "women's time."[20] According to Kristeva, although woman was mainly associated in western thought with space rather than with time, feminine subjectivity has also been conceived in terms of a certain type of temporality that can be distinguished from "male," historical time. "Women's time," she maintains, resists historical temporality as it is both "cyclical" and "monumental." In the first sense this temporality represents "the eternal recurrence of a biological rhythm which conforms to that of nature . . . whose regularity and unison with what is experienced as extra-subjective time, cosmic time, occasion vertiginous visions and unnamable *jouissance*."[21] In the second, "there is the massive presence of monumental temporality, without cleavage or escape, which has so little to do with linear time (that passes) that the very word "temporality" hardly fits: all-encompassing and infinite like imaginary space."[22]

In the following sections I will claim that the experiences of the immediate and sensible form of consciousness in its original form should be seen as unspeakable and as essentially transcending the scope of knowledge. In the course of this I shall examine both the nature of this type of experiences (or consciousness) and its place within Hegel's system of knowledge. On the basis of this I shall analyze the nature, place and function of the feminine in this system. In the latter analysis I shall primarily utilize temporal terms and in these terms I shall also finally contest the stability of sexual difference in Hegel's *PS*.

The unspeakable character of immediate sensibility is asserted in Hegel's text in both discussions of it, both explicitly and implicitly. To start with, the stated aim of the chapter on "Sense-Certainty" is overtly to make the case for this particular idea. But this idea is also implied in this chapter silently through the fact that the immediate and sensible consciousness in its *accurate* form is barely examined in it whereas the large part of Hegel's discussion already examines the subsequent concept-*mediated* consciousness, that is, "Perception" albeit in its immature form.[23] Thus, both explicitly and by implication, "sense-certainty" is shown to be an ineffable consciousness for which the knowledge of both self and other is impossible and that, accordingly, can articulate the contents of its sensible awareness only from a higher level of knowledge, that is, *retrospectively.*

In the fourth chapter, in turn, desire's inexpressible nature is similarly illustrated in a dual explicit and implicit manner yet by employing different literary means. The sections[24] that open the "desire" discussion and that are supposed to introduce its first (and relevant) phase focus on the whole with which consciousness as desire is unified rather than on the occurrences of desire itself. More specifically, these sections exclusively describe the transformation of the object as a whole from inanimate being into "Life," that is, the living natural world. Thus, the experiences that desire itself undergoes in this initial stage must be inferred by the reader from the description of the whole. By narrating the events in this manner, I suggest, Hegel wordlessly displays his fundamental idea according to which in its current condition desire is totally submerged in the living object without having the possibility to demarcate and express its sensible sense of "self." More generally, Hegel thereby shows that in certain preliminary stages of its development, such as desire, consciousness is simultaneously cognitively inaccessible to its alert self and inexpressible of its somatic and affective experiences *at the very time* of their occurrence.

Hegel directly alludes to this truth in the opening of the fourth chapter where he distinguishes between what is visible (or, knowable) "for *us,*" that is, his readers and what is knowable "for self-consciousness."[25] As he makes clear in the Introduction to his book, in such occasions he resorts to and depicts what is happening to self-consciousness from the omniscient "scientific"[26] vantage point that is, in fact, only historically accomplished in the final stage of the subject/Spirit becoming. In so doing, it should be added, Hegel makes visible the vantage point of the omniscient author (that evidently coincides with the viewpoint of the fully developed, Absolute Spirit). Hegel does so, I suggest, because it is important for him, for the clarity of his entire reasoning, to narrate his argument in a chronological order (that is, both "historically" and logically ordered). Thus, he simultaneously represents desire's experiences "in real time" and claims that these experiences can be depicted only retroactively, once superseded. He put forward the latter by directly addressing *his readers*, and narrating the occurrences (*for* them) from his own all-knowing vantage point, "behind the back of consciousness"—as he put it in the Introduction.[27]

Seeing that this type of experience evades direct cognition, knowledge of the unity with the object must be rendered as involving self-consciousness' *misplaced past* and, accordingly, be created retroactively via conjectured inference, while assuming the form of *memory*. The imagination is particularly required in this endeavor, seeing that when the protagonist is a representing being, in the second and third dialectical stages, he *always already* finds himself *different* from the object, either in opposition to it or as reconciled with it, in respect. This is just a more formal way to say again that the original unity with the object is beyond the protagonist's knowledge. Assumed to be utterly private and inexpressible, these bodily experiences can be seen, in Kristeva's terms, as *semiotic* or as *chora*. In the light of this, the subject's "knowledge" of his original immediate and sensible stage cannot be seen as knowledge in the proper sense of the term. Rather, it is more appropriately describable as a *fantasy* or, fantasized memory. Thus, rather than his object of knowledge, the lost unity with the other should be seen as the masculine subject's *object of desire*.

In moments of recollection, the subject is enthralled by his object of desire, engrossed in his own imagined past, and becomes momentarily unified with it. Hence, it can be suggested, in these moments man withdraws from historical time and immerses himself in "women's time." According to this suggestion, precisely because it is both "monumental" and "cyclical," "women's time" can also indicate the time of *desire*, as the time of recollection that is "intra-subjective" in nature and constitutes the subject's private sense of self: his singular subjectivity. Significantly, as Emmanuel Levinas asserts, recollection or memory exceeds history and, particularly, contests its totalizing determination by going against it: it moves *backward* toward the past and brings the past into the present.[28] This consideration discloses the intrinsic function of the "feminine" in the *self*-constitution of the Hegelian masculine subject. In these moments, I suggest, the feminine's particular significance is invoked in man; thus, the contents produced in "women's time" are projected onto woman and determine her significance.

As I have begun to claim, immediate sensibility cannot be directly articulated or acknowledged by Spirit's collective, self-conscious self-understanding, that is, by the Symbolic.[29] As Elizabeth Grosz explains with regard to semiotic experiences in general,

> [the semiotic] threatens to undermine and de-stabilize the rule-governed operations of the Symbolic, resisting its rules and norms. Governed by the primary processes, which seek immediate satisfaction of what may be anti-social impulses, the semiotic is the raw data of corporeal forces and energies organized by the law-abiding and rule-governed secondary-process activities of the Symbolic.[30]

Evidently, once superseded, man can neither straightforwardly identify himself with the notion of immediate unity with the other (but only as "negated," while suppressing it), nor express it or experience it in relation to his fellow men. Thus, such a sense of unity can only be experienced or, rather, fantasized or desired in the presence of woman, either as a notion in his mind or in his concrete encounter with her, not without an unconscious resonance, as feminist critics that draw on other texts avow, to the "primary identification" with the mother. In both cases, it is claimed, this unity is invoked as an idealization, as it is what is missing from man's (and woman's?) lived reality. Thus, Jessica Benjamin, for example, writes that:

> The vision of perfect unity...is an *ideal*—a symbolic expression of our longing—that we project on the past. The measures of this ideal expand in reaction to the experience of helplessness—in face of circumstance, lack of power, death—but also due to the distance from the mother's assistance that is forced since of denying her.[31]

Assuming expressly that "woman" is reduced to "motherhood," Kristeva puts forward a similar idea:

> If, however, one looks at it more closely, this motherhood is the *fantasy* that is nurtured by the adult, man or woman, of a lost territory; what is more, it involves less an idealized archaic mother than the idealization of the *relationship* that binds us to her, one that cannot be localized—an idealization of primary narcissism.[32]

Evidently, woman makes simultaneously an object of man's signification (rather than a self-signifying being) and an object of his desire (rather than of knowledge or recognition). But her signification, I suggest, is determined in the form of "re-presentation," so that her materialization of desire's object endures. That is, she is determined within and for Spirit to re-*present* the otherwise misplaced contents of immediate sensibility, in what can be identified as an "ontological" way: as a body, an object, or a place on which these contents are inscribed and by which they are *ineffably presented* in Spirit. In this way, the historical and rational Spirit promises, first, that (the memory of) its prehistorical origin in unity with the other, its material, "raw" condition or, its object of desire will not be forsaken but rather will endure for and continue to pulsate and enthrall it. Second, whereas women are determined to re-present these destabilizing contents in a living but *unspeaking* manner, Spirit becomes able to reflect on these contents while preventing their practical interference with or contesting of its own *self*-signification. Owing to the latter, rational Spirit also promises its possibility to create a *complete* self-understanding of its own historical self-constitution since its prehistorical stage—in the way that Hegel's narrative pretends to do.

Woman is thus constituted as the ahistorical place within Spirit's or the masculine subject's historical time. Or, woman is thus determined to re-present an ahistorical movement that is utterly immanent and so is rendered as a kind of temporality to which "the very word "temporality" hardly fits: all-encompassing and infinite like imaginary space." This suggestion shows Hegel's notion of woman in the *PS* to be in accord with what Luce Irigaray critically identifies in psychoanalytical literature, according to which

> [S]he will not represent "her" relation to "her" origin ... She is left with a *void*, a *lack* of all representation, re-presentation, and even strictly speaking of all mimesis of her desire for origin.[33]

Thus, in tune with my above reading into Hegel, Irigaray avers: "let us say that *in the beginning was the end of her story* and that from now on she will have one dictated to her: by the man-father."[34]

However, this reading of the feminine may well be seen to take on Irigaray's challenge, made through her famous claim that "in order to live and think through [sexual] difference we must reconsider the whole question of space and time."[35] Similarly to Kristeva, Irigaray identifies a linkage in western thought between woman and place or space, in *difference* from time. Thus, in this claim she encourages feminists to rethink woman's place so as to relocate her *within* the time of the masculine subject, whereas, according to her critique, time is interior to this subject alone. According to my suggestion, by identifying the practices of memory, desire, fantasy and recollection as *ahistorical*, the latter can be claimed to reside *within* the masculine subject's time. As I have shown throughout my analysis, Hegel confers on these practices a vital role in the constitution of the *knowledge* on which self-consciousness acts in the course of its becoming historical (as well as throughout its historical progression). Hence, these ahistorical practices can be claimed to *condition* the possibility of the sociohistorical subject. As my dual reading implies, Hegel includes these practices in the category of the theorizing form of action, and thereby their distinctive nature is concealed. But once it is acknowledged, Hegel's distinction between historical and ahistorical forms of self-constitution—which is the very foundation upon which his philosophical notion of sexual difference is built—is destabilized.

Notes

1. Henceforth *PS.* All the following citations are from A. V. Miller's translation (Oxford: Oxford University Press, 1977) unless otherwise is indicated.
2. Robert Pippin, "You Can't Get There From Here," in *The Cambridge Companion to Hegel,* ed. F. C. Beiser (Cambridge: Cambridge University Press, 1993).
3. *PS,* § 451, 268–270.
4. Ibid.
5. It should be stressed that according to this suggestion Hegel contends in these chapters that the conditions for the possibility of knowledge are neither given a-priori nor can be individual but are rather necessarily *constituted* in *relation* to the other.
6. I do this, however, in the first part of my unpublished dissertation *The Significance of Sexual Difference in and for Hegel's Phenomenology of Spirits.*
7. In the Introduction to the second part of the *Encyclopaedia* Hegel claims that when self-consciousness "withdraw[s] from natural things" by adopting a purely theoretical point of view, "the naturalness, individuality, and the immediacy of things vanish." G. W. F. Hegel, *Philosophy of Nature, Part II of the Encyclopaedia of the Philosophical Sciences,* trans. A. V. Miller (Oxford: Oxford University Press, 2004), 1, § 246Z., 197–198. Quoted from: Robert Stern, *Hegel and the Phenomenology of Spirit* (London: Routledge, 2002), 68.
8. Hegel's discussion of lordship and bondage in the fifth chapter restates and elaborates on this idea in negative terms, while claiming that it equally applies within a *social* form of life. Specifically, the lord's form of life consists in living on the slave's work while his mastery is established through a linguistic articulation of orders and demands. Thereby, Hegel claims, the lord retires from the world and leaves it untouched hence is determined to impotence. The slave, on the other hand, follows the lord's orders and satisfies his demands by cultivating the land and preparing goods that the first consumes. By this means

the slave expresses his individual sense of self in an objective manner that is vital for his becoming into an independent and free subject.

9. C.f. Hegel's *PS*, § 162, 100–102.
10. Pippin "You Can't Get There From Here," 63–71.
11. Slavoj Žižek, *Enjoy Your Symptom!* (London: Routledge, 1992).
12. Simone de Beauvoir, *The Second Sex*, trans. H. M. Parshley (Harmondsworth: Penguin Books, 1988).
13. Judith Butler, *Subjects of Desire: Hegelian Reflections in Twentieth-Century France* (New York: Columbia University Press, 1987).
14. In *Subjects of Desire* Judith Butler explicates this point in the following way: "At this stage of the dramatization of desire, unacceptable impoverishment seems to be its consequence; either as narcissism or as enthrallment with the object, desire is at odds with itself and dissatisfied" (Butler 1987, 34).
15. It should be remarked that Hegel's appropriation of the case of Antigone can be contended to exhibit a counterexample to this general claim. Hegel himself, however, does not acknowledge this.
16. As Hegel claims in his *Philosophy of Right* (henceforth PR): "The man's dominion is scientific universal cognition, and so art is the object of the man ... These are the man's provinces. There can be exceptions for individual women, but the exception in not the rule. Women, when they trespass into these provinces, put the provinces themselves in danger." Editorial Notes to Hegel *Elements of the Philosophy of Right,* trans. H. B. Nisbet, ed. A. W. Wood (Cambridge: Cambridge University Press, 1991): § 166, 439, from Hegel's lectures of 1822–1823, *Vorlesungen ¨uber Rechtsphilosophie*, 3, 1974, 525–526.
17. C.f. Terry Pinkard, *Hegel's Phenomenology: The Sociality of Reason* (Cambridge: Cambridge University Press, 1996), 306.
18. "In its external relations, the former [man] is powerful and active, the latter [woman] passive and subjective ... Woman, however, has her substantial vocation [*Bestimmung*] in the family, and her ethical disposition consists in this [family] *piety*" (Hegel, *PR*, § 166, 206).
19. Hannah Arendt, *The Human Condition* (Chicago. University of Chicago Press, 1998).
20. Julia Kristeva, Women's Time, trans. Alice Jardine and Harry Blake, *Signs: Journal of Women in Culture and Society 7*, no. 1 (1981): 13–35.
21. Kristeva, 1981, 16.
22. Ibid.
23. Terry Pinkard put forward this point in: *Hegel's Phenomenology*, 1996, 28.
24. Hegel's *PS*, § 166–171, 104–108.
25. "But *for us*, or *in itself*, the object which *for self-consciousness* is the negative element has, on its side, returned into itself, just as on the other side consciousness has done. Through this reflection into itself

the object has become Life" (Hegel, *PS*, § 168, 106. Latter italics added).

26. Hegel put this point in the following way: "Thus in the movement of consciousness there occurs a moment of *being-in-itself* or *being-for-us* which is not present to the consciousness comprehended in the experience itself. The *content*, however, of what presents itself to us does *for It* ... *For it*, what has thus arisen exists only as an object" (Hegel, *PS*, § 87, 56). "Because of this necessity," Hegel continues, "the way to Science is itself already *Science*" (Ibid., § 88, 56).

27. "But it is just this necessity itself, or the *origination* of the new object, that presents itself to consciousness without its understanding how this happens, which proceeds for us, as it were, behind the back of consciousness" (Hegel, *PS*, § 88, 56).

28. Emmanuel Levinas, *Totality and Infinity: An Essay on Exteriority*, trans. Alphonso Lingis (Pittsburgh, PA: Duquesne University Press, 1998), 57.

29. See: Elizabeth Grosz, Julia Kristeva, in *Feminism and Psychoanalysis: A Critical Dictionary*, ed. Elizabeth Wright (Oxford UK and Massachusetts USA: Blackwell, 1992), 195.

30. Ibid.

31. Jessica Benjamin, *The Bonds of Love: Psychoanalysis, Feminism, and the Problem of Domination* (New York: Pantheon Books, 1988), 199.

32. Julia Kristeva, Stabat Mater, in *Feminist Social Thought: A Reader*, ed. Diana T. Meyers (New York & London: Routledge, 1997), 303.

33. Luce Irigaray, *Speculum of the Other Woman*, trans. Gillian Gill (Ithaca: Cornell University Press, 1985), 42.

34. Irigaray, 1985, 42.

35. Luce Irigaray, "Sexual Difference," in *The Irigaray Reader: Luce Irigaray*, ed. and trans. Margaret Whitford (London: Wiley-Blackwell, 1992), 166.

CHAPTER NINE

Womanlife or Lifework and Psycho-technique: Woman as the Figure of the Plasticity of Transcendence

Susanna Lindberg

In what follows, I will reexamine the *figure* of woman found, reaffirmed, and reinterpreted by Hegel: I will present the woman as a figure of—to use a word coined by Nancy and developed by Malabou—the *"plasticity" of transcendence*. The importance for Hegel of "plasticity" was brought forth by Jean-Luc Nancy in his *La remarque spéculative (un bon mot de Hegel)*, and it has been further developed by Catherine Malabou since her *Avenir de Hegel, ou de la plasticité temporelle en dialectique*.[1] Nancy's work on plasticity is closely connected to his friend and colleague Philippe Lacoue-Labarthe's work on *figuration* and, more generally, on a kind of "malleability" of transcendence.[2] Nancy and Lacoue-Labarthe used a whole set of notions such that "plasticity," "malleability," "figuration," "rhythm," "scheme," et cetera, in order to go deeper into the question of *presentation* in philosophy that had been thematized by philosophers such as Jacques Derrida. Nancy's and Lacoue-Labarthe's terms are not late interpretations of Hegel, but rather a rediscovery of a thematic that was very important for German idealism and romanticism, namely the question of the presentation (*Darstellung*) of truth and its relation to art and fiction: if truth is to be not only *revealed* but also *presented*, then philosophy has to face the problematics of figurality and plasticity that enable presentation as such.

In this chapter I will study the "woman" as a privileged figure of such a transcendental plasticity. I will also show why the "woman" is, for Hegel, a major *figure* of an *absence* or of an *invisible* work of the negativity—a proposition that would be unthinkable without some kind of a figuration.

FIGURAL THINKING

Addressing the "woman" as a *figure*, I stress that the "woman," for Hegel, is neither an idea (like freedom) nor a real individual (like the heroes that form history). What does it mean to address a *figure* in Hegel's work?

In Hegel's work, a figure is a *phenomenological crystallization* of an intense complex of natural, historical, and symbolic circumstances, which is presented as an element of the process of philosophical knowing. A figure is *not an idea*, which comprises a timeless truth and can be exposed in a purely logical manner. A figure is already an articulation of sense and a sketch of truth—but it necessarily remains incomplete and obscure. A figure belongs to the domain of *particularity*. Because of their particularity, figures never contain the whole truth, but all of them are unilateral. Consequently, figures are *multiple* (for example, master and bondsman, Creon and Antigone). Particular figures are finite and modifiable, and that is why they are equally *historical*. One could describe a figure as being a kind of a historical idea, because it represents a possibility of coherence in the midst of a changing world.

Hegel's figures are often *fictions*, such as master and bondsman, Antigone and Creon, or the Mother of Christ. (Hegel's phenomenology differs from the contemporary phenomenology precisely because the former is based on figures, whereas the latter seeks a pure seeing of singular realities: one could approximately say that twentieth-century phenomenology starts from sensations, whereas early nineteenth-century German thinkers focus on phenomena of imagination.) In Hegel's work, however, a figure is not just any fiction, but only a figure that is capable of organizing an entire life-form; in this respect, figures resemble myths, only they do not propose divine *foundations* for the circumstances but just help in their *articulation*. Hegel's thinking is essentially figural and, at the same time, it claims to present truth in the most demanding sense: as absolute truth. This is how Hegel confronts us with a seemingly paradoxical idea of a *truth that is founded on fiction*.[3]

A figure is an instance of mediation—between universality and singularity, between concept and senses. We can trace such an idea of particular *figures* down to Kant's idea of the *"schemes* of imagination," that is to say, to the "secret activity of the soul," by which the sensibility is informed by the understanding and the understanding is incorporated in sensations.[4] Kant's schemes are particular traits that permit us to grasp unlimited, contingent reality and make sense of it. When Hegel examines figures instead of schemes, he pushes the same principle much further. To put it briefly, when schemes determine *objects*, figures determine *subjects* of knowledge and action. A figure does not present a true object but also a subject of certainty: the instance of a truth's discovery, articulation, birth, and invention.

Figures permit us to treat changing, historical, contingent realities in a philosophical manner. This is the important, positive side of figural thinking. However, figural thinking is very ambiguous. The principal danger of figures is their *normative* use—which has often been the lot of Hegelian figures (just remember the multiple, ideological uses of the dialectic of master and bondsman). Yet their very particularity and unilaterality should warn us against such temptations: at the very instant a figure is fixed it becomes a strain for the essential freedom of spirit. That is why in theoretical situations and in practical reality our aim should rather be to *shatter the figures*.[5] The same goes for the woman's figure in Hegel's work: myself, I examine it principally in order to bring out a destabilizing, if not straightforwardly deconstructive, effect on Hegel's thought, not in order to find a rule for any woman's concrete behavior.[6]

In what follows, I will examine woman as a single, rather unitary figure: a figure of life, death, and love. She appears as the figure of life mainly in the context of sexual difference.[7] She comes out as a figure of death through certain figurations of femininity, such as not only Antigone, who, being a theater *character,*[8] is the *figure par excellence*, but also the Erinyes, Ceres, Virgin Mary, and other Mother Goddesses. At the limit of life and death, the woman stands for the social affect as such—for love, which Hegel takes to be higher than simple animal sexuality and lower than genuine political recognition.[9] Female characters are not as frequent in Hegel's phenomenological account as masculine ones, but there are enough of them to bring out a "logic" of "femininity." On the contrary, even though Hegel analyses several female figures and characters, his account of history does not know women having really *existed*. Hegel's history is the suite of men, of the *geniuses* of art, philosophy, and politics, who together constitute the true plurality of men—a "republic of spirits." But there is no history of great women. Hegel knows female characters but no female geniuses—this too is in keeping with the concept of woman.

WOMAN AS A FIGURE OF LIFE

To start with, Hegel's woman would be a *figure of life*, insofar as life is interpreted as *soul*. Such an interpretation governs the transition between the *Encyclopedia*'s *Philosophy of Nature* and *Philosophy of Spirit*. This transition is one of the specific places of the femininity in the System.[10] She emerges with sexual difference, at the summit of the *Philosophy of Nature*.[11] Then she comes out in several passages of the *Anthropology*, which constitutes the first part of the *Philosophy of Spirit*: here we find notably the sexual relation,[12] the child's gestation in mother's womb,[13] and different pathological states such as sonnambulism, hypnotism, and magnetism (that seems to affect specifically "female friends with delicate nerves," *nervenschwachen Freundinnen*).[14] One could say that the whole of Hegel's *Anthropology* treats dispositions that were, at the time, regarded as being specifically feminine, for it is all about the soul's substantial, passive, unconscious, dreamlike, pathological states.

What are the philosophical stakes of this development that is specifically figured by femininity? The passage from parts two and three of the *Encyclopedia* is the transition from nature to spirit. For Hegel, nature and spirit are not sharply opposed, but spirit rises from nature and nature incorporates spirit. Hegel presents the transition between them—more precisely between the last moment of Nature (the animal) and the first moment of Spirit (soul)—by bringing out their original unity in the concept of *life*. Hegel thinks of this unity by going back to Aristotle, particularly to *On the Soul* (*Peri Psykhe*). In this treatise, life and soul are indeed intertwined, if not synonymous: Soul is the actuality of a body having life potentially within it: *psykhe* is the *entelechy* proper of the *zoon*, living being.[15] Soul occupies a crucial position: it is the common source of nature and spirit, of animal and human, and of sense and thought.

I want to stress the importance of this transition for Hegel. He does not think of the totality of being in terms of a simple opposition between the two *substances* of nature and spirit but rather focuses on the gradual transition and mediation between them through the *activity* of life. Such an idea of life has its origin in Kant's *Critique of Judgement*, and it inspired the whole of the Idealist and Romantic Movement. Kant faced the necessity of getting beyond the sharp division between *res cogitans* and *res extensa*, or between mechanist and spiritualist explications of nature, or between mechanism and freedom as principles of action. He understood that the solution lies in examining, instead of simple *substances* (such as *res extensa* and *res cogitans*), the *activity* that produces them. An archetype for such dynamic thinking is precisely Aristotle's principle of *entelechy* that Kant develops further in his idea of *teleology*.[16] Now, life is such a teleological principle. It is not nature as opposed to spirit, but the movement of becoming-self-conscious of nature and becoming-natural of self-consciousness. Life is not a domain of objects, it is a movement that constitutes an embodied subject; it is not a determining judgment but a reflexive one; it is a mediation, not a definition. Kant went as far as this. He studied teleology in works of art and in nature, in other words, in the domains of artificial and natural techniques. The German Idealists, especially Hegel, pushed Kant's discovery much further. They affirmed what Kant only proposed as an analogy: life is the very principle of subjectivity—not only in singular living beings but in the absolute subject itself. This is why life is the fundamental principle of Hegel's system—which is all about overcoming oppositions by mediations, transitions, passages, and syntheses. As such, life is a logical concept, but it also appears in several figures, the most famous of which are Dionysos (of the Great Bacchanal of Spirit)[17] and the Christ (who is "way, truth and life.")[18]

This is the context of the feminine figure of life. Woman is not the supreme figure of life: that would be God as the infinite life of the spirit. Instead, she figures life as soul: as the passage between nature and spirit, or between animality and humanity. Instead of representing one of the poles of this transition (nature), she *operates* the very movement of transition and makes it visible. And this is how *she stands for the birth of the spirit*.

WOMAN'S IDLE LIFEWORK

Woman really *makes* this transition, and the activity of synthesizing this passage and creating the transition is the woman's own work. To be suggestive, I might call it a *lifework*, a *psycho-technique,* and even a *bio-technique*—but these are not Hegel's words. Let us rather see how Hegel characterizes woman's work.

Hegel's woman is not a thing, she is an activity. At the simplest level, as a female animal, her most characteristic activity is childbirth. It has often been remarked that Hegel, like so many others ever since Aristotle, considers femininity as "matter" in respect to masculinity as "form."[19] Nevertheless, the matter described in Hegel's *Philosophy of Nature* is not an inert raw material (like the piece of wood that is the original sense of *hyle*, out of which the male would carve his offspring in his image). In Hegel's dynamic science of nature, even the abstract notion of matter describes an activity. Already in *Mechanics*, Hegel shows that what we generally take to be a material body is only an abstraction of the essential character of matter. In reality, matter is not a given entity that moves *in* a given, empty, indifferent space-time, because it *is* the temporalization of space and the spatialization of time.[20] In other words, matter *is* gravity, not a dead body submitted to external forces but a force in itself and, as such, already an outline of life.[21] Therefore, when Hegel compares the female to matter, he actually describes gravidity as the condition of gravity: the maternal instance provides the dimension of pure, restless differentiation that hosts the opening up of space and time.[22] Of course, the living being is much more than a simple piece of matter, but it still is essentially an originary spacing and temporalizing.[23] The female is the "place" in which this originary stretching out can take place. Furthermore, a concrete living being is more than a simple spatiotemporal existence: it has a form stemming from a gradual differentiation. The maternal instance does not *produce* this form, but she provides a ground of differentiation that allows the stabilization of the future child's figure, but that has no figure of her own.

Such a metaphysical idea of a place "before" real space and time and of a pure differentiation "before" real figures may seem strange. This idea of a "feminine" ground of life draws from a long tradition, however. It reflects Plato's notion of *khôra*, of a "maternal" "third genre" between the "paternal" idea and its "child," the existent thing. *Khôra* is no *thing* in itself but only the *mediation* between idea and reality: it is the receptacle of all forms that has no form of its own, and a source of all reality with no reality of its own.[24] Or to put it in another context, the maternal ground of life is the material version of what Kant called the transcendental imagination: a blind work of schematization, out of which a figure (a child) can come.[25]

Sexuality is a higher manifestation of the same logic in the domain of life itself: the animal's offspring comes out of a sexual *difference* instead of simply reduplicating the male model. The female is, then, the very *locus* of this differentiation when it is considered as such: as *pure* differentiation where the identity does not affirm itself, yet.

The "materiality" of the female in reproduction also describes her *relation* to the male: she is supposed to be the "passive" element of conception. No doubt, woman remains "passive" in the sense that in order to give birth she cannot but *receive* semen and carry the child as if *despite* of herself. Nevertheless, she is powerless not so much in regard to the progenitor's will as in regard to the child's specific identity: also for Hegel, the child is absolutely new and unknown (and we can note in passing that the child is a stranger to the father, too, who will have to educate it in order to know himself in it). I will return to the question of childbirth below. For now, I just resume: woman's passivity is not that of an object, but *passivity is her own activity*, her way of being. Woman is the *capacity* to *give* oneself to *be taken* by a form. She is the figure of abandon and exposition, but in the sense that giving oneself is an action. The principle of the feminine action is that of "espousing a form" and "embodying an idea."

Because femininity is this capacity of exposing oneself to forthcoming forms, figures, impulses, or events, it is the very figure of the plasticity of transcendence—of capacity for modification, regeneration, and change. The woman's position in regard to the "male form" or the "rational idea" is oblique. To be exact, the principal process of the formation of spirit goes on as an "education" (of young males), and the female principle assists this process sideways and occasionally. The young male is formed *in view* of the idea, the female just undergoes diverse impulsions without a specific direction. This difference is significant. Whereas the young man's negativity is productive, the woman's negativity remains purely negative.[26] It also means that the woman has a purer way of being-in-relation-with-something-other, and that her teleology is different from that of man's.

First we consider the being-in-relation-with-something-else. In a Hegelian context, all knowledge and action presuppose a relation with something other and, henceforth, a capacity to be *affected* by the other (thing, person, idea, et cetera). Generally, spirit is supposed to gather itself after such affection, or to *appropriate* the other. A young man's education is just another figure of this capacity to be affected (by the master)—in view of the end of the education in the act of an auto-affirmation (that suppresses the master in a victorious "*Aufhebung.*") On the contrary, femininity figures a being-under-influence and a being-affected *without* appropriation of the other, and without affirmation of the autonomy of self. Femininity is the pure being-affected-by-something. This is illustrated by the process of reproduction, where woman conceives and delivers the child who, so to say, swims through her. It is illustrated even better by the logic of the "genius" described in the §405 of the *Encyclopedia*.[27] Genius is a subject who supplants and subjugates another subject: genius is an alien subjectivity that *possesses* somebody. Hegel says that a mother is a child's genius when she has psychic influence on the baby in her womb. He also believes that young women are particularly sensitive to the so-called magical relations, where somebody is possessed by another subjectivity (that is why it is supposedly easy to hypnotize them). In both cases of "magical relations" a person's subjectivity is outside of herself: her subjectivity is alien, it is another subjectivity. Whether she possesses somebody or is possessed herself, woman is the very figure of such a possession. She is what *rests* open to the other and incapable of gathering herself: she is the very figure of division and scattering.

The general Hegelian logic of recognition presupposes such a possession, such a contact with another subjectivity, but it equally presupposes a turning back from the other, so that each subject can affirm its autonomy at its place, *bei sich*: it presupposes a separation and a conscious confrontation, which is not the case in the feminine possession. Motherlove is the very figure of pure recognition of the other as such, even before language and before the combat of recognition that will return each self-consciousness to itself.[28]

And yet, woman's passive, influenceable, and scattered being, her constant being-outside-of-herself, remains an *activity*. The external impulse, male or genius, does not just *impress* the woman, it gets a genuine *response*; it is not only *reflected* from the woman but also undergoes a process of *gestation* and *maturing* (instead of the simple digestion and consumption that define the animal metabolism). Something *else* comes out after woman's intervention. She enables an activity of which she is neither the subject nor the object but the ground (fundus and heart...). Now, such an activity describes very exactly the logic of the internal *teleology* of the finite beings. Generally scholars evoking Hegel's teleology pay attention only to the absolute and in any event give a very voluntaristic account of it. Teleology is understood as an eminently conscious and quasi-intentional process, the sense of which is the realization of a preexisting idea. This amounts to thinking of teleology as if it was a method for fabricating objects, beings, or truths according to a subject's will. I maintain, however, that Hegel's teleology—following Kant's—does not *proceed* from a self-consciousness or from any intentionality—even if a self-consciousness may *follow* it. The hero of the world history is the archetype of a finite being's teleological action: now, he is taken by the *ruse* of the world spirit and remains absolutely *unconscious* of what he does.[29] Teleology is an action that has an aim, not a production that has a model—knowing that an aim belongs to the future, when a model belongs to the past. A subject's aim does not preexist his or her action: on the contrary, it is possible to show that the Hegelian teleology is a way of being open to an *alien* will, *exterior* event, or other impulse, so that it may *become* an *aim* directing an action and, thus, modifying the form of its agent. I know this is a very complicated idea and goes against some of the toughest preconceptions of action and of teleology.[30] But that is precisely where the woman's figure may be helpful. A finite being can act in a teleological manner since it is open to chance, suggestion, and hazard (like semen, beloved, hypnotizer). When such an external event starts to direct somebody's action, she (or he) is taken into an activity of which she (or he) is neither the subject nor the object but an agent. The subject and the object do not precede the agent's action but follow from it: the agent's activity produces the object and transforms him/herself into a subject.

Hegel's woman stands for a specific activity: a teleology whose aim is outside of its agent. Her activity is neither a simple mechanism (such as the life of the Cartesian animal-machine) nor a self-conscious activity (such as "man's" productive work and creative action). It is teleology without intention or consciousness, a work that she does not will or provoke but still happens only through her. Such would be the woman's work that I have tentatively called it *lifework* and *psycho-technique*. To put it very briefly, lifework produces a child and psycho-technique produces a language, and I will show why these two works should be feminine and why they describe a production that is none.

Woman's Unconscious Psycho-technique: The Guardian of the Cradle and of the Tomb

The human being as such is, for Hegel, a finite spirit (this expression is already a contradiction as such). His finitude has everything to do with time. *Lifework* and *psycho-technique* are also *timework*. To explain the woman's relation to time, I leave the *Encyclopedia* and move toward the *Phenomenology of Spirit*.

It is easy to reckon that Hegel's conception of time is made out of several layers. The idea is *eternal* and, even for Hegel, essentially timeless. A God is different: he is not timeless but *immortal*, not outside of time but outside of death or capable of overcoming it. *Death* is the fate of the human being. Certainly other living beings too perish, but only the human being relates to his death as to his destiny. The phenomenological account of the so-called dialectic of master and bondsman shows us that according to Hegel, human consciousness becomes a true self-consciousness when it meets death as its "absolute master."[31] More specifically, death is the affair of human males, insofar as the public confrontation with death (in duel, war, crime, punishment, and sacrifice) is constitutive of the human community, which remains a predominantly masculine matter in Hegel's account. Men risk their lives,[32] set off for war,[33] have their heads cut off like cabbage,[34] lay scattered on the ground, and need to be buried[35] and resurrected,[36] et cetera. Men's work forms the permanent world that resists the immediate negativity of natural time, of which death gives a glimpse; their action tears a given world apart, so that another configuration of the world might take place. Different ways of defying the "absolute master" determine the "spiritual presence" (*geistige Gegenwart*)[37] of human self-consciousness and community.

What is the woman's place in this history? She is not immersed in the pure life of the animals, who do not question the coincidence of the individual death with the species' reproduction.[38] The woman is not unaware of death—and yet she does not reside in the "spiritual presence" either.[39] In Hegel's account, the woman intervenes just before birth and just after death. She assists in these two passages between humankind and the natural condition. Either she gives life, in the figure of mother, or she buries dead corpses, mourns them, and stops the work of death, in the figure of Antigone and certain other characters evoked by Hegel. In these ways, she resists the work of nature and its time of pure disappearance, by opening a dimension in which the human being can *rest*. This is how the femininity dwells just below self-consciousness, before life, after death. Her lifework is giving birth and stopping death. Contrary to the bondsman, she does not give permanence to her own self in the objective world. Instead, she protects others from natural consumption and human oblivion by preserving them in the inner space of her memory. In this sense, she is the very figure of what Hegel calls "subjective time": time as memory, oblivion, hope, and fear.[40] This is how the "woman" marks the birthplace of human time: she is the figure of the transcendental synthesis of human time (that can become objective history when it is seized by a "male" action).

No doubt, the figure of such a *mater dolorosa* is old and narrow—but it is a *figure*, a powerful and terrifying myth. What is its speculative sense? But first, what is the speculative sense of childbirth? That human life is event-like. It is coming to be and going to nothingness, an incandescent point of becoming, countless points scattered in instantaneous, finite jolts. For Hegel, a child is not a product of either of its parents, but it comes out of the obscurity of a sexual *difference*.[41] Birth is a speculative event par excellence, a qualitative leap, where an entire new possibility appears.[42] Of course, it has conditions. A child has a genealogy, and it is submitted to the "unconscious influence" of the maternal, and to the conscious education of the paternal. Yet birth and the end of the education are analogous moments, where a subject emancipates itself from such influences and claims its own freedom. The child needs to be ungrateful in order to be autonomous, and this is the condition of all historical change, artistic creation, and spiritual life.

The mother's work, or what I called the woman's *lifework*, consists in simply letting this happen. On the one hand, however hard her labor, her work is nevertheless "idle" in the sense that her conscious will and knowledge cannot produce the child. Her subjectivity does not count in the becoming of the child. She can only be *hospitable* to the future child, receive the future subject to herself (*bei ihr, chez elle*), open her interiority ("womb," "heart") to house the alien subject.

On the other hand, the woman's apparent passivity "does" something. Her "lifework" is really a "psycho-technique" that prepares the birth of the spirit. It is best understood in terms of temporality: in this sense one could say that the woman's work consists in *giving time*. She synthesizes the primary human time, which could be called an "immemorial time": Hegel associates the feminine time with custom, tradition, and the conservation of the immemorial ethical inheritance figured by Antigone's "Penates." In the *Phenomenology of Spirit*, Hegel grants a right of its own to the immemorial time of the tradition, but in the *History of Philosophy* he scolds it for being incapable of the change and the newness required by history.[43] A child's birth is a virtual possibility of change; only the man's historical action realizes it. None of these tears the natural time itself, but only the ethical time of "tradition"—which would not exist if the woman did not create it as her "im-memory."

The feminine "im-memory" already deals with the past, and this is why its operation is always already a work of mourning. What is the speculative sense of mourning and of the funeral service that stands for it? Hegel quotes a surprising amount of figures of mourning. Everybody knows the case of Antigone, who is the exemplary figure of a funeral ritual that is needed so that a citizen could rest in the memory of the city.[44] But Antigone is not the only such figure. She is closely preceded by the Erinyes, goddesses of vengeance who mourn the loss of Iphigenia and Clytemnestra.[45] Ceres is equally important for Hegel (she is the goddess of corn and also mother of Koré, who died and became Persephone, goddess of the Underworld: Ceres is the very figure of an inconsolable mother who mourns the loss of her daughter).[46] Naturally Hegel also refers to Virgin Mary.[47] Both Mary and Ceres are mothers who each lost her child, double figures of motherlove and mourning, birth and death, cradle and tomb; Antigone and the Erinyes just mourn, but in the Greek context, they also mourn their childlessness. When these figures of mourning mothers abound, other possible female figures are absent from Hegel's speculative discourse. He gives practically no place to erotic figures such as Aphrodite, or to muses such as Eurydike, or to heroines such as Penthesilea. For him, the woman's speculative role is above all to be the guardian of birth and death.

These figures show the Hegelian woman's relationship to death. Unlike the masculine figures of Hegel's phenomenological account, these women do not meet the absolute master personally: they neither die nor kill, and they do not shiver for themselves. Instead, they mourn dead parents, and this is the woman's work. The description of the ethical world in the *Phenomenology of Spirit* shows most clearly that woman's work consists in the funeral service that stops nature's mindless work, which aims at returning the dead body to organic nature.[48] Once again, burying a beloved person is not essentially a production or a fabrication (the material construction of the tomb belongs to artisans and artists and has nothing to do with the dead person). One essentially buries a beloved person in one's "heart," so that, once again, woman gives hospitality to someone else, opens her intimacy to an exterior person.[49] This is woman's second work or what I called earlier her *psycho-technique*: it is a *work of memory* that consists in dealing with dead people and lost moments, keeping them in mind and forgetting them, preserving them and mourning for them. The funerary service is a work of memory where a person's disappearance is made up for by a representation (*Vorstellung*): the lost person is replaced by his sign.

One could compare this funerary work with the creation of linguistic signs in Hegel's *Psychology*, which is another science of the "soul." Hegel compares representation with a *"tomb"* in which an "alien soul" waits for its resurrection in the process of speculative comprehension.[50] But before such a comprehension, the representation is created and conserved in a long process of memory and imagination outside of the conscience in what Hegel calls the "night-like abyss"[51] of the unconsciousness. Woman's "psycho-technique" seems to correspond to the unconscious work of the imagination that first creates representations and signs, that is to say, that creates language as such—perhaps, the mother tongue. Which is a necessary, if not sufficient, condition for speculative philosophy.

So, woman's work would be nonproductive, nonconscious hospitality to the child (who will be a finite spirit capable of freedom) and to the language (which will become thought). Such being-under-influence was already her role in the *Anthropology* where we examined woman's relation to an alien genius. Now she is possessed by the future and by the past: indeed, she loves absent people, unborn children and dead kinsmen, and if her society is often wordless this is because you cannot really talk with people who are not *here*. Lifework is called fertile, psycho-technique is called sterile, but both are works of gestation, rumination, conservation, and maturation. Woman slows down the natural time, gives time to nightly processes of maturation. This is how "woman" is presented as a hollow space where an invisible work takes place: she is the figure of the transcendental imagination as far as it is "invisible"; but contrasting the *purity* of the Kantian faculty of imagination, the Hegelian woman figures a *concrete* imagination that schematizes the time of real, contingent events without knowing whether the concept is to seize them or not.

FIGURE OF ABSENCE

To conclude, I propose to consider Hegel's woman as a *figure of absence*. She is almost an absent figure. Femininity does not constitute a moment of its own in the system. Sexual difference is treated in scattered remarks in the transition between the *Philosophy of Nature* and *Philosophy of Spirit*. Hegel's analysis of the family in the *Phenomenology of Spirit* and in the *Philosophy of Right* mainly reveals the woman's curious status as a non-political condition of politics. Because "femininity" is not a clear-cut category of its own but rather a subterranean "logic" that contributes to several conceptual constellations, my preceding presentation necessarily remains somewhat speculative too. However, I do not think that "real" women ought to be offended by the fact that "femininity" is not a moment of the system but a figure that haunts it: after all, "the human being" is not a concept either, but the operator of all concepts.

On the other hand, woman is very clearly a figure of absence on the real, political scene. Her work belongs before or after the bright "presence of spirit" that opens up the political space. She assists the spiritual daylight by maturating and delivering its two conditions: the individual human being and language. But she does not participate in it. She has no presence, no present work, no capacity for regular political, artistic, and philosophical action.

But most profoundly, woman is the figure par excellence of the retreat of the conditions of thought. She *makes visible the transition* between nature and spirit, animal and man, sense and thought. She is the visibility of the work of negativity in this particular, crucial transition.

Woman is the figure of *absence*. But on the other hand, she *is* the *figure* of absence. She makes absence visible. Her figure permits us to observe the functioning of the mediation. Mediator par excellence, embodied or incarnated mediation, the "woman" maybe does not see but is visible to us—exposed, seen, seen seeing what is not there.

NOTES

1. Jean-Luc Nancy, *La remarque spéculative (un bon mot de Hegel)* (Paris: Galilée, 1973), in particular the "Préambule." English translation by Céline Surprenant, *The speculative remark. One of Hegel's bons mots* (Stanford: Stanford University Press, 2001), "Préambule." Catherine Malabou, *L'Avenir de Hegel: Plasticité, Temporalité, Dialectique* (Paris: J. Vrin, 1996). English translation by Lisabeth During, *The future of Hegel. Plasticity, temporality, dialectic* (New York: Routledge, 2005).

2. See, in particular, Philippe Lacoue-Labarthe, Philippe «Typographie». In *Mimesis des articulations*, ed. Sylviane Agaçinski (Paris: Flammarion, 1975). Translated as «Typography» in *Typography, Mimesis, Philosophy, Politics*, trans. Christopher Fynsk (Cambridge: Harvard University Press, 1989). I explain the stakes of Lacoue-Labarthe's work in my "Ontorythmie," forthcoming in *Revue philosophique de Louvain*.

3. For instance, *tragedy* has been shown to be "the origin or matrix...of speculative thought" in particular by Philippe Lacoue-Labarthe in *Typography, Mimesis, Philosophy, Politics*, 208. For a general presentation of the interpretation of Hegel's thought through tragedy, see Theodore D. George, introduction to *Tragedies of Spirit* (New York: State University of New York Press, 2006). I might just add: not all figures of Hegel's *Phenomenology* are tragic, but all of them are figural.

4. Immanuel Kant, *Kritik der reinen Vernunft*, 1 (Frankfurt am Main: Suhrkamp, 1974), A141/B181, 190. Translated as *The Critique of pure Reason*, by N. K. Smith (London: Macmillan, 1952).

5. Following the "imperative" of Philippe Lacoue-Labarthe, formulated in his *Heidegger—la politique du poème* (Paris: Galilée, 2002), 152.

6. In this article, my approach will be different from Luce Irigaray's in the chapter "The Eternal Irony of Community" of *Speculum of the Other Woman*, trans. Gillian C. Gill (New York: Cornell University Press, 1985), and from Judith Butler's in *Antigone's Claim. Kinship Between Life and Death* (New York: Columbia University Press, 2000), because I will not examine the political potential of Antigone. Apart from that, my approach of Hegel is close to theirs.

7. According to Hegel, sexual difference is an essential determination of animal life, and it is particularly marked in the human species. In the human beings, sexuality determines both the habitus and the spiritual nature. See Hegel, *Enzyklopädie der philosophischen Wissenschaften 2, Werke 9* (Frankfurt am Main: Suhrkamp, 1970), § 355 *Zusätze*, 459,

translated as *Hegel's Philosophy of Nature 3,* Michael John Petry (London and New York: George Allen and Unwin Ltd. and Humanities Press, 1970), 131.

8. Hegel analyses Antigone as a "character," which is also a psychological type or a character, but above all the character in theater. G. W. F. Hegel, *Phänomenologie des Geistes, Werke 3* (Frankfurt am Main: Suhrkamp, 1970), 343. Translated as *Phenomenology of Spirit by* A. V. Miller (Oxford: Oxford University Press, 1977), 280.

9. For a comprehensive presentation of the notion of love in Hegel's work, see Laura Werner, *The Restless Love of Thinking* (Helsinki: University of Helsinki Press, 2007).

10. As Kimberly Hutchings says, the Hegelian woman makes the transition between spirit and nature: Kimberly Hutchings, *Hegel and Feminist Philosophy* (Cambridge: Polity Press, 2003), 45. Correlatively, it is possible to interpret the Hegelian man as the transition between human and divine.

11. Hegel, *Enzyklopädie der philosophischen Wissenschaften 2, Werke 9* (Frankfurt am Main: Suhrkamp, 1970), § 367 Zus, 499; § 369 Zus, 519 translated as *Hegel's Philosophy of Nature 3,* by Michael John Petry (London and New York: George Allen and Unwin Ltd. and Humanities Press, 1970), 172. Sexual relation is the highest point of nature: Hegel, *Enzyklopädie der philosophischen Wissenschaften 3, Werke 10* (Frankfurt am Main: Suhrkamp, 1970), § 381 Zus, 20. Translated as *Hegel's Philosophy of Subjective Spirit 1,* by Michael John Petry (Dodrecht and Boston: D. Reidel Publishing Co., 1979), 33.

12. Hegel, *Enzyklopädie der philosophischen Wissenschaften 3, Werke 10* (Frankfurt am Main: Suhrkamp, 1970), § 397, 86. Translated as *Hegel's Philosophy of Subjective Spirit 2,* by Michael John Petry (Dodrecht and Boston: D. Reidel Publishing Co., 1979), 125.

13. Hegel, *Enzyklopädie der philosophischen Wissenschaften 3,* § 405 Anm, 125. *Hegel's Philosophy of Subjective Spirit 2,* 221.

14. Hegel, *Enzyklopädie der philosophischen Wissenschaften 3,* § 405 Anm, 126. *Hegel's Philosophy of Subjective Spirit 2,* 223.

15. Aristotle, *De anima, in The Works of Aristotle,* vol. 3 (Oxford: Clarendon Press, 1931), 2, 1, 412a. On Hegel's theory of the living being, see my "Vivant à la limite." *Les Études philosophiques,* n° 1/2006, 107–120.

16. Immanuel Kant, *Kritik der Urteilskraft* (Frankfurt am Main: Suhrkamp 1974), § 65. Translated as *The Critique of Judgment* by J. C. Meredith (Oxford: Oxford University Press, 1982) 2:19–24.

17. Hegel, *Phänomenologie des Geistes,* 46. *Phenomenology of Spirit,* 27.

18. See *e.g.* Hegel, *Wissenschaft der Logik 2, Werke 6* (Frankfurt am Main: Suhrkamp, 1970), 549. Translated as *Hegel's Science of Logig* by V. Miller (London and New York: George Allen and Unwin Ltd. and Humanities Press, 1969), 824.

19. Hegel, *Enzyklopädie der philosophischen Wissenschaften 2,* § 369 Zus, 519. *Hegel's Philosophy of Nature 3,* 175.

20. Hegel, *Enzyklopädie der philosophischen Wissenschaften 2*, § 261, 56–60. *Hegel's Philosophy of Nature 1*, 237–240.

21. Hegel, *Enzyklopädie der philosophischen Wissenschaften 2*, § 262, 60–63. *Hegel's Philosophy of Nature 1*, 241–244.

22. See the common origin of space and time in the pure negativity of the "point" and in the pure differentiation that the point concretizes: Hegel, *Enzyklopädie der philosophischen Wissenschaften 2*, § 256–257, 44–48. *Hegel's Philosophy of Nature 1*, 226–229.

23. On the living being as an originary spatialization and temporalization, see: Hegel, *Enzyklopädie der philosophischen Wissenschaften 2*, § 351, 431–435. *Hegel's Philosophy of Nature 3*, 103–107.

24. Plato, *Timaeus*, 48e–52e. See the insightful commentary by Jacques Derrida, *Khora* (Paris: Galilée, 1993), Translated as "Khora," in *On the Name*, by David Wood, ed. Thomas Dutoit (Stanford: Stanford University Press, 1995).

25. The structural analogy between the Platonic *khora* and the Kantian imagination is also brought forth by John Sallis in *The Force of Imagination*, 29, 45, 66, 70.

26. This is to be understood in the sense of the two negativities described in the last chapter of the *Great Logic*: there is a negative negativity and a positive one, one that is just unthinkable, the other one gives to think. Hegel, *Wissenschaft der Logik 2*, 563. *Hegel's Science of Logic*, 835.

27. See also Jean-Luc Nancy, "Identité et tremblement."

28. For Hegel like for the whole of his epoch, the most ideal representation of motherlove is Rafael's Sixtine Madonna although wordless and without desire, Mary's love of the Child is supposed to manifest the summit of spirituality. See Hegel, *Vorlesungen über die Ästhetik 3*, *Werke 15* (Frankfurt am Main: Suhrkamp, 1986), 21, 49. On the other hand, the love between man and woman is the recognition of the other human being as such, in his/her entire subjectivity: it remains unilateral and incapable of universality precisely because it remains bound to subjectivity. See Hegel, *Vorlesungen über die Ästhetik 2*, *Werke 14* (Frankfurt am Main: Suhrkamp, 1986), 182.

29. On the hero of the world history as a victim of the "cunning of reason," see Hegel, *Vorlesungen über die Philosophie der Geschichte*. *Werke 12* (Frankfurt am Main: Suhrkamp, 1986), 49. Translated as *The Philosophy of History* by J. Sibree (New York: Cosimo Classics, 2007), 33. For the logical explanation of this situation, see Hegel, *Wissenschaft der Logik 2*, 452. *Hegel's Science of Logic*, 746.

30. This kind of an interpretation of Kant's and Hegel's teleology was developed in particular by Gérard Lebrun. In his interpretation of Kant, he urges us to think teleology as an art that is not artificial or as a technique that is not producing. See Gérard Lebrun, *Kant et la fin de la métaphysique. Essai sur la "Critique de la faculté de juger"* (Paris: Livre de poche/Armand Colin, 1970), 389. In his *Hegel et la*

patience du concept (Paris: Gallimard, 1962), 354 *s.q*, he impressively refuses the idea that Hegel's teleology could simply be the rolling forth of a pre-established program.

31. Hegel, *Phänomenologie des Geistes,* 153–154. *Phenomenology of Spirit,* 117–118.

32. Hegel, *Phänomenologie des Geistes,* 145 *s.q. Phenomenology of Spirit,* 111 *s.q.q.*

33. Hegel, *Phänomenologie des Geistes,* 353. *Phenomenology of Spirit,* 288.

34. Hegel, *Phänomenologie des Geistes,* 436. *Phenomenology of Spirit,* 360.

35. Hegel, *Phänomenologie des Geistes,* 332. *Phenomenology of Spirit,* 269–270.

36. Hegel, *Phänomenologie des Geistes,* 555 *s.q. Phenomenology of Spirit,* 462.

37. Hegel, *Phänomenologie des Geistes,* 145. *Phenomenology of Spirit,* 111.

38. Hegel, *Wissenschaft der Logik 2,* 486. *Hegel's Science of Logic,* 774. Hegel, *Enzyklopädie der philosophischen Wissenschaften 2,* § 370 & Zus, p. 519 *s.q. Hegel's Philosophy of Nature 3,* 177 *s.q.q.*

39. Because the woman does not "present" or show herself in terms of the speculative dialectic, Hegel's system cannot "digest" her, as Derrida puts it in his *Glas* (Paris: Galilée, 1974); *Glas* trans. John P. Leavey and Richard Rand (Lincoln: University of Nebraska Press, 1990). I simply add that this is precisely what she *figures*: an inassimilable impresentable non-ground of presentation.

40. Hegel, *Enzyklopädie der philosophischen Wissenschaften 2,* § 259, 52. *Hegel's Philosophy of Nature I,* 229.

41. This is the sense of the famous "death of the parents in the child," Hegel, *Wissenschaft der Logik 2,* 485–486. *Hegel's Science of Logic,* 773–774.

42. That is why a child's birth is Hegel's metaphor for the very development of the spirit. Hegel, *Phänomenologie des Geistes,* 18. *Phenomenology of Spirit,* 6.

43. Hegel, *Vorlesungen über die Geschichte der Philosophie I* (Frankfurt am Main: Suhrkamp, 1986), 21.

44. "The law of the family" that guides Antigone's action precisely directs the *work, Arbeit,* that is proper to the family. Hegel, *Phänomenologie des Geistes,* 330–334. *Phenomenology of Spirit,* 268–271.

45. Hegel, "Über die Wissenschaftlichen Behandlungsarten des Naturrechts, seine Stelle in der praktischen Philosophie und sein Verhältnis zu den positiven Rechtswissenschaften," in Hegel, *Jenaer Schriften 1801–1807, Werke 2* (Frankfurt am Main: Suhrkamp, 1986), 495. See also Hegel, *Phänomenologie des Geistes,* 340, 536–541. *Phenomenology of Spirit,* 277, 445–450.

46. See in particular Hegel, *Phänomenologie des Geistes,* 91, 523. An excellent explication of the Greek goddesses that mourn the loss of their children is Nicole Loraux's *Les mères en deuil* (Paris: Seuil,

1990), translated as *Mothers in Mourning, trans.* Corinne Pache (Ithaca: Cornell University Press, 1998).

47. In the *Phenomenology of spirit*, Mary's role is short but important. Hegel, *Phänomenologie des Geistes*, 574, *Phenomenology of Spirit*, 478.

48. Hegel, *Phänomenologie des Geistes*, 332, *Phenomenology of Spirit*, 270.

49. This idea is curiously reflected in Levinas's *Totalité et infini. Essai sur l'extériorité* (La Haye: M. Nijohoff, 1961; *Totality and Infinity: An Essay on Exteriority, trans.* Alphonso Lingis, [Pittsburgh, PA: Duquesne University Press, 1998]), where the principle of "interiority" as "home" (maison) is "illustrated" by the feminine "welcome" or "reception" (*accueil*) of the "same," whereby the feminine instance neither speaks nor thinks, but houses the "same" so that it could later go out to face the "other." The feminine is neither the "same" nor the "other," but the "home" where each one retires.

50. Hegel, *Enzyklopädie der philosophischen Wissenschaften 3*, § 458, 270–271, see also § 457 Zus, 269. *Hegel's Philosophy of Subjective Spirit 3*, 177, 175. The classical analysis of Hegel's sign as a "tomb" is Jacques Derrida's "The Pit and the Pyramid," in *Margins of Philosophy, trans.* Alan Bass (Chicago: University of Chicago Press, 1982). See also Christophe Bouton, "L'épitaphe et le tombeau," *Philosophie* 52 (1996), 54–76. The association between burial and unconscious imagination is also noted by Irigaray: "Their inherent duty is to ensure the *burial of the dead*, thus changing a natural phenomenon into a spiritual act. One more step (into negation) and we see that it is the task of womankind, guardian of the blood tie, to gather man into his final figuration, beyond the turmoil of contingent life and the scattered moments of his Being-there. Man is thereby raised into the peace of simple universality" (*Speculum of the Other Woman*, 214). "*She ensures the Erinnerung of the consciousness of self by forgetting herself*" (op. cit, 225).

51. Hegel, *Enzyklopädie der philosophischen Wissenschaften 3*, § 453 Anm., 260. *Hegel's Philosophy of Subjective Spirit 3*, 153.

CHAPTER TEN

The Gender of Spirit: Hegel's Moves and Strategies

Laura Werner

The figure of Hegel as a thinker as well as the image, however distorted, of "the Hegelian system" have proved to be a constant target of criticism as well as a point of reference for feminist theorists and philosophers of the twentieth and twenty-first centuries. Simone de Beauvoir's appropriation and creative re-conceptualization of Hegel's dialectics of lordship and bondage to depict the origins of gender inequality in *Le Deuxième Sexe* is arguably her most well-known encounter with Hegelian dialectics, although it is her earlier *Pour une morale de l'ambigüité* that contains Beauvoir's clearest confrontation and critique of Hegel's thought. For Luce Irigaray, Hegel is an explicit conversation partner in *Speculum* as well as, more emphatically, in *J'aime à toi*. In Judith Butler's latest works, she openly posits her thought in the Hegelian tradition—a situating that is perhaps not very surprising considering her doctoral dissertation *Subjects of Desire* that examined the philosophical reception of Hegel's concept *Begierde* (desire) in twentieth-century French thought from Kojève and Hyppolite through Sartre and Lacan to Deleuze and Foucault.[1]

In recent years, feminist scholars have made several important contributions to understanding Hegel's views on gender, sexual, and family relations.[2] Hegel's discussion of the relation between family and political life through Sophocles's tragedy *Antigone* has been examined and challenged by a multitude of feminist philosophers and political theorists. Though by now well known among feminist theorists, Hegel's treatment of gender difference in the context of *Antigone* in the *Phänomenologie des Geistes* (*Phenomenology of Spirit*) and the

Grundlinien der Philosophie des Rechts (*Philosophy of Right*) is, however, not his only text of interest for contemporary feminists intrigued by the historical formation of gender concepts and categories.[3]

The late eighteenth and early nineteenth centuries were important turning points in this process. In Hegel's lifetime, new conceptual theorizations of "woman" were developed both in the sphere of biological discourse and in literature and philosophy. My focus in this chapter is on how Hegel constructs gender identity and gender difference philosophically and conceptually. In contrast to Rousseau, whose influence was tremendous in introducing the historically new conception of romantic child-centered motherhood,[4] he does not lay any special emphasis on mothering for the construction of adult women—or for their education. While Rousseau famously presented in *Émile* a program of education for girls that was designed to enforce restriction of movement, passivity, docility, and playing with dolls in order to make them good future mothers, Hegel showed no such concerns in terms of instilling proper womanhood in girls. Indeed, he was not concerned with the education of women at all, claiming in an addition to *Philosophy of Right* that

> the education of women takes place imperceptibly, as if through the atmosphere of representational thought, more through living than through the acquisition of knowledge, whereas a man attains his position only through the attainment of thought and numerous technical exertations.[5]

If female children need not be especially educated into being "women," where does the identity of the gender category stem from in Hegel's philosophy? Despite the fact that feminists have rarely found much in his work to commend him, one of the main problems with which feminist theorists have been concerned—how to conceptualize identity and difference or, in the case of feminism, how to reconcile political action in the name of "women" as an identity category with the multiplicity of differences between individual women—was one he could have shed light on, as Patricia Mills has pointed out.[6] Hegel's understanding of identity as always involving difference and differentiation, and of difference as containing identity, is one historical but often unacknowledged root of contemporary feminist endeavors to understand political and personal identities as relational and non-essential.[7] He suggests in *Phenomenology of Spirit* that "womankind" [*Weiblichkeit*] as the inner enemy of the state is created by its attempt to subjugate it.[8] This argument was later echoed by feminist theorists who pointed out that only a group excluded from universality could have an identity as "women," "black," or "gay," whereas the corresponding categories conceived of as universal or "the majority"—"man," "white," or "heterosexual"—were not seen to constitute an identity at all.[9] Thus group identity is not the result of an inherent unity but is only a consequence of repression or exclusion.

Although the dialectics of the state and "womankind" presented in *Phenomenology of Spirit* could be read as pointing toward a nonessential theory of gender differentiation, Hegel's theorization of gender differences elsewhere in his work does not evince such a theoretical direction. I suggest that if we are to understand the construction of gender difference in Hegel's philosophy we need to distinguish two separate but interconnected "differences" that function on the two separate levels of "realness" he distinguishes in his thought, *Wirklichkeit* (actuality) and *Realität* (reality). My argument is that he constructs gender difference conceptually, first as "actual" differences between men and women (the level or viewpoint of the acting concept or absolute spirit) and second as "real" or "concrete" differences (the level or viewpoint of everyday, concrete differences), the latter being based on the former ones. This differentiation conforms neither to the classical nature/culture divide in modern philosophy nor to the much debated feminist theoretical differentiation between "sex" and "gender" according to which "sex" is understood as a biological category and, by extension, the unchangeable material basis of sexual differences, and "gender" is understood as a cultural construction of what being "a woman" or "a man" is like.[10] Although I argue that there are two levels of gender differentiation in Hegel's thought, for him the "actual" basis is not biological but conceptual, based on the spirit's self-movement. The concrete differences that Hegel ascribes to men and women are evinced equally in the sphere of material bodies and in social and political life, but neither of these spheres is the cause of the other. Instead, they both result from the spirito-conceptual actual difference he perceives on the basis of unity [*Einheit*] and difference or self-differentiation [*Unterschied*].

In the following, I argue that, in order to understand Hegel's construction of the categories "men" and "women" and his political differentiation of gendered spheres of action, we need to understand two moves or strategies he uses. He constructs gender difference first through a conceptual, *actual* difference regarding "difference" itself and self-differentiation, and second through *concrete* differences resulting from the first, actual difference. To understand the logic behind these differentiations, I will first look at the way in which the concepts *Identität* and *Unterschied* (identity and difference) are interlinked in Hegel's thought.

"Identity" in the Hegelian Context

"Identity" has several common uses in contemporary theoretical discussions. The basic philosophical and logical meaning indicates "sameness," or being "one and the same," and originates from the Latin *idem*. However, there have been two clearly separate phases of usage. From Aristotle on, most philosophers before Leibniz and Locke considered two entities to be identical, or "one and the same," if they had the same substance or essence. Socrates, for example, was one and the same at different times as he always had the same substance or essence. From Locke and Leibniz on, there was a radical change: two entities were considered identical based not on their substance or essence but on their properties. If x had every property y had and vice versa, x was one and the same as y, and if x and y were one and the same, every property of x was also a property of y.[11]

A second discourse of "identity" is the "self-identity" used in the context of (social) psychology. In this case, the identity or oneness and sameness of an individual is linked to her or his experience of her- or himself as one and the same. There is often a normative element included: a person may have an underdeveloped self-identity and should ideally have a well-developed one, in other words, he or she should experience him- or herself as one.[12]

The third common use of "identity" is the social or communal identity often encountered in sociological discourse. In that context, having a "German identity" or the "identity of a philosopher" connotes an experience of identifying with a certain group or community, a given "we." On the one hand, social identity is understood as a quality—a person may or may not have a particular identity—and, on the other, it could be considered a new and separate entity with certain properties it may or may not have.[13]

"Gender identity" as a concept is rather new, having been introduced in the 1950s in the context of medical research on what is now commonly called "transgender." The psychoanalyst Robert Stoller determined "gender identity" as the sense of knowing to which sex one belongs, the ability to say "I am a man" or "I am a woman." It is not knowledge of being one-and-the-same or knowledge of one's qualities, but rather one's idea of *what* one is—a man or a woman.[14] The term that came to be used in different ways in later feminist discussions, "gender identity" can be used to refer to the unity of a gender, in other words, the unity of one's self-identity as a man or a woman, or to identify (politically or otherwise) with a gender group. Thus the term "gender identity" carries with it similar alternative uses as its root concept "identity": to describe having knowledge of being one gender, the unity of one's self-identity as man or woman, or social or political identification with a gender group.

Hegel's treatment of identity is to be found in the doctrine of *Wesen* or "Essence" in *Science of Logic* and the *Encyclopaedia* logic.[15] As is characteristic of his logic, although he used the term *Identität* as a logical concept, it is also a stage of the self-movement of spirit—a view that brings together logical identity and self identity. He defines "identity" as reflexive self-relation but distinguishes between the two notions of formal and concrete. The first, *formal identity* or identity of understanding [*Verstandesidentität*], is *abstract*, all difference is abstracted and closed out from it. It is also purely *formal*, it can be expressed with the empty formulations "a planet is a planet," "magnetism is magnetism," or "spirit is spirit." *Concrete identity*, in contrast, does not close out the concrete manifold of differences from its concept.[16] Accordingly, Hegel sometimes preferred to use *Einheit* (oneness, unity) for the second, non-abstract meaning, and to associate *Identität* with the first notion of the abstract identity of understanding.[17]

The dialectic counter-concept to *Identität* in Hegel's logic is *Unterschied*, the general word for "difference" or "distinction." As identity is a self-relation, he thought of difference as the result of a process of active self-differentiation within the self-relation of being. He determined *Unterschied* as a process or development in terms of differentiating one or itself, a process attested to by the reflexive form of the verb *sich unterscheiden*.[18] Thus he conceptualized "identity" in connection with and in contrast to "difference" or "distinction" understood as active self-differentiation.

However, neither identity nor difference is a stable, unchanging concept in his logic. They are always interrelated in the movement of thought, and in a way that emphasizes *action*, the active process of self-differentiation rather than *being*. Hegel points out that identity would have no interest for the movement of thought if it did not lead to distinction, and difference or distinction itself always includes identity. He makes clear the mutual dependence of the concepts in the Addition to §116 of the *Encyclopaedia* logic:

> The question "how does identity arrive at distinction?" presupposes
> that identity, taken as a mere (that is, abstract) identity is something on

its own account, and that distinction, too, is something else that is equally something on its own accord. But this presupposition makes it impossible to answer the question raised, for when identity and distinction are regarded as diverse, then what we have in fact is only distinction; and for that reason the advance to distinction cannot be demonstrated, because what the advance is supposed to start from is not present at all for the one who is asking about the "how" of the advance. So when we look more closely, the question proves to be a completely unthinking one and whoever raises it should be asked first of all what he understands by "identity." It would then turn out that no thought underlies the word he uses and that identity is just an empty name for him.[19]

He thus considered each of the two terms "identity" and "difference" (or "distinction") to be an empty term without the other. The question of movement from one to the other presupposes their original distinctness—a presupposition he thought false.

Hegel never used the term "identity" in the sense of gendered self-identity in any discussion of either "male" or "female" identity. However, I will show that he did formulate gender differences in a way that constructed the determinations of "men" and "women" through the conceptual space of "unity" [einheit] and "difference" [Unterschied]. He states in Philosophy of Right that a man has to fight his way to "self-subsistent unity with himself" through his original self-differentiation. He may have a "tranquil intuition of this unity" in the family, but he can find self-conscious "unity with himself" only outside of it, after work, and struggle with the world and with himself.[20] In this sense, Hegel's definition of identity as a reflexive self-relation [reflektierte Beziehung auf sich][21] clearly points to a conception of gendered self-identity as the unity of self. However, I suggest that the unity of "man" is concrete identity, that is, identity not closing out difference but necessarily connected to it, whereas the identity of "woman" is characterized as formal, abstract identity and unity without the reflexive process of self-differentiation.

The question of how Hegel constructed sexual and gender categories is often looked at in terms of his description of bodily sexual and reproductive differences in his Encyclopaedia philosophy of nature, or through his account of the gendered spheres of Sittlichkeit in Phenomenology of Spirit and Philosophy of Right. I nevertheless argue that we must look carefully at the complete body of his works in order to understand the logic behind his sexual and gender differentiation.

DIFFERENCE FROM DIFFERENCE

Hegel did not treat gender explicitly in his earliest Frankfurt and Jena writings. In the *System of Ethical Life*, he mentions "the two sexes" that find themselves in the other through labor and love, but it is not until the Jena *Lectures on the Philosophy of Spirit* that he deals explicitly with spirit or the subject dividing itself into "the man" [*der Mann*] and "the feminine" or "femaleness" [*das Weibliche*]. With the appearance of "female cunning," the ability to harness nature's powers into tools that serve purposes that are completely different from nature's original goals, spirit also doubles itself and splits into two "characters." Hegel's description of these two characters is very obscure, but he refers to the first, apparently the male one, as "open, straightforward, driving," "confronting," and "blind," and to the second as "evil," "subterranean," and using reason against something that it does not take with full seriousness, utilizing the thing's own efforts to accomplish its destruction like a bullfighter offering a cape to the bull, which hits nothing but is hit itself. Of the two characters, Hegel calls the first universal and the second particular.[22]

These characterizations are certainly similar to the way in which Hegel described the law of the state and *Weiblichkeit* a year or so later in *Phenomenology of Spirit*, in which the open daylight law of the state that actualizes itself in men and kings is confronted by the subterranean "divine law" represented by women. However, instead of fixing universality to just one law, he emphasizes the fact that both laws contain in themselves moments of both universality and particularity. Still, his final description of "womankind" [*die Weiblichkeit*] as the eternal irony of the community, which works to change and pervert the universal aims of the community for its own private and particular aims, echoes the Jena lectures' description of the female character as a cunning bullfighter and representative of particularity.[23]

Hegel's most well-known and most compact depiction of gender difference is to be found in *Philosophy of Right*. In the often quoted paragraph 166, he defines "man" as spirit that *divides* itself into personal self-sufficiency and the knowledge and volition of free universality. He states that a man lives and acts substantively in the state, in learning, laboring, and struggling with the external world and with himself. He defines "woman," however, as spirit *maintaining itself in unity* in the knowledge and volition of concrete singularity [*Einzelheit*] and feeling [*Empfindung*]. She is passive and subjective in her external relations and has her substantial determination [*Bestimmung*] in the family.

Hegel thus conceptualizes gender difference as the difference between spirit holding itself in unity and spirit struggling and dividing itself. This basic contrast differentiates maleness from femaleness at the level of both spirit and body. He portrays the way in which the difference expresses itself bodily most clearly in the *Encyclopaedia* philosophy of nature's description of the sexual organs of the male and the female. According to Hegel, in the adult female, the sexual organs stay in their undeveloped unity and do not gain the outward differentiation into the penis, testicles, and scrotum as they do in the adult male. The ovaries of the female do not develop into testicles, which Hegel calls the "active brain," but stay inactive. Likewise the penis, the "swelling heart" or the "external heart," represents active feeling in the male, whereas the woman's clitoris harbors "inactive feeling in general." Males thus have an extra pair of active brains and a heart between their legs, whereas in the female the possibility for this doubling has not been realized.[24]

Hegel's description of the genitals of males and females expresses precisely the hierarchical one-sex model that had been prevalent in Western medical thought since classical antiquity, but which was challenged strongly by the complementary two-sex model at the end of the eighteenth century. Thomas Lacqueur describes the one-sex model as one in which two genders correspond to only one sex, and in which the boundaries between male and female are understood as ones of degree, not of kind. The Greek medical thinker Galen, who formulated the most powerful and enduring model of the identity of the male and female reproductive organs in the second century, argued that women were essentially men in whom a lack of vital heat—a sign of greater perfection—had resulted in the retention of structures that in the male were visible outside. He compared female genitalia to the eyes of the mole, which have the same structure as the eyes of other animals except that they do not open or project but are left imperfect in not allowing the mole to see. Similarly, the female genitalia "do not open" and, therefore, remain an imperfect version of what they would be were they thrust out.[25]

As Lacqueur points out, neither Galen nor his theoretical predecessor Aristotle made any effort to ground social roles in nature. They rather considered social categories themselves to be "natural" and on the same explanatory level as twenty-first-century readers would take physical or biological facts to be. The biological is not even in principle seen as the foundation of particular social arrangements. Rather, the immutable, "natural" truths concern principles: male activity and female passivity, male form and female materiality, male perfection and heat and female imperfection and coldness. The biology of penises and vaginas, testicles and ovaries, expresses only contingently and rather uninterestingly the self-evident conceptual hierarchy of men and women.[26]

Hegel's theorization of sexual difference in male and female genitals similarly expresses a principle of male outer differentiation and female staying-in-unity that is based on a structure of spirit, not on "nature" seen as previous to or separate from spirit. It must be remembered that Hegel's *Geist* and *Natur* are not the same as "culture" and "nature" seen as opposite, independent categories. Hegel's "nature" is "spirit estranged from itself," the place in which spirit lets itself go as a "Bacchic god" but in which its essence is nevertheless concealed. He describes nature as the "process of becoming spirit, of sublating its otherness."[27] The processes and divisions of nature point toward its finding itself as spirit while it develops from mechanics and physics to organics. Hegel's examination of "the terrestrial organism," plant life, and the animal organism in his *Encyclopaedia* philosophy of nature culminates with "The Process of the Genus" in which he deals with sex and death, the reproduction and self-destruction of the individual. The end of his philosophy of nature is hence reached when nature attains the dialectics of life, reproduction, and death. The dialectics of life, sex, and death is the junction between nature and spirit where nature becomes spirit, and spirit can find itself in nature. Hegel's *Geist* is described throughout his work above all as alive [*lebendig*], a description linking it to natural life in Hegel's multitudinous descriptions of "spirit" as a bud, a flower, birth, and, indeed, (sexual) love. As could be inferred from the importance of the process of the genus as the acme of the philosophy of nature, the relation of spirit and nature is not indifferent to sex. Hegel's metaphor for the relation is carnal and clearly gendered: "Spirit has the certainty which Adam had when he looked on Eve: 'This is the flesh of my flesh, and bone of my bone.' Thus Nature is the bride which Spirit weds."[28]

The importance of sexual differentiation to the individual becomes clear when Hegel contrasts sexual difference in animals and in plants. In fertilization, the plant "endows its moments with an abstract existence in which they exist separately, and posits them as a unity again through contact [*Berührung*]."[29] In general, the whole process happens within the plant itself and even in the few such as the *Dioecia* where "the separate sexes are distributed in two separate and distinct plants," the differences often change as the plants are growing. Thus a hemp plant may show an early disposition to be female and yet sub-sequently become male. Hegel states that

> the different individuals cannot therefore be regarded as of different sexes because they have not been completely imbued with the *principle* of their opposition—because this does not completely pervade them, is not a universal moment of the entire individual, but is a separated part of it—The sexual relationship proper must have for its opposed moments entire individuals whose determinateness, completely reflected into itself, spreads through the whole individual. The entire habit [*habitus*] of the individual must be bound up with its sex.[30]

Hegel concludes that plants are asexual because their sexual parts form a closed circle unconnected to their individuality. In contrast, in animals the "force of sexuality" has penetrated and saturated the individual, right from the beginning. Different sexes are thus the result of being completely imbued by the universal principle of sexual difference and opposition. Unlike Rousseau, who postulated that "the male is only a male now and again, the female is always a female—everything reminds her of her sex,"[31] Hegel constructs no difference in terms of how tied males and females are to their sex.

In the philosophy of nature, he thus determines animal males and females as completely bound up with their sex. He makes the vital distinction between both animal males and females as well as human men and women through the operations of self-differentiation and distinction. Although the female and the male are made of the same stuff, they represent diverse stages of differentiation. What character-izes both adult women and female reproductive organs is indiffer-ence, whereas adult men and the male reproductive organs are characterized by self-division and opposition. It is through this differ-ence, claims Hegel, that a man is active and acting, while the woman is passive and receptive, as her genitals and she stay in undifferentiated unity.[32] The ideal of unity versus differentiation is echoed in an apho-rism Hegel wrote in his Jena period: "A mended sock is better than a torn one; not so with self-consciousness."[33] For self-consciousness, it is clearly better to be torn than whole.

Consequently, I suggest, Hegel actually constructed sexual and gender difference as a *difference within the male*. Rather than locating sexual difference between "male" and "female," he situated differ-ence within the male as torn, self-differentiated consciousness. In both *Philosophy of Right* and the *Encyclopaedia* philosophy of nature, males and men have a dynamic, productive difference within that leads to action whereas "woman" and *Weiblichkeit* are *without difference*. Accordingly, he defines sexual and gender difference as the difference between (active) difference and (passive) non-difference.

Hegel observes in *Science of Logic*, "that which is different from difference is identity."[34] When "identity" is understood in the first sense that Hegel differentiates, as being one-and-the-same and conceptualized in contrast with *Unterschied* as primarily self-differentiation, it would seem to follow that only women could logically have identity in Hegel's philosophy—since only they do not include self-differentiation within themselves and are hence "different from difference," one-and-the-same. The passive unity Hegel assigns to "woman" and "femaleness" is contrasted to the dynamic movement of self-differentiation of spirit that is evinced by both male genitals and men in the state.

Furthermore, this self-unity of females transforms into their identity and unity as a group. He appears to claim in *Philosophy of Right* that women cannot truly attain separate individuality as men do, since they lack the necessary capacity to self-differentiate and the inner complexity that results from the labor of first dividing and opposing themselves and only after that finding themselves again. His quotation from *El Cid* in his handwritten notes to §165 connects the non-difference and self-identity of women to their identity as a group: when at the Last Judgement God looks at women, he must find them all guilty or all innocent because their hearts are so interwoven.[35] Thus, men are for Hegel logically necessarily differentiated both within themselves and from other men, whereas women are logically undifferentiated, all the same—in their bodies, in themselves, and in relation to other women.

Thus the actual [*wirklich*], meta-level basis of women's identity in Hegel's work is not just their difference from men, but also their *difference from difference*. Dialectically this could be seen as a negation of a negation: differing from difference itself transforms into the group identity of "women."

CONCLUSION

In the above I have delineated the way Hegel grounded his account of gender difference and gender identity on the conceptual difference between difference and non-difference. I have suggested that the actual [*wirklich*] basis of the category "women" in his work is their *difference from difference*, their unreflexive unity within their bodies, their spirit, and as a group. He also used this conceptual idea of unity to define women's political place as persons who do not split their lives between political life in the state and life in the family but remain in the undifferentiated unity of the family. Dialectically, this difference from difference transforms into something "positive"—unity and abstract identity.

Hegel's theorization of gender occupies an interesting mediating position with respect to the models of sexual and gender differentiation existing in the late-eighteenth and early-nineteenth centuries. On one hand, in terms of bodily sexual organs, his philosophy of nature represents the earlier one-sex model that was prevalent from classical antiquity to the turn of the nineteenth century. According to this model, there was only one sex, the male, which was left undeveloped in women because their reproductive organs remained within their body and did not gain outward doubling into "an active brain" (the testicles) and the "up-swelling heart" (the penis). On the other hand, Hegel supported the theory of two separate spheres for men and women that had become prevalent after the French Revolution but usually utilized the newer two-sex model to justify the strict separation of men's and women's spheres of action as "public" and "private." Nevertheless, the same dialectical logic of spirit's self-movement allowed him to argue for both the older one-sex model and the newer gender theory of two separate spheres. Behind both the female body and the position of women as belonging to only one domestic sphere of action lies for Hegel the undifferentiation of spirit, the incapacity for active self-differentiation and torn self-consciousness. He defined the male body and the position of man as citizen, however, in terms of their inner and outer negativity, struggle and differentiation. "Family," for men, remains the place to which they can return from their divided life in the public sphere to have "a peaceful intuition of unity."

Many feminist scholars have noted and commented upon Hegel's assignment of a stable, ahistorical identity to women.[36] I think that this is the logical consequence of his exclusion of "women" as a category from the sphere of the self-differentiation of the spirit, and consequently of spirit's movement as history. It seems to me that the fundamental problem in Hegel's account is the fact that "women" have too much identity conceived of as one-and-the-sameness, without difference. Thus the clear gender identity he conceptualized for women results in their incapability to change and their confinement within the family unit. Women's theorized unity and sameness necessarily leaves them outside history and the dialectical movement of the spirit. Since their self-consciousness is not torn, they remain the ones repairing the torn socks and the torn self-consciousnesses returning home to find wholeness.

NOTES

1. Simone de Beauvoir, *The Second Sex,* trans. H.M. Parshley (Harmondsworth: Penguin Books, 1988[1949]); *Ethics of Ambiguity,* trans. B. Frechtman (New York: Citadel Press, 1976 [1947]). Luce Irigaray, *I Love to You. Sketch for a Felicity within History,* trans. Alison Martin (New York & London: Routledge, 1996 [1991]); *Speculum of the Other Woman,* trans. Gillian C. Gill (Ithaca: Cornell University Press, 1985 [1974]). Judith Butler, *Undoing Gender* (New York & London: Routledge, 2004); *Subjects of Desire. Hegelian Reflections in Twentieth-Century France* (New York: Columbia University Press, 1987).

2. In addition to those already cited, see Seyla Benhabib, "On Hegel, Women and Irony," in *Feminist Interpretations of G. W. F. Hegel* (University Park, PA: Pennsylvania State University Press, 1996); Carole Pateman's discussion of Hegel in *The Sexual Contact* (Cambridge: Polity Press, 1988); Kimberly Hutchings, *Hegel and Feminist Philosophy* (Cambridge: Polity Press, 2003).

3. This essay will employ the following abbreviations in references to G. W. F. Hegel's texts:

EL: *The Encyclopaedia Logic. Part One of the Encyclopaedia of the Philosophical Sciences with the Zusätze,* trans. T.F. Geraets, W.A. Suchting and H.S. Harris (Indianapolis/Cambridge: Hackett Publishing Co., 1991).

EN: *Hegel's Philosophy of Nature. Part Two of the Encyclopaedia of the Philosophical Sciences (1830),* trans. A.V. Miller (Oxford: Oxford University Press, 2004).

JLPS: *Jena Lectures on the Philosophy of Spirit* (1805/06) in trans., *Hegel and the Human Spirit,* ed. and trans. Leo Rauch (Detroit: Wayne State University Press 1983), 83–183.

JRP: *Jenaer Realphilosophie* (1805/06) in *Hegels frühe politische Systeme,* ed. Gerhard Göhler (Frankfurt am Main and Berlin & Wien: Ullstein 1974), 201–289.

MW: Jon Stewart, ed., *Miscellaneous Writings of G.W.F. Hegel* (Evanston, IL: Northwestern University Press, 2002).

PR: *Elements of the Philosophy of Right,* trans. H.B. Nisbet (Cambridge: Cambridge University Press, 1991).

PS: *Phenomenology of Spirit,* trans. A.V. Miller (Oxford: Oxford University Press, 1977).

SL: *Hegel's Science of Logic,* trans. A.V. Miller (London: Allen & Unwin, 1969).

W3: *Phänomenologie des Geistes,* Werke in 20 Bänden 3 (Frankfurt am Main: Suhrkamp, 1986).

W6: *Wissenschaft der Logik 2,* Werke in 20 Bänden 6 (Frankfurt am Main: Suhrkamp, 1986).

W7: *Grundlinien der Philosophie des Rechts,* Werke in 20 Bänden 7 (Frankfurt am Main: Suhrkamp, 1986).

W8 *Enzyklopädie der philosophischen Wissenschaften 1,* Werke in 20 Bänden 8 (Frankfurt am Main: Suhrkamp, 1986).

W9: *Enzyklopädie der philosophischen Wissenschaften 2,* Werke in 20 Bänden 9 (Frankfurt am Main: Suhrkamp, 1986).

4. Lynn Abrams, *The Making of Modern Woman: Europe 1789–1918* (London: Longman/Pearson, 2002), 29–32, 103. Barbara Caine and Glenda Sluga, *Gendering European History 1780–1920* (London & New York: Continuum, 2000), 11–13.

5. Hegel, §166A, W7, 320; PR, 207.

6. Patricia Jagentowicz Mills, "Hegel's *Antigone,*" in *Feminist Interpretations of G. W. F. Hegel,* ed. Mills (University Park, PA: Pennsylvania State University Press, 1996), 21, 84.

7. Tuija Pulkkinen "Identiteetti ja ei-identiteetti. Alkuperästä ja ykseydestä moneuteen ja toistoon identiteettipolitiikassa" (Identity and Non-Identity. From origin and oneness to multiplicity and repetition in identity politics), *Ajatus* 56 (1999), 213–236.

8. Hegel, W3, 353; PS, 288.

9. Tuija Pulkkinen, "Naisyhteisö: Subjektius, identiteetti ja toimijuus" (Women as Community: Subjectivity, Identity, and Agency), in *Yhteisö,* ed. Jussi Kotkavirta and Arto Laitinen (Jyväskylä: SoPhi, 1998), 239–251; "Political Identity—An Inquiry into the Concept," in *La passió per la llibertat/Passion for Freedom. Action, Passion and Politics—Feminist controversies,* ed. Fina Birulés and Maria Isabel Penã Aguado (Barcelona: University of Barcelona, 2004), 484–487.

10. Moira Gatens, *Imaginary Bodies. Ethics, Power and Corporeality* (London & New York: Routledge, 1996), 3–20; Sara Heinämaa *Ele, tyyli ja sukupuoli Merleau-Pontyn ja Beauvoirin ruumiinfenomenologia ja sen merkitys sukupuolikysymykselle* (Gesture, Style, Sex. Merleau-Ponty's and Beauvoir's phenomenology of the body and its meaning for the question of sexual difference) (Helsinki: Gaudeamus, 1996), 110–131; Joan Wallace Scott, *Gender and the Politics of History,* rev. ed. (New York: Columbia University Press, 1999), 28–50, 199–222; Judith Butler, *Gender Trouble,* 10th Anniversary Edition (New York & London: Routledge, 1999).

11. Kuno Lorenz, "Identität," in *Historisches Wörterbuch der Philosophie Band 4* (Basel: Schwabe & Co., 1976), 144–148. T. Pulkkinen, "Naisyhteisö: Subjektius, identiteetti ja toimijuus" (Women as Community: Subjectivity, Identity, and Agency) op. cit., 243–244; "Political Identity—An Inquiry into the Concept," op. cit.

12. Pulkkinen, "Naisyhteisö," op. cit., 243–244; "Identity and Non-Identity," op. cit.
13. Ibid.
14. Robert J. Stoller, *Sex and Gender* (New York: Science House, 1968); Gatens, *Imaginary Bodies,* op. cit., 5–6.
15. Hegel, W6, 38–64; SL, 408–431; W8, 234–247; EL, 179–188.
16. § 115, W8, 236–238; EL, 179–181.
17. Michael Inwood, "Identity, difference and otherness," in *A Hegel Dictionary* (Oxford: Blackwell, 1992), 131.
18. Ibid.
19. W8, 239; EL, 181–182.
20. §166, W3, 319; PR, 206.
21. §115, W8, 236; EL, 179.
22. JRP, 221; JLPS, 104–105.
23. W3, 352–3; PS, 288.
24. §369; W9, 518–519; EN, 412–413.
25. Thomas Lacqueur, *Making Sex: Body and Gender from the Greeks to Freud* (Cambridge, MA: Harvard University Press, 1990), 25–28.
26. Ibid., 28–29.
27. W9, 24; EN, 14.
28. W9, 23; EN, 13.
29. §348, W9, 420; EN, 344.
30. §348, W9, 421; EN, 344.
31. Jean-Jacques Rousseau, *Èmile,* trans. P. D. Jimack (London: Phoenix/ Everyman, 1993 [1762]), 388.
32. §369, W9, 518–519; EN, 413.
33. Karl Rosenkranz, *Georg Wilhelm Friedrich Hegels Leben* (Darmstadt: Wissenschaftliche Buchgesellschaft, 1998 [1844]), 552; Hegel, MW, 251.
34. W6, 47; SL, 417.
35. W7, 318.
36. For example, Seyla Benhabib "On Hegel, Women and Irony," op. cit.; P. J. Mills, "Hegel's *Antigone*," op. cit.

CHAPTER ELEVEN

Matter and Form: Hegel, Organicism, and the Difference between Women and Men

Alison Stone

Infamously, Hegel in his 1821 *Elements of the Philosophy of Right* maintains that it is an essential feature of modern European societies—and in accordance with the principles of right—that women are confined to the family, excluded from the public spheres of work and politics. "Woman [*die Frau*] . . . has her substantial vocation in the family, and her ethical disposition consists in this *piety*."[1] Feminist scholars have offered a range of interpretations of Hegel's philosophical rationale for making these claims. For instance, according to Carole Pateman in *The Sexual Contract*, Hegel makes these claims because he retains classical social contract theory's male-defined conception of the civil individual.[2] Others see these claims as rooted more broadly in Hegel's philosophical system. Genevieve Lloyd thinks that his relegation of women to the family reflects a hierarchical opposition between life (gendered female) and self-consciousness (gendered male) that structures his whole philosophy of mind. Even more broadly, Luce Irigaray thinks that Hegel's claims about women and family reflect the nature of his dialectic: he places whatever is oppositional and other to (male) subjectivity at the service of that self-same male subjectivity, thus having women serve men within the family.[3]

In this chapter I will put forward my own reconstruction of Hegel's reasons for confining women to the family, drawing on Frederick Neuhouser's argument that Hegel endorses a form of political organicism. According to this organicist position, the modern state (in the sense of politically organized society as a whole) is subdivided into three functional spheres: (1) the family, embodying the principle of "immediate unity" or "undifferentiated unity" between its members; (2) civil society, embodying the principle of "difference" between its members; and (3) the strictly political state, embodying the principle of "differentiated unity."[4] Since, in his philosophies of nature and mind, Hegel also holds that the female body is organized upon a principle of "immediate unity" between the female individual and the species, especially as embodied in the child, the essential principles that organize the female body and the family correspond to one another, so that for Hegel women are preeminently suited to family life. In sections 1 to 3 I will elucidate these Hegelian views.

Moreover, as I will examine in section 4, Hegel's interpretation of the female body as organized by a principle of self/other indistinction, and of the male body as organized by a principle of self/other difference, forms part of a broader set of symbolic equations that we can trace in the sections of his *Philosophy of Nature* (1817, 1827, 1830) that precede and prepare for the account that he gives in that work of the difference between the sexes (*Geschlechtsdifferenz*). Hegel conceives of nature as consisting of two basic elements, matter and concept, which exist in an initial opposition that is progressively overcome. Following a philosophical tradition that goes back to Plato, Hegel symbolizes matter as female and the concept as male. Moreover, since he identifies matter as the being-outside-itself of the concept, he implicitly understands the female as the being-outside-itself of the male—as an inverted and inferior form *of* the male, rather than as a sexuate identity in its own right.[5] Given that Hegel symbolizes matter as female, it is unsurprising that in his account of sex difference he reciprocally identifies females *as* comparatively "material": in his view, the lack of self/other difference characteristic of the female sex represents a form of relationship to the species that is relatively "material," compared to the more "spiritual" relationship to the species that distinguishes the male sex.

Given Hegel's sexual symbolism, the process that he narrates in his philosophy of nature—whereby the concept re-emerges from matter and progressively remodels matter in its own image—amounts to a progressive mastery of the female by the male. The philosophy of mind—which includes Hegel's political philosophy—narrates the continuation of this process once the concept has assumed the form of mind. Thus, the progression of male citizens beyond the family and their entrance into spheres of economic and political life from which they exercise jurisdiction over the family represent a culminating stage in this progressive domination of (female) matter by (male) mind. Ultimately, then, Hegel's exclusion of women from civil and political existence reflects hierarchical, gendered oppositions that are fundamental to his system—as Lloyd and Irigaray suggested. But unlike Lloyd and Irigaray, I think that the key opposition that structures Hegel's system of nature and mind is not between self-consciousness and life or subjectivity and alterity, but between concept and matter, as I will try to show.

1. Hegel's Political Organicism

For Hegel, modern states are rightly organized into functionally differentiated subsystems in the same way that organisms are. In his *Philosophy of Right* Hegel defends this prima facie unfashionable position through an immanent critique of contractarian views that derive the legitimacy of states from the consent actually or hypothetically given them by free individuals. Hegel begins from the contractarian premise that individuals have free will in the sense of the capacity to choose between options, including between their own desires.[6] He then argues that freedom requires private-property ownership, through which the individual embodies and realizes his or her freedom in material things, something that in turn requires contractual relations in which property-owners recognize and respect one another as persons of equal standing.[7] Yet since property-owners will whenever possible try to obtain recognition without conferring it upon others, relations of right (*Rechtsverhältnisse*) are ever-liable to degenerate into crime.[8] Overcoming this problem requires that individuals learn to be moral, to heed the interests of others for their own sake—which depends on individuals being morally educated by an appropriate set of social institutions,[9] namely, the family, civil society, and the state, collectively called "ethical life" (*Sittlichkeit*) or "ethical substance" (*sittliche Substantialität*).

Within the family, individuals relinquish their sense of having purely individual interests and identify their good with the common good of the entire family. Individuals experience their identification with the family's common good in the form of love for their family members. The family thus instills in individuals a direct concern with the interests of others, in the form of the interests of the family as a whole. However, this kind of immediate identification with the common good is possible only in small-scale, emotionally intense communities—such as nuclear families—whereas modern societies are large and complex. Civil society, then, plays a crucial role in educating individuals to pursue their personal economic interests in ways that profit the common weal. The strictly political state is necessary, in turn, because it educates citizens to consciously identify their interests with those of the whole community and to see themselves as essentially members of society.

For Hegel, this family/civil society/state constellation, found more or less fully realized in modern European societies,[10] accords with right because it provides the conditions for secure contractual relations, therefore, secure property-ownership, and thus individual freedom. Immanently criticizing contract theory, Hegel has established that voluntary relations between individuals (and, *a fortiori*, between individuals and states) can be coherently maintained only if those individuals already belong to and are educated by certain social institutions, institutions to which those individuals must, therefore, belong *non*-voluntarily.[11] Ultimately then, for Hegel, individuals can have freedom of choice only if they also have what Neuhouser calls "social freedom": the freedom to act in accordance with social roles and positions (for example, the role of a family member) that they embrace as essential to their identities.[12]

Moreover, for Hegel, individuals can attain social freedom only if the social order is structured into the interlocking set of basic institutions (family, civil society, state) that he finds to be present, or at least emergent, in modern European societies. A social order that is structured into these distinct but mutually supporting spheres is organized *organically*, for Hegel. Here Hegel takes it that an organism is an entity that has its own purposes (above all, it aims to reproduce itself) and articulates itself into specialized subsystems (for example, the digestive system, the reproductive organs) that support one another so that they collectively realize the organism's purposes.[13] Hegel also thinks that every organism is self-determining—that is, free—in the sense that it develops and articulates itself in accordance with its *own*, inbuilt, purpose or plan. For Hegel, then, individuals cannot have freedom of choice unless they first have social freedom, and they can achieve social freedom only within a social order that is *itself* free in the sense of being organically articulated. Societies ordered in this way are to be found more or less fully developed in modern European countries.

When Hegel describes the elements of the modern social order within the *Philosophy of Right*, he takes it that this kind of social order is a living system: "As living spirit, the state exists only as an organized whole, differentiated into particular functions which proceed from the *single* concept . . . of the rational will and continually produce it as their result."[14] Hegel is using the word "state" here, as he sometimes does, to mean a structured social order as a whole.[15] The overall purpose of the modern social order is to reconcile people's sense of having individual interests—and, correspondingly, their sense of being different from one another as individuals—with concern for others and commitment to the collective good, corresponding to a sense of "unity" with others. As a purposive entity, the social order must be subdivided into specialized spheres, each with a function and character that flow out of the purpose of the social order as a whole. Specifically, then, the social order must be subdivided—as in modern European states—into three spheres: (1) one sphere that fosters a strong sense of unity between people (the family); (2) one sphere that fosters a strong sense of difference between people (civil society); and (3) another sphere that reconciles the two (the state).

Hegel's organicist conception of modern society seems to imply that the individual should have access to all three spheres, because each sphere represents an essential aspect of membership in a modern society. But Hegel instead declares that women may participate only in the familial sphere. This is because, as Allen Wood explains, for Hegel "differentiated institutions require a social differentiation among individuals. Each principle [that is, each sphere] must have its proper representative and guardian."[16] Given specialized institutions, certain individuals must be permanently based in and responsible for each of them. This conclusion follows from Hegel's idea that modern societies are rightly structured like organisms. Each of the functionally specialized subsystems within an organism is realized by a specific range of organs: for instance, the stomach, bowels, et cetera realize the digestive system; the gonads, genitals, et cetera realize the reproductive system. Similarly, Hegel assumes that each social subsystem must be populated and maintained by a dedicated set of people who serve as its "organs" or functionaries.

However, even if we accept Hegel's position that there must be some people who are permanently based in and responsible for their families, it does not automatically follow that those people must always be women. Why should it be contrary to right for men to play this role in some families and women in others, depending on individual preferences? To answer this, Hegel introduces the further idea that women as a sex must play the familial role because their bodily and psychical nature uniquely suits them to do so: "The *natural* determinacy of the two sexes acquires an *intellectual* and *ethical* significance."[17] In particular, this "natural determinacy" is that women's nature is to embody an "immediate unity" of self and other, both corporeally and psychically, while men's nature is to embody "difference" between self and other. Hegel expands on this in his *Philosophy of Nature*, to which I now turn.[18] We can subsequently return to clarify exactly how natural sex difference becomes translated into a socio-political differentiation in roles.

2. HEGEL ON THE DIFFERENCE BETWEEN THE SEXES

In his *Philosophy of Right*, Hegel indicates that the "natural determinacy of the two sexes" arises out of "life in its totality, . . . as the actuality of the *species* and its process,"[19] thereby referring us to his discussion of the "species-process" (*Gattungsprozess*)—that is, reproduction— within §368–369 of his *Philosophy of Nature*. Paragraphs §368–369 of the latter, however, discuss reproduction without referring to sex difference. Hegel's account of sex difference is in the addition to §368. This, like the other additions to the *Philosophy of Nature*, was assembled by Hegel's editor Jules Michelet from various sources including student transcripts, Hegel's Heidelberg and Berlin lecture notes on nature spanning from 1819 to 1830, and his Jena lecture notes on nature and mind from 1805 to 1806. It is from the Heidelberg, Berlin, and, especially, the Jena notes that Michelet drew Hegel's account of sex difference.[20]

It might seem that we cannot wisely interpret Hegel's mature conception of men, women, and their social roles based on passages largely composed of material dating back to 1805–6. Yet the very fact that Hegel did not include an account of sex difference in the main paragraphs of his mature *Philosophy of Nature*, and that he did not in his maturity give sex difference the same prominence as he did at the time of his Jena drafts (for instance, sex difference is mentioned only very briefly in the transcript of Hegel's 1823/24 nature lectures made by K. G. J. von Griesheim),[21] suggests that he saw no need to qualify or revise his Jena account of sex difference. He presumably remained satisfied with this account, as is also suggested by the fact that the Jena account ties in with those comments on sex difference that he did make during the Berlin and Heidelberg years, as well as with his treatment of women in the *Philosophy of Right*. So we may, after all, rely on the addition to §368 as presenting Hegel's considered and continuing view of sex difference.

The context of this view is Hegel's account of "sexual relationships" (*Geschlechtsverhältnisse*)—the reproductive activities of animals, including human beings considered solely in respect of the characteristics they share with animals. "Sexual" relationships arise when one animal encounters another of the same species. These encounters are the first case that Hegel finds within nature where there exists a relationship of one subject to another—in effect, a primary and nonconscious relationship of mutual recognition. In any such encounter, the animal senses that the two are both "identical"—insofar as they belong to the same species—and "different" as individuals. The animal senses a tension between the identity and the difference: it "has the *feeling* of this defect [or tension]. The species [*Gattung*] is therefore present in the individual as a straining against the inadequacy of its single actuality."[22] The animal acquires an urge to realize the identity of the two animals by copulating with the other and producing offspring in which this identity will be embodied: "In the natural state the identity of the sexes is...a third, that is, *produced*, in which both sexes intuit their identity as a natural actuality."[23] Ultimately, though, reproduction (*Begattung*) is futile, because the offspring are still individual animals who differ from their parents as yet more separate individuals, and who will become compelled to pass back through the same reproductive process in their turn.

To see how Hegel's account of sex difference flows from this theory of reproduction, we must spell out certain assumptions that Hegel makes at this point. (He does not make these assumptions explicit, but we may legitimately impute them to Hegel insofar as by doing so we can make intelligible the logic of his ensuing approach to sex difference.) He assumes that in any reproductive process the two participant animals must play different roles. Reproduction is a process with a purpose: the purpose of producing a third entity that incarnates the identity of the two animals who have contributed to it. Just as every purposive organism must articulate itself into specialized subsystems, likewise the two individuals who are carrying out the purposive activity of reproduction must assume specialized roles within that process. The entity to be produced must be a "third," different from the parents, and so one parent must be responsible for producing the child as a distinct individual. Yet the offspring is also to be nothing more than an embodiment of the identity between the parents. In this respect, the offspring must itself be identical with the parent(s). It falls to the second parent to produce the offspring as something that is identical with the parent(s).

Each parent animal develops a specific reproductive anatomy that enables it to play one or the other of these roles: "The *formation* [that is, anatomical shape] *of the differentiated sexes* must be different, their determinacy against each other which is posited by the concept [i.e., which is rationally required] must exist."[24] Notably, then, Hegel does not think that different animals play different roles in reproduction because they have different anatomies. He thinks that there are different roles in reproduction, of which each animal must assume one, and that the anatomy of each animal develops accordingly. Sex difference is primarily not a biological difference, for Hegel; it is rather a difference in reproductive role where reproduction (*Begattung*) is conceived, in metaphysical rather than narrowly biological terms, as the process of resolving the difference between individual and species (*Gattung*) by producing a third in whom this difference is— temporarily, imperfectly—overcome. Since reproduction is this metaphysical process of joining the individual and the universal, sex difference too, for Hegel, is ultimately a metaphysical difference and is only secondarily anatomical.

Regarding the reproductive anatomy of male (*männliche*) animals, Hegel states that by lying on the body's exterior, these genitals embody "the moment of duality [*das Entzweite*], of opposition."[25] It is distinctive of male genitals that they are located primarily on the outside of the body. Hegel believes that "external" organs and limbs generally enable animals to engage and interact with items in the external world. He holds that the outward development of an animal's anatomical shape reflects its "connection with an other outside it."[26] The "other" to which male animals are related in the reproductive process is the species as-it-is-to-be embodied in the offspring. Thus, male genitals have the form they do because these genitals enable the animal to play the role of relating to its offspring as to something that is other to or different from it. It is not that males so relate to their offspring because their anatomy causes them to adopt certain attitudes. Rather, for Hegel, it is in the nature of any reproductive process that one of its participants must relate to its offspring as to a different individual, and these participants develop male reproductive anatomy as the necessary expression and realization of their reproductive role. This anatomy enables male animals to contribute to the offspring in a way that treats that offspring as something different from the male parent—by expelling it outside that parent's body, as semen.

However, those animals whose role is to produce the offspring as something identical with them develop female (*weibliche*) anatomy. The female genitals are located on the inside of the body: "The male testicle remains enclosed in the ovary in the female, does not emerge into opposition."[27] The females' internal anatomy allows them to contribute to their offspring in a way that treats the offspring as some-thing identical to them—a part of their own bodies—and to retain their offspring in their wombs, within their own bodies, as part of their own bodily processes. Thus, "the female remains in her unde-veloped unity."

Hegel sums up his picture of sex difference as follows: "in one or other of these genitals, one or the other part is essential; in the female this is necessarily the undifferentiated element [*das Indifferente*], in the male, the moment of…opposition."[28] Hegel's idea is that female bodies are organized by a principle of self/other unity. Female anat-omy reflects and realizes a reproductive role in which the mother and her offspring form an undifferentiated unity, with no firm boundary cordoning off the mother's body from that of her offspring. The female body embodies immediate unity between self and other. The male body, for its part, embodies difference between self and other.

Moreover, since the other to whom both animals are related is—as well as being a distinct individual—the species, the self/other unity around which the female body is organized is simultaneously a unity of individual and species. This implies that for Hegel the female body is placed at the service of the species in a way that the male body is not—interestingly, a position that survives in Simone de Beauvoir's Hegel-inspired account of woman's alterity: "woman [undergoes] subordination to the species…in no other [mammalian female] is enslavement of the organism to reproduction more imperious."[29]

Hegel's account of sex difference in the *Philosophy of Nature* feeds through into his *Philosophy of Mind*. He holds, now with respect spe-cifically to human beings as the unique bearers of mind, that female embodiment transmutes into a specific maternal-female form of psy-chical organization in which no firm distinction exists between the mother's self and the self of her fetus or child. Hegel discusses this in the section of his *Philosophy of Mind* on the "feeling soul."[30] The con-dition of being a "feeling soul" (*fühlende Seele*) is one through which each individual human being must pass at an extremely early stage in his or her life. As a feeling soul, one is overwhelmed by the flux of one's sensations, not yet having the cognitive and conceptual skills to organize and comprehend these sensations. As a feeling soul, one is not yet conscious, having not yet developed the capacity to take one's sensations to be one's own—to attach these sensations to oneself as a subject, a capacity that is a precondition of being able to organize and comprehend those sensations (and, therefore, to be conscious, taking it that someone is conscious if they have experience as a specifically cognitive state).

According to Hegel, other subjects and, above all, the individual's mother are principal sources of these sensations that overwhelm the feeling soul. In fact, Hegel suggests that this condition of being swamped by sensations that emanate from the mother begins while the child is still a fetus in the womb. At this time "opposition is completely absent" and the fetus is utterly "dominated" by its mother, who is the source of all its sensations.[31] A trace of this domination continues after birth, with the psyche of each young child being fundamentally imprinted by sensations that are simultaneously the sensations of its mother too. "The mother" (*Mutter*), Hegel says, "is the genius of the child"[32]—the presiding spirit who fundamentally stamps the child's personality. Unable to distinguish its own sensations from those of others, the child is in a state where the sensations of others—particularly those of the mother with whom the child's life is so entwined—can be literally transmitted into the child: "The child is...infected in a preponderantly *immediate* manner by the mind of the adults it sees around it," chiefly its mother.[33] Hegel concludes that in any child's early life there is a lack of psychical opposition between the child and its mother, prolonging the physical indistinction that obtained when the child was still in the womb.

Evidently, Hegel has described the psychical mother/child relationship from the child's perspective, but we may extrapolate that his point applies to mothers as well. Just as in pregnancy no firm physical boundary demarcates the child from its mother's body, in the early stages of the child's life no firm psychical boundary demarcates the sensations of the mother from those of the child. This psychical indistinction recapitulates the physical lack of distinction that obtained during pregnancy. For Hegel, the self/other fusion that expressed itself in women's anatomy during reproduction transmutes, postnatally, into the psychical form of a self/other fusion at the level of sensations. Although the mother, unlike the very young child, is conscious, it seems that in her relationship with the child she undergoes a kind of regression to an infantile state of indistinction (Hegel remarks that individuals may "relapse" from higher to lower stages of mind).[34]

The essence of the female body and of the maternal-female psyche—Hegel draws no distinction between maternal and female here—is immediate self/other unity and, simultaneously, immediate individual/species unity. Let us now see how these Hegelian claims inform his relegation of women to the family in the *Philosophy of Right*.

3. THE POLITICAL IMPLICATIONS OF
SEX DIFFERENCE

As we saw in Section 1, Hegel believes that modern European states are becoming increasingly organically structured, and rightly so. These states are on their way to being articulated into three subsystems or social spheres: the "immediate unity" of the family; the "difference" of civil society; and the "mediated unity" of the political state.[35] Hegel also believes that some people must be permanently based in each of the earlier spheres, that is, in the family and in civil society, and that it is and should be women who always remain in the family. For Hegel this lot falls to women because, corporeally and psychically, to be female is to draw no self/other, individual/species distinction—women are suited to a familial role because their bodies and psyches are organized by the same principle of "immediate unity" that regulates the family. How precisely does Hegel think that this (ostensible) fact about what it is to be female equips women for the familial role?

Contrary to what one might initially assume from his reference to the "natural determinacy of the sexes," Hegel's form of argument is importantly different from that of biological determinism. Biological determinist arguments take the following form: women's and men's biological traits—perhaps their hormones or energy levels—predispose them toward certain kinds of activities and away from others, toward the domestic realm and away from the public realm in women's case, and vice versa for men. Women and men should (the biological determinist claims), therefore, stick to the activities for which they are each predisposed, and society should be so arranged as to encourage men and women to do this, because anything else would be futile, would lead to frustration and unhappiness for both men and women, and would be damagingly inefficient for society.

Actually, though, Hegel's approach to sex difference differs from a biological determinist approach, first, because he does not understand the "natural" difference between the sexes to be biological in the standard modern sense. That sense, which became current following the French revolution, is that differences in anatomy cause men and women to think and act differently.[36] Hegel, though, believes that men's and women's different biological traits reflect and realize a difference in reproductive roles that is required by the metaphysical character of reproduction. Because the two sexes are defined by their different ways of relating species and individual, universal and particular, the natures of the two sexes are primarily metaphysical rather than biological. If Hegel is an essentialist with respect to sex, he is a metaphysical rather than a biological essentialist.[37]

Second, Hegel's approach departs from biological determinism because he does not think that women must remain in the family because their nature causally predisposes them to do so, by disposing them to prefer family-focused activities or to perform poorly in the public world. Instead, Hegel's view is that women's bodily organization around "immediate unity" *corresponds* to the organization of the family around the principle of "immediate unity." He writes,

> The *natural* determinacy of the two sexes acquires an *intellectual* and *ethical* significance by virtue of its rationality. This significance is determined by the difference into which the ethical substantiality, as the concept in itself, divides itself up in order that its vitality may thereby achieve a concrete unity.[38]

To paraphrase, the "ethical substance" of society subdivides itself into family, civil society, and state because this substance is a "vital"—that is, organic—whole. The resulting difference between family and public sphere (the latter encompassing both civil society and state) gives ethical meaning—a socio-political dimension—to natural sex difference. Once arisen, the higher-level, more spiritual difference between the social spheres of immediate unity and difference imparts a new layer of meaning to the lower-level, more natural difference between bodies organized by immediate unity and difference. On the one hand, then, when sexually differentiated human beings find themselves living within (modern European) societies that are organically subdifferentiated, their natural sex difference becomes enfolded within the higher-level domestic/public difference. On the other hand, the natural sex difference *should* be enfolded by the domestic/public division in this way, because, through this enfolding, that which is more spiritual—the social order—takes up what is more material—bodily sex difference—and renders this material functional for its own ends, thereby imparting to this material an enhanced level of rationality.

As a result of this enfolding, men's and women's different natures take on a new significance, with male "difference" assuming the form of "personal self-sufficiency" and female "immediate unity" assuming the form of "spirituality which maintains itself in unity as knowledge and volition of the substantial in the form of concrete *individuality* and *feeling*."[39] Naturally, women's bodies are not differentiated from those of their offspring, and psychically, too, women-mothers experience sensations that are indeterminately those of their offspring. These characteristics now gain added spiritual significance by being rendered into the basis for women's familial role of identifying their interests with those of their families—where women, unlike men, do not re-emerge from this identification into the renewed individualism of civil society. Thus, the enfolding of the natural sex difference into the social domestic/public difference gives women's natural fusion with their children and with the species a new socio-political function. Equally, women's female (*weibliche*) nature is made into the basis of the socio-political identity of woman-as-wife-and-mother (*Frau*). Hegel's position here is not that women's bodily and psychical fusion with their children directly *causes* them to identify their interests with those of their families at the political level. Rather, women's natural character of bodily and psychical fusion "acquires" (*erhält*) or "receives"[40] the further character of domestic identity when that natural character is enfolded into the social sphere of the family.

Hegel's rationale for excluding women from the public world lies in his theory of nature, then, but this does not mean that his is a biological determinist mode of argument. Rather, his argument is that women's nature corresponds—at a lower, relatively natural level—to the more spiritual structure of the family and that, as part of the process of spiritualizing what is natural, women's nature should (and in modern Europe largely does) assume the further spiritual form of a domestic identity. As Kimberly Hutchings has noted, then, Hegel joins together his accounts of women's place in social life (the family) and of mind's emergence from nature (an emergence that he nonetheless insists is non-natural, because mind "over-grasps" nature, enfolding nature into its own higher-level functioning). Woman becomes the hinge where this enfolding of material nature by mind takes place, so that for Hegel "women only [ever] appear at a point of mediation or transition between natural and spiritual existence."[41]

My reconstruction of Hegel's rationale for consigning women to the family is not yet complete, however. His account of sex difference in the *Philosophy of Nature* emerges out of and represents the culmination of a broader pattern of sexuate symbolism that informs his entire theory of nature—a pattern in which matter is symbolically female while the concept and mind are symbolically male. To fully appreciate Hegel's account of sex difference and of how that difference takes on socio-political significance, then, we need to trace the sexuate symbolism with which he imbues his theory of nature.

4. FEMALE MATTER, MALE CONCEPT

To see how sexuate symbolism informs Hegel's *Philosophy of Nature*, we must briefly review that text's basic structure and contents. The text begins by presupposing that nature has emerged from the "idea," itself the highest form of the "concept"—the whole rationally inter-connected sequence of basic ontological principles and forms, as nar-rated in Hegel's *Logic* (being, nothingness, becoming, determinacy, et cetera). The Hegelian concept, then, is nothing subjective but is "the true, objective, actual being of things themselves. It is like the Platonic Ideas, which... exist in individual things as their substantial kinds."[42]

The idea comes out of itself or externalizes itself to constitute nature (by a process that we need not examine here). As the product of the idea's self-externalization, nature initially exists as sheer "externality," *partes extra partes*—that is, as pure matter. Hegel traces how nature's matter becomes permeated by thought in a "series of stages consisting of many moments, the exposition of which constitutes the philosophy of nature."[43] First, the concept re-emerges within nature in the form of the unifying principles that hold portions of matter together into individual bodies. Second, the concept increasingly reshapes matter into forms that express and reflect it, so that material bodies acquire increasingly complex properties—first mechanical, then electrical, then chemical—in respect of which their matter progressively comes to manifest the complex, articulated character of the concept. At the pinnacle of nature's hierarchy stand animals, whose bodies are com-pletely conceptually permeated: "the whole [of the animal's body] is so pervaded by its unity that... in the animal body the complete untruth of [material] being-outside-one-another is revealed."[44] This presages the emergence of mind within human beings, an emergence that represents the concept's completed return-to-itself from its self-externalization in the multiplicity of material nature.

We can now appreciate how Hegel symbolizes matter as female, a symbolic equation that surfaces in several passages from the Introduction to the *Philosophy of Nature*. Consider the following:

> The study of nature is thus the liberation of spirit in nature... This is also the liberation of nature... Spirit has the certainty which Adam had when he looked on Eve, "This is flesh of my flesh, and bone of my bone." Thus Nature is the bride which spirit weds.[45]

By tracing how nature's material side becomes increasingly permeated by its conceptual side, eventually to the point where the concept assumes the form of spirit or mind, we the Hegelian philosophers "liberate" nature. At the same time, we confirm that the nature that we are studying is of the same "flesh" as us: nature is not pure matter standing over against ourselves as beings of pure mind; rather, we are composed of concept-permeated matter and so is nature. This places nature in the same relation to human beings as the biblical Eve stands to Adam: Eve/nature shares Adam's/humanity's concept-permeated materiality. Nonetheless, nature remains *relatively* material compared with humanity—for in much of nature, the concept struggles to express itself within matter, succeeding only partially. By implication, Eve too is relatively material compared to Adam. As a woman Eve is more material than Adam; implicitly, her greater materiality is what *makes* Eve female and not merely another man, another instance of spirit. Matter is, then, symbolically female, so that it confers womanhood on those in whose flesh it predominates.

Pursuing the same train of associations, Hegel writes, "The inscription on the veil of Isis, 'I am that which was, is, and will be, and no mortal has lifted my veil' melts away before thought."[46] Once again, his point is that when we recognize that nature is conceptually permeated we remove the illusory appearance that nature is merely material, which corresponds to the philosopher's lifting of the veil of Isis, his symbolic marrying of Isis, whereby (according to Hegel's account of marriage) he identifies with what they have in common—the status of being concept-permeated matter. But the fact that Hegel figures nature as Isis—a quintessentially *female* goddess, traditionally depicted as many-breasted[47]—reflects his view that nature remains *relatively* material compared to the human inquirer, and so this figuration confirms that he associates matter with the female.

The same associations emerge when Hegel claims that traditional Christian doctrine offers a merely "representational" grasp of the relations between nature, concept, and matter—that is, a grasp of these relations that partially attains to the level of conceptual thought but remains infected with pictorial, imaginary thinking. The process by which the idea, at the end of Hegel's *Logic*, transforms or inverts itself into pure matter corresponds to God's creation of the world.[48] The stage at which the concept has returned to itself from matter and has assumed the form of mind corresponds to the appearance of Christ. Nature, Hegel writes, corresponds to "the son of God, but not as the son, but as abiding in otherness... Nature is spirit estranged from itself; in nature, spirit lets itself go, a Bacchic god unrestrained."[49] Nature corresponds, then, to a dead, dismembered Dionysian God—in other words, to the concept dispersed in materiality. Insofar as Christ is born from out of this materiality of nature, this materiality occupies the symbolic place of Christ's mother Mary—so, once more, of the female. Interestingly, in a fragment from his Bern period (1793–97) Hegel suggests that Bacchanalian festivals existed to satisfy "female temperaments."[50] He implies that the condition of God being dismembered in matter is a peculiarly "female" condition, so that the cult of the dismembered God would have appealed especially to women—perhaps alluding to Euripides' tragedy *The Bacchae* in which it is female revelers who, possessed by the Dionysian spirit, tear apart king Pentheus.[51]

Since Hegel symbolizes matter as female and since he also considers matter to be the being-outside-itself of the concept ("nature is the idea in the form of otherness"),[52] he implicitly understands the female to be the being-outside-itself *of* the male. The female ranks as an inadequate, self-alienated form of the male, rather than being a sexuate identity in its own right. Moreover, the progression that occurs in nature whereby the concept re-emerges and progressively reshapes matter is a progression wherein that which is symbolically male re-emerges and increasingly converts the symbolically female into the vehicle of its own self-expression.

One might wonder whether this sexuate symbolism is inessential to Hegel's philosophical thought, and whether his basic claims regarding matter, the concept, and nature can be (re)stated independent of this symbolism, permitting Hegel's latter-day readers to retain those claims while discarding their symbolic wrapping. That is, one might suspect that Hegel's symbolism is merely superficial, not deep—not constitutive of the substance of his theories. Yet the historical character of Hegel's thought militates against ready classification of his sexuate symbolism as either deep or superficial. Hegel's philosophical system is explicitly formed as a working-through of previous philosophies. But throughout the history of philosophy, as feminist philosophers have documented, matter has been symbolized as female—from Plato's idea of the maternal *chora* (χωρα) or "receptacle" in his *Timeaus* through to Descartes' theoretical reconstitution of the living, maternal cosmos of medieval times as bare extended matter.[53] Because Hegel draws openly on this heritage of thinking about matter, structuring his own account of matter/concept relations as corrective of the deficiencies within this heritage, he necessarily imports the tradition's sexuate symbolism into his system. So, regardless of whether the metaphor of matter-as-female is deep or superficial in Plato, Descartes, and other philosophers, the fact that this metaphor has become historically sedimented means that that metaphor inescapably becomes embedded in Hegel's thought, since this thought is constituted *as* a reworking of the history of philosophy. Sexuate symbolism might not be necessary to Hegel's account of matter and the concept if it is considered in abstraction from its historical provenance and precursors, but that symbolism *is* necessary to Hegel's account when it is considered—as he intended it to be—in its historical concreteness.

Hegel's account of sex difference in the *Philosophy of Nature* is the consequence of the symbolic equation between female and matter, male and concept, that has informed his entire preceding account of nature. Although Hegel has described male and female reproductive anatomies as organized respectively around differentiation and its absence, he adds that the female and the male respectively contribute "the material element" and "subjectivity" to their offspring.

> *Procreation* must not be reduced to the ovary and the sperm, as if the new product were merely a composition of the forms or parts of both sides; the truth is that the female contains the material element, but the male contains the subjectivity.[54]

Because the female retains the fetus within her own body, as part of her own physical processes, she exchanges bodily materials with the fetus on an ongoing basis, and in that respect she contributes to the fetus materially. On the other hand, the male expels his semen outside him and thereafter has no further material, corporeal relationship with the fetus. In what sense, though, is the male thereby bestowing subjectivity upon the fetus? Hegel explains: "The seed is…[a] simple representation…—simply a *single* point, like the name and the entire self."[55] That is, because the male's contribution to the fetus takes the form of one single emission of semen (rather than many material exchanges over time), the male is providing matter in a shape suited to represent the individuality of the fetus: the single emission of semen "represents" the child-to-be as a single individual. As such, the material aspect of the emission of semen carries a meaning: its matter is concept-permeated. Hegel can, therefore, extrapolate that the male is contributing to the fetus matter that is fully concept-permeated—that is, subjectivity.

Since Hegel has tacitly equated matter with the female and the concept with the male throughout his system, it is unsurprising that when he has come to theorize sex difference he has mapped the man/woman difference onto the concept/matter opposition. And since the progressive domination of the concept over matter is, symbolically, a progressive domination of male over female, it is equally unsurprising that, when this process of spiritualization of matter continues through the *Philosophy of Mind* into the *Philosophy of Right*, this process results in women being placed in subservience to men. As we have seen, women are—rightly in Hegel's estimation—confined to the family because their immediately unified nature corresponds, at a lower, more material level, to the immediately unified structure of the family, which enfolds women's nature into its own higher-level functioning. This enfolding of women's nature by the family is part of the broader process of the spiritualization of matter: the process whereby the (symbolically male) concept renders matter into forms that express and reflect the concept's sovereignty. Since the concept is symbolically male, the spiritualization of women's nature simultaneously renders that nature into a vehicle of service to male citizens. Spiritualized, women's nature becomes the wellspring of women's devotion to the reproduction and tending of the male citizens who exercise economic power and legal jurisdiction over the family and its female inhabitants. Women's spiritualized nature thus expresses and reflects the mastery exercised by the male citizens for whom that nature has been made functional: so that, as Hegel concludes in one of his Jena drafts, "The *sexes* are plainly in a [hierarchical] relation to one another, one the universal, the other the particular; they are not absolutely equal."[56]

The deeply gendered structure of Hegel's philosophy that I have described is hardly likely to enhance the appeal of his philosophy to feminist readers. Nonetheless, it is important for we feminist readers of Hegel to acknowledge that his thought does have this deeply gendered structure, and for our efforts to use and reconstruct Hegelian ideas to be informed by this acknowledgment. Otherwise we run the risk of inadvertently reproducing in our own thinking the very gendered schemata that we aim, as feminists, to expose and challenge. Arguably, for instance, Simone de Beauvoir does this in *The Second Sex* when she takes up Hegel's master/slave dialectic as a way of understanding the relations between men and women. She argues that women's oppression has its historical roots in hunter-gatherer conditions when women's reproductive burden prevented them from participating in the struggle for recognition by risking life. She does not ask whether Hegel's master/slave dialectic was conceived all along as a struggle between men—as Lloyd argues, suggesting that Hegel conceives the struggle to risk and transcend life *as* a struggle to transcend the feminine.[57] Because Beauvoir ignores this and simply takes over the value of transcendence, she concludes that those things that seem most "female" and life-related about women—reproduction, mothering, menstruation, et cetera—are inherent obstacles to

transcendence (as we saw earlier, she regards women as being alien-
ated from their own projects in the service of the species). Thus,
unhelpfully, she attributes part of the blame for women's oppression
to women's own biology, rather than to what society has made of that
biology. By attending to the gendered structure of Hegel's philosophy we can avoid simply reproducing it as Beauvoir ends up doing.

Understanding this gendered structure need not make it impossible for feminists to use parts of Hegel's philosophy, but it suggests
that if we do so then we need simultaneously to reconstruct and rein-
terpret that philosophy, or the parts of it that we are using, in a more
gender-egalitarian form. An example of this kind of simultaneous
use-and-reinterpretation is Irigaray's position in *I Love to You* that
each sex should have its own dialectic—rather than only the male sex
undergoing a dialectical development in which it enfolds and incorporates the female. In particular, for Irigaray, both sexes should
undergo a negative dialectic, whereby they learn to limit themselves
out of respect for the alterity of the other sex. If, like Irigaray, we
want to transform rather than reproduce Hegel's gendered schemata
when we use his ideas, we need first to identify how those schemata
are at work within his thought, as I have tried to do here.

Notes

1. Hegel, *Elements of the Philosophy of Right* (henceforth *Elements*), trans.
   H. B. Nisbet (Cambridge: Cambridge University Press, 1991), §166,
   206. Translations of Hegel are sometimes corrected without special
   notice in light of Hegel, *Werke in 20 Bänden*, ed. Karl M. Michel and
   Eva Moldenhauer (Frankfurt am Main: Suhrkamp, 1972).
2. Pateman sees Hegel as criticizing contract theory by putting forward
   his conception of marriage as a contract to transcend the standpoint of
   contract; see Pateman, *The Sexual Contract* (Cambridge, UK: Polity
   Press, 1988), 174. But she notes that he allocates women just enough
   civil personality to make the marital contracts whereby they relinquish
   any (further) civil personality. This, she thinks, is because Hegel inher-
   its from classical contract theory a conception of the contracting individual as someone who owns their own body. But because women have
   uncertain bodily boundaries (emblematically in pregnancy) they cannot unproblematically own their own bodies, so that the contracting
   individual is implicitly male—for Hegel as for classical contractarians.
   I find Pateman's interpretation unconvincing because Hegel criticizes
   the individualism of classical contractarianism, re-conceiving property-ownership as predicated on social relations of mutual recognition
   rather on sovereign self-ownership. Thus, he re-conceives the status of
   the contracting individual in a way that renders this status potentially

compatible with being female. His reasons for consigning women to the family must lie elsewhere.

3. See Lloyd, *The Man of Reason: "Male" and "Female" in Western Philosophy* (London: Routledge, 1984); Irigaray, *I Love to You: Sketch for a Possible Felicity in History*, trans. Alison Martin (London: Routledge, 1996).

4. Neuhouser, *Foundations of Hegel's Social Theory: Actualizing Freedom* (Cambridge, MA: Harvard University Press, 2000), 133.

5. Here Hegel's view of sexuate difference exemplifies what Irigaray sees as the pattern in western philosophy whereby "The 'female' is always described as deficiency, atrophy, lack of the sex that has a monopoly on value: the male sex"; Irigaray, *This Sex Which Is Not One*, trans. Catherine Porter (Ithaca: Cornell University Press, 1985), 69.

6. Hegel, *Elements* §4, 37; §11, 45.

7. Ibid., §71, 102.

8. Ibid., §82, 115–116.

9. Ibid., §153, 196.

10. Hegel is not offering a prescriptive account of the right form of society in the way that (for instance) Plato does in the *Republic*. As Michael Hardimon has made clear, Hegel is describing what he sees as the essential tendencies within modern European societies in a way that is intended to bring out the rationality of these tendencies (hence Hegel's notorious equation of the actual with the rational) and so reconcile us (modern Europeans) to the societies we live in. See Hardimon, *Hegel's Social Philosophy: The Project of Reconciliation* (Cambridge: Cambridge University Press, 1994).

11. On this anti-contractarian argument of Hegel's, see Drucilla Cornell, Michael Rosenfeld, David Gray and Carlson, "Introduction," in *Hegel and Legal Theory*, ed. Cornell, Rosenfeld, and Carlson (London: Routledge, 1991), x-xi.

12. Frederick Neuhouser, *Foundations of Hegel's Social Theory: Actualizing Freedom* (Cambridge, MA: Harvard University Press, 2000), 33.

13. Hegel, *Philosophy of Mind*, trans. W. Wallace (Oxford: Clarendon Press, 1971) §381A, 9 10.

14. Ibid., §539, 265.

15. On this use by Hegel of the term "state," see Z. A. Pelczynski, "The Hegelian Conception of the State," in *Hegel's Political Philosophy: Problems and Perspectives*, ed. Z. A. Pelczynski (Cambridge: Cambridge University Press, 1971), 14.

16. Wood, *Hegel's Ethical Thought* (Cambridge: Cambridge University Press, 1990), 244.

17. Hegel, *Elements*, §165, 206.

18. Surprisingly there has been very little sustained examination of Hegel's theory of natural sex difference at all, although feminist thinkers have regularly mentioned it: Irigaray, *Speculum of the Other Woman*, trans. Gillian C. Gill (Ithaca: Cornell University Press,

1985), 214–226; see also Simone de Beauvoir, *The Second Sex*, trans. H. M. Parshley (Harmondsworth: Penguin Books, 1988), 40–41; and Tina Chanter, *Ethics of Eros: Irigaray's Rewriting of the Philosophers* (London: Routledge, 1995), 82–84. None of these three authors situates this theory of sex difference in the *Philosophy of Nature* more broadly.

19. Hegel, *Elements*, §161, 200.
20. The relevant passages from the Jena drafts can be found in Hegel, *Jenaer Systementwürfe 3: Naturphilosophie und Philosophie des Geistes*, ed. Rolf-Peter Horstmann (Hamburg: Felix Meiner, 1987), 160–161.
21. See Hegel, *Vorlesung über Naturphilosophie Berlin 1823/24, Nachschrift von K. G. J. v. Griesheim,* ed. Gilles Marmasse (Frankfurt: Peter Lang, 2000), 259.
22. Hegel, *Philosophy of Nature, Part 2 of the Encyclopaedia of the Philosophical Sciences*, trans. A. V. Miller (Oxford: Oxford University Press, 2004), §368, 411.
23. Hegel, *Lectures on Natural Right and Political Science: The First Philosophy of Right, Heidelberg 1817–1819, with Additions from the Lectures of 1818–1819*, trans. J. Michael Stewart and C. Hodgson (Berkeley: University of California Press, 1996), §75, 139.
24. Hegel, *Philosophy of Nature*, §368A, 412.
25. Ibid., §368A, 413.
26. Ibid., §355A, 376.
27. Ibid., §368A, 413.
28. Ibid., §368A, 413.
29. Beauvoir, *The Second Sex*, 64. As Kimberly Hutchings explains, "Beauvoir follows Hegel's analysis of sexual difference in his *Philosophy of Nature*, in which male sexual and reproductive roles are associated with a principle of activity and individuation and female sexual and reproductive roles with passivity and species identification. Moreover, Beauvoir argues that the individual/species alienation is carried into the lives of women as an experienced reality"; Hutchings, *Hegel and Feminist Philosophy* (Cambridge, UK: Polity Press, 2003), 66.
30. Hegel, *Philosophy of Mind*, §403-§406, 92–122.
31. So Eric O. Clarke puts it on Hegel's behalf in "Fetal Attraction: Hegel's An-aesthetics of Gender," in *Feminist Interpretations of G. W. F. Hegel*, ed. Patricia J. Mills (University Park, PA: Pennsylvania State University Press, 1996), 158.
32. Hegel, *Philosophy of Mind*, §405, 95.
33. Ibid., §405A, 97.
34. Ibid., §405A, 96.
35. Neuhouser, *Foundations of Hegel's Social Theory*, op. cit., 133.
36. See Londa Schiebinger, *The Mind Has No Sex?: Women in the Origins of Modern Science* (Cambridge, MA: Harvard University Press, 1989).

37. I take the distinction between biological and metaphysical essential-ism from Cressida Heyes, *Line Drawings: Defining Women Through Feminist Practice* (Ithaca: Cornell University Press, 2000), chap. 1.
38. Hegel, *Elements*, §165, 206.
39. Ibid., §166, 206.
40. Ibid., §165, 206.
41. Hutchings, op.cit., 45.
42. Hegel, *Philosophy of Nature*, §246A, 9.
43. Hegel, *Philosophy of Mind*, §381A, 13.
44. Ibid., §389A, 10.
45. Hegel, *Philosophy of Nature*, §246A, 13.
46. Ibid., §246A, 10.
47. For a history of the long-standing figuration of nature as Isis, see Pierre Hadot, *The Veil of Isis: An Essay on the History of the Idea of Nature*, trans. Michael Chase (Cambridge, MA: Harvard University Press, 2006).
48. Hegel, *Philosophy of Nature*, §247A, 14.
49. Ibid., §247A, 14.
50. In *Miscellaneous Writings of G. W. F. Hegel*, ed. Jon Stewart (Evanston, IL: Northwestern University Press, 2002), 98
51. See Euripides, *The Bacchae*, trans. Geoffrey S. Kirk (Englewood Cliffs, NJ: Prentice-Hall, 1970).
52. Hegel, *Philosophy of Nature*, §247A, 15.
53. See Plato, *Timaeus and Critias*, trans. Desmond Lee (Harmondsworth: Penguin Books, 1971), 67–73; for this interpretation of Descartes, see Susan Bordo, *The Flight to Objectivity: Essays on Cartesianism and Culture* (Albany: SUNY Press, 1987).
54. Hegel, *Philosophy of Nature*, §368A, 413.
55. Ibid., §368A, 413–414.
56. Hegel, *System of Ethical Life (1802/3) and First Philosophy of Spirit*, ed. H. S. Harris and T. M. Knox (Albany: SUNY Press, 1979), 110.
57. Lloyd, *The Man of Reason: "Male" and "Female" in Western Philosophy* (London: Routledge, 1984), 92.

CHAPTER TWELVE

Debating Hegel's Legacy for Contemporary Feminist Politics

Nancy Bauer, Kimberly Hutchings, Tuija Pulkkinen, and Alison Stone

This book has focused primarily on the *philosophical* implications, for both feminism and Hegelianism, of engagements between Hegel and feminist thought. Traditionally, however, a key concern of feminist engagements with Hegel has had to do with the *political* implications of using his work for feminist purposes. In this final chapter, we revisit this traditional concern, in a debate over Hegel and feminist politics. We decided to do this by inviting four feminist philosophers with a long-term, active, and diverse engagement in feminist politics to exchange views on the question of the relevance of Hegel's work for contemporary feminist politics. In doing this we hope to highlight the very different ways in which philosophical and political concerns intersect within feminist thought on Hegel.

The text that follows was produced in an email exchange in three rounds within one month. The discussants were asked to respond to the initial question and then, in turn, to the successive rounds of responses, as if in face-to-face dialogue with one another. The question posed to the discussants was: *Does Hegel's work have any significance for contemporary feminist politics?*

ROUND ONE

Alison Stone:

I think it's not a question of Hegel potentially having a significance that feminists have yet to appropriate, because the reception of Hegel has always been important for feminism. After all, the master/slave dialectic and the concept of recognition are fundamental to Simone de Beauvoir's formulation in *The Second Sex* that woman is man's other, surely a founding insight for second wave feminism. As this illustrates, it is particularly Hegel's concept of recognition that many feminists have drawn on. A more recent example is Nancy Fraser's view that gay/lesbian/queer politics is first and foremost a struggle for cultural recognition, while class politics concerns economic redistribution, and feminism and anti-racism combine both. Recognition isn't understood in a very precisely Hegelian way here, but without Hegel we couldn't even formulate the notion of a politics of recognition. Without Hegel, one couldn't think of recognition as constitutively necessary for someone to be a subject at all and, therefore, as vitally necessary for everyone, and as something of which one can be deprived (as is the slave in Hegel's master/slave dialectic, who works without receiving any recognition as a subject, an autonomous agent and maker of meaning). If everyone needs recognition, then being deprived of it must count as unjust, so that recognition becomes a political matter. Indeed, based on Hegel's account, it can be argued that cultural recognition is just as vital a need as economic justice.

Another aspect of Hegel's thought that feminists have used is not a specific Hegelian concept but his dialectical logic: his way of showing how one concept, when isolated or separated from its antithesis, tends to collapse back into or become invaded by the antithesis—in a return of the repressed (as in Adorno's and Horkheimer's application, the more enlightenment tries to separate itself from myth the more barbaric and mythical it becomes).

Irigaray uses this form of argument to theorize the psychical difficulties that individuals face under patriarchy. She argues that daughters are forced to separate themselves from their mothers and to identify with and idealize their fathers, because only by so doing can they accede to independent subjectivity; but because this kind of separation is impossibly sharp, daughters are endlessly sucked back into fusion with their mothers. Likewise she thinks that sons try to separate from their mothers but remain unconsciously locked into Oedipal desire for their mothers and reenact this in their relationships with other women but then attempt to reestablish separation through violent breaks with the feminine, and so on. Irigaray's arguments follow a Hegelian logic: trying to separate from immediate unity reproduces it; we need instead to redefine being a subject as being related-to but distinct-from one's maternal origin. These issues—about conceptions of subjectivity, their different impacts on men and women—may seem very abstract but they are still matters of recognition, which following Hegel we can recognize to remain politically important.

Kimberly Hutchings:

I don't think that there's a straightforward answer to this question. I would say that Hegel's work, in substantive ideological terms, is of minimal significance for contemporary feminist politics in its various forms. In other words, Hegel doesn't set out specific political ideals that share ground with feminism, except perhaps insofar as he saw the idea of self-determination as the key motif of modernity. In general, he wasn't a thinker who set out specific political blueprints; furthermore, his time and place, though sharing ground with aspects of the present, were also very different from ours. To the extent that feminism was a nascent political ideology in Hegel's time, he was clearly not sympathetic to it, as Benhabib's "On Hegel, Women and Irony" demonstrates. It's pretty clear that as a matter of fact Hegel did not rate the claims of women particularly high, he denigrated them in his philosophy of nature and they play a highly subordinate role in both his philosophies of spirit and of right. But, of course, the story doesn't end here, I think that Hegel's work does have some importance for feminist politics in two respects: first, as a diagnostician of an emergent modernity in early nineteenth-century Europe, Hegel had some insightful things to say about the structural position of women within the modern state, which still resonate in the contemporary world, in particular given the globalization of capitalism. Here I am thinking of Hegel's account of the private sphere and the family and its relation to civil society in *Elements of the Philosophy of Right*. In many ways more explicitly than Marx, it seems to me that Hegel shows how the realm of productive labor, property, and exchange depends on the realm of reproductive labor and care, and how the latter needs to be defined as a noneconomic sphere in order for the whole thing to work. I take seriously Hegel's claim not to be arguing for this as what *ought* to be, but rather as extrapolating the logic of what *is*. We are still, it seems to me, in a world in which the specifically modern distinction between reproductive and productive labor is essential both to keeping capitalism going and to the subordination of women— most obviously when it comes to their share in global wealth. Second, more abstractly, Hegel was, above all, a critic of binary thinking. In this respect he shares a great deal of ground with feminists who argue that binary thinking underpins the taken for granted legitimacy of a gendered social order. Whether he would like it or not, I think that taking Hegel's logic and phenomenology seriously is fundamentally troubling to any set of political convictions that rely on mutually exclusive categories of male/female or masculine/feminine. My hope, as a feminist philosopher, is that Hegel can help us to think *differently* about the meanings and implications of categories such as sex and gender.

Tuija Pulkkinen:

Some say there is no such thing as contemporary feminist politics, since the moment of a unified feminist movement is over. If Hegel is considered to have left his strongest inheritance through Marx in thinking of politics in terms of united goal-oriented collective sub- jects, such as nations and movements, whether socialist or feminist, it would be right to say that Hegel, although historically significant, is of diminishing significance to contemporary feminist politics. If this was the case, I would not find it a deplorable state of affairs.

However, if Hegel is considered as a thinker for whom concepts turn over and over incessantly, for whom there is no end point in his- tory, and who does not engage with eternal concepts but concepts in time, he is of growing significance to feminist politics. This signifi- cance comes through being an inspiration for feminist thought, and I would consider profound thought always to be the most effective and radical of politics.

I see Hegel as inspirational in at least three acute dimensions of contemporary feminist thought and politics. The first dimension is the very contemporariness. Unlike most philosophers Hegel was a contemporary thinker, he thought with time (*con tempus*) and was aware of the change of thought in time. Contemporary feminist poli- tics are diverse and have no one goal, they react constantly to their surroundings; what is feminist depends on what happens in the world, there is no program to be carried out. I would see Hegel as extremely significant as an inspiration of contemporariness of thought.

The second related dimension is Hegel's embracing of incessant, restless motion of thought. I have always had difficulties in seeing how Hegel can be read as a philosopher of the end of history, stag- ing a particular state as the endpoint. I read him as exactly the opposite, as someone who thinks in terms of endless movement, constant change, with no definite knowledge of what is to come, only that there is relentless change, which is driven by what has come before, through a perpetual movement of thought and the force of negation.

Contemporary feminist politics involve, I think, a similar sense of constant motion. Simultaneously, feminism is a resolute call for change, motivated by a feeling of injustice and perhaps an idea of justice in terms of the gender to come. There is a certain faith involved in bringing about change, and in this sense feminism is energetic involvement in change that does not know its endpoint in the future. This reminds me of a Hegelian trace that I think Derrida has captured in his writings on "to come." The "to come" character is the third dimension in which I see Hegel as significantly inspirational to contemporary feminist politics. There is a structure of hope and faith that surfaces in much of contemporary feminist politics, which transforms the content of the name "feminism" in a regular pulse. Feminism and feminist prevail while their meaning is altered through the constant turning up of another side of the issue.

Consider, for example, the politics around transsexuality, or the complexities around the politics of the headscarf and the veil. What exactly the feminist point of view in these struggles is remains undecided and easily turns from one point to the opposite, but it is clear that these are feminist struggles worth struggling for. Hegel offers no guidance on these issues, precisely because he was a thinker in his own time and this is a long time ago, but reading him prepares one to accept the evident complexity, the constant turning of the case, and not letting go the desire to move on.

Nancy Bauer:

The other day I was reading a paper on J. L. Austin, the mid-twentieth-century ordinary-language philosopher who's famous for reminding his colleagues and their progeny that to speak is not, or not just, to remark on the passing show; it's to *do* something. The author of the paper was arguing that Austin's denunciation of what he called the "true-false fetish" ought to draw our attention to the rich vocabulary we have for describing the ways in which utterances can fail to do what people set out to do with them. An utterance may be false, yes; but more often we fail to do things with words because what we say is, to name just a few ways we can go astray, beside the point or insincere or unwarranted or unauthorized or misconstrued by its audience. The author concludes his discussion of Austin by claiming that, though many philosophers are guilty of the crime, Hegel's investment in dialectic epitomizes the deplorable tendency to reduce all these rich terms of criticism to the single dimension of *contradiction.*

Now, as it happens, I'm quite sympathetic to this author's interpretation of and admiration for Austin. But his denunciation of Hegel brought me up short. For it seems to me that, far from being reductive, Hegel's conception of dialectic draws our attention, as no other theory before or since has, to the *conditions* under which our words can and cannot do things. What counts as insincerity or lack of authorization, for example, is a function in any given society of the values of that society, including what it values as the truth. What Hegel teaches us—and, really, given his own politics, probably despite himself—is that our subtler terms of criticism can go only so far. What's often required in order to induce substantial changes in the world is making vivid precisely the blatant contradictions between what a society says it values, that is, the ideology it preaches and the terms in which it expresses this ideology, and what it actually values: what specific policies and practices it sanctions, what sorts of suffering and injustice are and are not on its radar screen. These contradictions sometimes become evident all by themselves. But often, they come into clear view and induce a substantial shift in ideology only when enough people are brave and resourceful enough to reject the old terms of criticism and develop new ways of speaking that change a society's conception of what counts as the truth and so push the dialectic in a new direction.

This, I think, is what Simone de Beauvoir took herself to be attempting in *The Second Sex.* Beauvoir re-describes the absolutely ordinary, everyday experience of women in a way that unmasked—I think it *still* unmasks—the gross inadequacy of our conceptualization of women's situation in the world. She appropriates Hegel's master/slave dialectic to develop the idea that there is something fundamentally twisted about our views on sex difference. The fundamental problem is not, according to Beauvoir, that there are legal or political or social or economic inequities between the sexes, although those inequities are indeed intolerable. Rather, the problem is that people are invested in ways of understanding themselves as women and men that ensure that both sexes—but especially women—live less than fully human lives. What Beauvoir wants to do is a quintessentially Hegelian thing: to make us unbearably uncomfortable with this newly articulated truth, to see the contradiction between it and our socially sanctioned fantasy that sexism can be erased merely by tinkering from within the present system.

One of the things that Beauvoir makes vivid is just how invested people are in *not* having the system come tumbling down. We all benefit in various ways from the present terms in which we construe ourselves as men and women. I think this shows up in the wildly contradictory lives that many young women find themselves leading these days. On the one hand, they are staunch post-feminists. They think that sexism is a thing of the past and that there need be no limit to their ambitions for themselves. On the other hand, they are as concerned as ever—from what I can tell perhaps *more* concerned than ever—to ensure that they are sexually pleasing to men, both in the ways they comport themselves and in their commitment to men's (but, too often, not their own) sexual satisfaction. They try to negotiate this contradiction by construing their own sexiness as a kind of social power, as a sign of their strength and success.

Meanwhile, most feminists, at least that I know, continue to talk as though Beauvoir had never existed. We denounce the obvious inequities. We decry or praise pornography. We do lots of good work socially—for example, supporting shelters for women victims of domestic violence and struggling to preserve "our right to choose." But we're not, for the most part, making serious attempts to shift the ways that people construe themselves as gendered beings. As a result, we've made ourselves irrelevant to actual women. This is why for years I've been calling for a return to Beauvoir—which amounts, of course, to a return to Hegel.

ROUND TWO

Tuija Pulkkinen:

I am interested in the issues of "contemporary feminist politics" that our first round of entries produced, wondering which of these were feminist issues in Hegel's time and which are contemporary, and whether Hegel has anything to say in each of them.

First, there is the question of "ideology" that Nancy takes up: young women trying to please men, thinking of their sexiness as social power. A similar, maybe the same, problem was addressed by two feminists in Hegel's time—Olympe de Gouge and Mary Wollstonecraft. They assumed that *coquetterie* was caused by circumstances, which gave hardly any other choice, and they thought it alterable by feminist politics. Hegel was, in a way, in agreement with Wollstonecraft on this issue, as he also promoted "the sensible mother" model instead of the sexy, aristocratic flower-like woman— although this, of course, did not make him a feminist, but a gender politician. A similar, again maybe the same, problem emerged in the early 1970s when feminists identified it as existing within women themselves and thought that solving it needed the hard work of consciousness raising and politicizing of the private. I think Nancy is right in diagnosing that today there is less courage than before to criticize people's personal choices and make politics of them.

But is Beauvoir really a good guide here? Is she really a critic of ideology, a rebel, and in favor of turning the "system" as the early 1970s women were? I think she has been read in a much more revolutionary direction than she, as an existentialist philosopher, actually was.

I also have trouble with the distinction between "we" (the feminists) and the "ordinary women" that the politics of critique of ideology easily produces, and I think some of this may well be Hegelian inheritance through Marx, and connected to certain messianism. Although I do see the sexiness problem and worry about it too, I think there are subtleties in these politics. It is very hard to say whose satisfaction is in question in these performances of sexiness. The femininity and femmeness are not always simply what they seem to be-pleasing to men. Sometimes, also, the sexiness of young feminists is but one more turn in the internal dialectic of the history of feminist politics of appearance. Nevertheless, the issue clearly has been and is a feminist political issue, so it seems, and an undecided one.

A second persistent feminist issue, which I think is really important, relates to Kim's observation that Hegel saw the role of the private, the family and the care within it, as providing the condition for productive labor, property, and exchange. Hegel incorporated this into the structure of *The Philosophy of Right*, which also makes him a gender politician.

A contemporary Hegelian point to add here is that public political discourse often turns the fact of gendered labor awkwardly around. The underpaid work in schools and social care as well as the free care work in homes are regularly presented as something that merely consumes the fruits of productive economic activity, when, in fact, it is exactly this work that conditions and makes the economic activity possible. This dialectic is really worth watching!

Other contemporary feminist political issues mentioned in our exchange are struggles for recognition of sexual minorities, the questions of the scarf and veil, and transgender politics. It is worth noticing that these issues were not considered to be feminist ones in Hegel's times. They were not there in the late eighteenth century, the late nineteenth century, and not even really in the 1970s in feminist politics. This has to do with the contemporariness of feminism. I think Hegel might have had something interesting to say about transgender if he had had a chance; the idea just fits his way of turning over the seemingly inevitable palette of choices. Going beyond and turning the two sexes into something new, this could have been a welcome opportunity for Hegel, I could imagine, had it been on the agenda in the contemporary gender politics of his time.

Alison Stone:

I want to pick up on three things from the first round. First, Nancy's claim that most feminists tackle obvious gender inequities but are not "making serious attempts to shift the ways that people construe themselves as gendered beings. As a result, we've made ourselves irrelevant to actual women." I agree that many women, perhaps especially young women, don't find feminism relevant. This could indeed be because they are unaware that feminism raises questions about the gendered structure of our basic self-understandings and not merely about concrete socio-political issues. Perhaps, indeed, it's when one sees that feminism raises these deeper questions—that feminism has an existential and psychical as well as a socio-political side—that one can get really excited about feminist projects. But if women are unaware of this side of feminism, I think this, in the UK at least, is more the fault of the media than of feminists themselves. The British media very rarely portrays feminism as having any existential/psychical dimension but rather seems to oscillate between assuming that feminism is concerned solely with gender equality (especially at higher professional levels) and criticizing the feminism thus constructed for ignoring women's difference, the value of mothering, et cetera. I see how this narrow representation of feminism makes it seem irrelevant to most women, but I think the problem is with the public representation *of* feminism, not with what feminists themselves are doing.

Perhaps another reason why many younger women don't find feminism relevant is that gender inequities usually become sharper for women after they have children. As Kim says, perhaps Hegel can help us to think about how family structure oppresses women. Kim says "Hegel shows how the realm of productive labor, property and exchange depends on the realm of reproductive labor and care, and how the latter needs to be defined as a non-economic sphere in order for the whole thing to work. I take seriously Hegel's claim not to be arguing for this as what *ought* to be, but rather as extrapolating the logic of what *is*." I agree that Hegel gave a prescient account of the emerging division between productive/public and reproductive/private spheres. But I think he regards that division as rational and right: it is *and* it ought to be. Hegel colludes in the view that (what is largely) women's reproductive and emotional labor within families is not pro-ductive, not labor at all. Yet, he also provides a way to understand how that view has become entrenched. If, as he suggests, (male) chil-dren need to separate themselves from their families to enter civil society, then in order to define themselves *as* separate individuals and as productive workers these citizens presumably need to define the family in contrast as a non-productive, still quasi-"natural" sphere.

Finally, I only partly agree with Tuija that "profound thought [is] always the most effective and radical of politics"—which does seem a very Hegelian stance: that one must comprehend one's society before one can hope to change it, otherwise one's attempts to bring about change will be futile, misplaced, or mistimed. But I'd want to add that radical politics can also be the source of the profoundest thought (for example, the impact of Paris 1968 on recent French philosophy). I wonder if this is also a Hegelian view, thinking especially of the Hegel of the *Phenomenology*: if forms of social life are forms of spirit, of collective thought, then to change social life is necessarily to pro-duce upheavals in thought.

Nancy Bauer:

I agree with Alison that a vital part of Hegel's legacy to feminism is the idea that recognition is an absolutely fundamental part of being human. I really like the way that Alison, *pace* Nancy Fraser, appropri-ates the concept of recognition politically. In *The Phenomenology of Spirit*, and even, I think, in *The Second Sex*, recognition is something that individuals confer on other individuals. It occurs when two peo-ple mutually acknowledge that each is both a subject (for both Hegel and Beauvoir, this means a being who has desires that go beyond the animal given and the capacity to give shape and voice to these desires) and an object (a being who cannot control the inevitable judgments that other people inevitably bring to bear on him or her, which some-times manifest themselves menacingly, in both psychological and material ways). What Alison is suggesting—wonderfully, to my mind—is that we can transpose the notion of recognition to the political level and argue that a person's not being recognized consti-tutes a violation of his or her humanity. Given what I've claimed about how Hegel and Beauvoir construe recognition, this would mean that an individual's aspirations deserve prima facie political respect and that the risks that internally acknowledging and then publicly expressing these desires entail must be mitigated politically. Here we have an instance of the sort of thing I was getting at in my first-round comments: a new, rich way of understanding our current circumstances, one that has the potential both to change the way that real people think about their lives and the lives of others and, thereby, to work against sexism and other sorts of oppression.

I also agree with what Kim says about Hegel's unmasking the logic of "the specifically modern distinction between reproductive and productive labor," whereby reproductive labor, ignored economically and, therefore, ensuring a certain oppression of women, is a necessary condition for the success of capitalist forms of production. Of course, something like this insight was very much on the minds of feminists a generation ago and showed up in, most notably, the wages-for-housework movement. And yet, as it turned out, this way of appropriating the insight was, ultimately, quite alienating for many women. The idea that husbands should pay housewives a formal salary is in tension with various ideals that lead people to marry in the first place. And the idea that governments should tax workers to fund pay for housewives seemed both unworkable and unwarranted: too much of an invasion into the privacy of the home. If we are to revive Hegel's insight, then, we need to start by taking seriously people's investment in understanding, first, marriage as a relationship of friendship, companionship, and romance and, second, the home as a sphere of privacy. History shows that insisting that "the personal is the political," as we used to do, will not motivate real women to understand themselves as deserving of better than they have now. All this said, however, I think that it's of the highest importance for feminists to think seriously about the costs to women of uncompensated reproductive labor, since, if anything, those of us who work full-time and run households full-time are being run even more ragged than we were 30 years ago.

Tuija claims that a valuable aspect of Hegel's legacy for feminism is his "embracing of incessant, restless motion of thought," one that "does not know its endpoint in the future." For Tuija, if I understand her correctly, what this means is that a Hegelian feminist is obliged to keep struggling against injustice while at the same time remaining mindful that the struggle will always be ongoing and indeed that what we're struggling for—what counts as the feminist point of view at any given time—is bound to be unstable. Tuija cites transsexuality and Muslim women's wearing of the headscarf/veil as obviously feminist issues about which, nonetheless, there cannot be something called "the" feminist position. Theoretically, I'm in agreement with this claim. However, I do not want to lose sight of the fact that both old-fashioned feminist dogmatism (for example, the position that pornography is the root of all evil) *and* a certain wishy-washiness (for example, the idea that all generalizations about women are "second-wave" and, therefore, by definition hopelessly racist, ethno-centric, and class-insensitive) have hamstrung feminist theory for at least the last decade. The challenge here for feminists, I imagine, is to dare to make judgments about whether various women's desires for themselves and visions of the meanings of and possibilities for their lives are woefully attenuated or not. This will require, above all, taking seriously what actual women say about their lives. But it will then require—and, once again, Beauvoir is *the* model here—daring to search for the right words in which to speak for other people and then actually to do the speaking, which means risking being wrong, even perhaps disastrously so, about what other people want and need and deserve.

Kimberly Hutchings:

The first round of comments is interesting, both in terms of what it says about Hegel and for what it says about contemporary feminism. Both Nancy and Alison point to the significance of Beauvoir's adaptation of Hegel's master/slave dialectic for feminism but highlight different aspects of this significance. Nancy stresses the ways in which Beauvoir's treatment of this dialectic demonstrates the degree of investment that both men and women have made in the conditions of their own oppression. Alison makes the point that contemporary feminism is, to some extent, a politics of recognition, and that it was Hegel who first put recognition on the political agenda. In terms of the implications for feminist politics, Nancy's emphasis is on the *radical* nature of the change required by feminism and she points to the problems of contemporary feminist actions that address specific political issues of significance to women but don't make "serious attempts to shift the ways that people construe themselves as gendered beings." In Alison's case, however, it is suggested that the master/slave dialectic demonstrates how we rely on recognition to operate as subjects, and that insofar as we are deprived of recognition we are treated unjustly, suggesting, following Fraser, that feminism as a politics of recognition is one of the ways in which this injustice can be addressed. For me, this raises the question of what a politics of recognition means, and whether it can meet the requirement for *radical* change set out by Nancy. This question obviously takes us into familiar ground in debates between different forms of feminism, but it also takes us back to questions about the interpretation of the political implications of Hegel's writings, and whether the Hegel of the *Phenomenology* was a much more radical thinker than the Hegel of *Elements of the Philosophy of Right*. Are feminist goals compatible with liberal, market societies and states?

Although I see some difference in emphasis between Nancy and Alison, it seems to me that nevertheless both of them share the view that in the master/slave dialectic Hegel draws attention to the ways in which human being, living a human life, is warped and distorted in a world structured around hierarchical sex/gender difference. For both, I think, there is an aspiration to what it might mean to live an undistorted, fully human life. And in both cases this is about thinking/ defining human being in different kinds of ways, drawing on Hegelian/Beauvoirian insights to do so. Nancy refers to the idea of construing oneself as men and women differently, Alison refers to defining the subject, following Irigaray, "as being related-to but distinct-from one's maternal origin." This seems to me to be in contrast with Tuija's commitment to the sheer openness of both Hegelian philosophy and feminism as a political project. To what extent is the link Nancy and Alison make between feminist politics and the call to think the subject differently compatible with the link Tuija makes between feminism and a Derridean "gender to come"? I am somewhat uncomfortable with the quasi-religious language of "faith" and "hope" in relation to both Hegel and feminism, although I accept the point that history cannot end for either. I'd like to know more about how, if we construe both Hegel and feminism in Tuija's terms, we understand the continuity and identity of feminist politics as well as its discontinuity and difference. How do we know that feminist fights are worth fighting, or what counts as a feminist fight?

All of the comments in the first round, including my own, make a link between feminist politics and different ways of thinking— suggesting that radical political change for feminists is bound up with thinking dialectically about gender. Nancy makes an interesting point at the end of her comments in suggesting that feminists have made themselves irrelevant to actual women *precisely because* not enough attention has been paid to gendered self-understanding. In some ways this seems to run counter to the regular complaint made by feminist activists about academic feminism that the latter is all about *thinking* and not enough about *practice* and *materiality*. In Hegelian terms, actualizing a politics of rethinking cannot happen in abstraction from the realms of either spirit or nature. This means, I think, that Nancy is right, when she suggests that feminists need to pay much closer attention to the gender fault lines in contemporary ethical life, such as the lack of fit between a presumed achieved equality on the one hand, and the reproduction of hierarchically gendered sexual norms on the other. Of course, such fault lines will be different in different contexts, which would mean that feminist politics would have to be plural, diverse, and changing in the way that Tuija suggests. In a world in which "gender mainstreaming" is beginning to be enforced in international regimes, Hegelian feminists will always have reason to remember not only that gender is not equivalent to "women" but also that "women" are not straightforwardly equivalent to each other.

ROUND THREE

Alison Stone:

Kim asks whether the politics of recognition can ever be a politics of *radical* change. Presumably it isn't if what is to be recognized is pre-existing social identities, and/or if the state is to confer the recognition (for example, legal rights to protection for cultural identities), and/or given that in Hegel's *Philosophy of Right* mutual recognition means property-owners respecting one another within a market economy. I think, though, that ultimately the politics of recognition needs to be radical. We could fully recognize one another as subjects only by transforming our identities, especially our gendered identities, and thereby transforming the kinds of subject as which we are to recognize one another. This, I think, also requires radical change to the social and economic structures that are currently bound up with our gendered identities. Plausibly the market economy rests on instrumental rationality and on a model of the instrumentally rational economic actor, both gendered male. Thus I think a feminist politics of recognition has to be socialist feminist. But a problem for socialist feminism is that (without defending the former "communist" regimes) since 1989 it seems increasingly hard for people in most of the world to imagine alternative economic arrangements to capitalism. Perhaps, if feminism indeed has affinities with socialism, then this is another reason why many people now find feminism irrelevant. Has any of this got anything to do with Hegel? Hegel conceptualizes particular social and economic structures as connected to particular forms of recognition—that is, never as narrowly economic structures (as Marx sometimes seems to think) but always as having an ideational/psychical aspect as well. And we can pit the "young" Hegel against the "old"—even if the old Hegel thinks the definitively right set of arrangements is a market society, for the young Hegel of the *Phenomenology* there is no such end of history: to reach "absolute knowing" is just to recognize one's inescapable historicity, to "absolve" oneself of the burdensome illusion that one thinks as an ahistorical detached individual.

Maybe this stress that Hegel places on our historicity can shed light on feminine norms of appearance, which Tuija discusses. These norms are historically instituted, we as historical beings are caught up in them; we may criticize them but that doesn't take away their hold over us. And these norms hold us partly because they mediate our (distorted) ways of recognizing one another: by (trying to) conform to these norms we position ourselves in gender, class, and race terms— for example, as a more or less close approximation to the idealized rational-actor-in-control-of-her-own life.

We all seem to agree on what Nancy calls "the costs to women of uncompensated reproductive labor." I also agree with Nancy that this burden seems to have grown over the last 30 years or so, since (for financial reasons and because they are intrinsically committed to paid work) many more women now work while their children are young, despite still being presumed to have sole or main responsibility for childcare. There is a collective failure to conceive fathers as nurturers who could potentially bear the main or equal responsibility for looking after young children. I doubt Hegel has much to offer here. After all in the *Philosophy of Right* he sees the father's role as head-of-household who represents the family in the external, civil world—in effect, the breadwinner.

Nancy Bauer:

What unites the second-round contributions is an implicit question about what it is to do philosophy—a question that, of course, looms large in all of Hegel's writings, particularly in *The Phenomenology of Spirit*. In the first round I suggested that Hegel bequeaths to us the proposal that the role of the philosopher in the production of social change is to describe the *Zeitgeist* in terms that bring to light its internal contradictions and their intolerableness. I also suggested that we find a model of how to do feminist philosophy in this spirit in Simone de Beauvoir's *The Second Sex*.

In this final round, I want to press this suggestion again, which means that I must begin by taking issue with Tuija's suggestion that Beauvoir, as an "existentialist philosopher," was less revolutionary than I and others have taken her to be. Elsewhere, I've tried to show that it's at best very misleading to think of Beauvoir as existentialist, since, by the time she wrote *The Second Sex*, she had come to disagree starkly with some of Sartre's most deeply held positions—for example, his view that the idea of reciprocal recognition is metaphysically incoherent or his extreme voluntarism. Here, I will just ask the skeptic to reflect on the question of how *The Second Sex* became, hands-down, the most influential text ever written in the service of advancing feminist aims. The answer, it seems to me, has little to do with existentialist tenets and much to do with Beauvoir's rich and compelling description of women's everyday lives in terms that transform the reader's sense of how things are and how they ought to be.

This brings me to Alison's claim that feminism has gotten a bad rap from younger women not, or not primarily, because of a failure on the part of feminist philosophers to engage in a sort of Beauvoirian re-description but because of the distorted representation of feminism endlessly proffered by the media. There's no doubt that the mainstream media are not on our side. One reason, though, that feminist views are twisted in media representations is that we feminist academics rarely stop to think about what J. L. Austin urged philosophers to heed, namely, what *our* words are doing. Disdaining ordinary discourse—our common cultural currency—we close off the possibility of transforming it. Instead, we write almost exclusively to and for each other, restricting our mode of discourse, at least *as philosophers*, to what befits a journal article or scholarly monograph. One reason I admire Beauvoir so much is that she aspired in her writing to speak with full philosophical depth and rigor to ordinary women—a concept that makes Tuija uneasy but that, for me at least, doesn't so much imply that there are two distinct groups of people, one plain and one fancy, as it upbraids feminist academics for failing to keep their own ordinariness in view as they write. (Here, it goes without saying, Beauvoir did *not* take Hegel as a model.)

In her later years, Beauvoir also grasped a closely related truth, one that Alison presses on us, which is that taking action when you find that you must—going out in the streets, or onto the magazine page, and doing what you have to do because you cannot do otherwise, even when you cannot produce a story about what justifies your action—is sometimes, perhaps paradoxically, the best way to put yourself in a position to tell just such a story. In acting, and sometimes only in acting, you may figure out why what you're doing makes sense; the action itself may speak transformative volumes to others. (This can be true in love as well as politics.) Kim raises the thorny epistemological question of how we can know which feminist fights are worth fighting. The answer, it seems to me, is that we often won't be able to know in advance of the fight, especially if it's a fight for recognition. It's a mark of Hegel's brilliance that his slave can't explain, even to himself, why he waves the white flag until well after his particular fight is over. And it's a mark of Beauvoir's brilliance that she does not compromise with respect to the liberatory vision she lays out in *The Second Sex*, despite being sure that she was inviting trouble and despite not knowing whether she was prepared to bear up under it or to take responsibility for her own words without regret.

Tuija Pulkkinen:

Commenting on some of the issues taken up in the second round, I think Kim is right in detecting my deep suspicion toward claims of knowledge about the goal of the future perfection, whether in the name of a good life, human perfection, or full recognition. My commitment is, rather, to complete openness of the future. In this respect, I think Kim rightly analyzes in the first round discussion a difference of orientation in the background of some of the disagreement between Alison and Nancy on the one side, and me on the other.

In the second round Alison raised some doubts about the effective "profound thought" that I had mentioned and wondered whether it is a Hegelian stance that one must comprehend one's society before one can change it. I would find this more of a Marxian or Engelsian stance than a Hegelian one: Hegel does not pose such a dualism of thought and action. My proposal of profound thought as radical action and vice versa rests exactly on the refusal to accept the juxtaposition of the two, which I think is more of a Hegelian stance.

Nancy's worry in the second round is about feminists today not taking the risk of speaking for others. There is a rich history of speaking for others and of teaching others in feminism, and my additional worry would be whether there is actually any risk at all involved in teaching other people. My heroes are those 1970s radical feminists who changed, more than anything else, their own lives and took enormous risks in social terms in doing it. People such as Kate Millett and others were not nice girls, they were not publicly liked. Feminism always had to do with one's personal life.

Personally, I could not take de Beauvoir as a primary model here. In my adolescent memories she was the publicly celebrated female part of a heterosexual couple. For me this also has a connection to her philosophy. I believe there is a deep heterosexuality embedded in her existential project, which builds on the human as a couple—as does

Luce Irigaray's thought. This is not a direction that is necessarily taken starting from Hegelian premises. I think it derives, for both, much more from the phenomenological tradition. Hegel could inspire feminist thought more toward change and an open future, instead of maintaining the aspiration of revealing the human condition.

This is related to the opposition that Kim mentioned between Alison's idea of feminism looking for recognition and Nancy's idea of feminism connected with the radical change. On this issue I strongly take Nancy's side: I think a valuable tradition of feminist politics has been continuously confronting the existing gender norms, and in this sense it has been for radical change rather than for recognition. Hegel's is a tricky heritage in this respect: on the one hand he claims only to mirror, and he has a serious investment with the prevailing norms of a culture; on the other hand the dynamic of *Sittlichkeit* calls for an image of permanent change, triggered by constant individual confrontation of those norms.

Kim poses the problem of continuity and identity of feminism. But, do we really need to worry about conserving an identity? There is something disconcerting about putting the question in the form of "how do we know what counts as feminist." Who are "we"? Is it really possible to posit such a point of view of a general "knowing," and is it desirable? Instead of worrying whether the name feminism continues to act as a name for good politics in the unforeseeable future, I would recognize that it obviously does at the moment. This could be a kind of quasi-Hegelian analysis of the present, digging out what is important and future oriented in the present, for the future that nevertheless remains open. There is a lot of space for imagination in politics of gender, and yet any politics of change cannot be radically effective without an acknowledgment of both gendered norms and of feminisms that have challenged them. I agree with Kim that Hegelian thought also encourages the insight that politics of rethinking cannot happen in the abstract.

I think that there is, in feminist inheritance, something more than the recipe for implementing gender mainstreaming, of completing the project once set. There is a spirit of continuous change, a spirit that seems to renew itself and always challenge the gendered norms radically and in unexpected ways.

Kimberly Hutchings:

I'm intrigued by several points in the last round of comments. I'd like to start with the "politics of recognition" argument that both Alison and Nancy have put forward. Nancy, in her latest response, endorses Alison's argument that denial of recognition constitutes a violation of humanity, and that this means that all individuals' aspirations should be accorded prima facie respect. Yet this seems somewhat at odds with Nancy's points in the last round about the ways in which women experience their sexuality in relation to men. I think this points again to the difficulty of working out quite what a politics of recognition means. Does it depend on an ideal of what it means to be a flourishing human being, or is it about a *process* of interaction in which the outcomes are unspecified and unspecifiable? I think I would lean to the latter understanding and would see this as very much the message of Hegel's own account of the struggle for recognition in the *Phenomenology.* The trouble is that it's not clear what the implications of this would be for actual politics. How does one address politically the consciousness of young women who perceive themselves to be free agents if one doesn't have an ideal of what it means to be truly human that can act as the ground for critique? I also thought that Nancy was quite right to point to the problems of previous feminist attempts to address the issue of reproductive and caring labor. The commodification of such labor doesn't seem like a helpful route to go down to improve women's position, in particular given the degree of affective investment in the loving relationships that are so often bound up with it. At the same time, however, I think we have to be careful not to assume that we can address the issue solely at the level of self-understandings about the private sphere. We have to remember the cleaners, nurses, nannies that so often enable the companionate marriages of middle class people in Western societies. This is a socioeconomic issue as well and needs to be addressed as such.

I take Alison's point about Hegel being perfectly happy with the gendered division of labor explicated in *Elements of the Philosophy of Right.* But I think we have a philosophical difference in interpretation here, in that, in the context of that text, I read Hegel as claiming to extrapolate the logic of what "is" rather than what "ought to be." But this is less important, I think, than our agreement that his analysis remains useful and insightful. I'd also like to echo Alison's point in her concluding paragraph, about the interrelation of thought and spirit in Hegel's argument. I think this is quite right and I think it is the clue to how we may put Hegel fruitfully to work for feminism, in a way that is pragmatic and contextual. In this respect, I think Tuija's point about feminism's "contemporary" nature is right. Because of this, I am concerned that we are all tending to read feminism in terms of the issues that have dominated feminist theory and practice in

Western societies over the past few decades. Feminism has always been a transnational movement, and we currently inhabit a complex situation in which there are indigenous feminisms and international feminisms that are differently institutionalized in domestic and international law, movements, and organizations. I referred to "gender mainstreaming" in my previous comments. UN Resolution 1325, which requires gender mainstreaming in conflict resolution, peacemaking, and peace-building processes, was a massive victory for feminist lobby groups, but it also represents a major challenge for feminism as clashes between "top down" and "bottom up" understandings of what it means to address gendered relations of power are fought out on the ground in situations of profound political contestation. A Hegelian approach, it seems to me, is one that is committed to two things: first, what Nancy refers to as "risking being wrong," that is, being willing to speak and act on the basis of one's judgment and experience; second, however, and perhaps more importantly, it seems to me that a Hegelian feminism obliges one to work on one's listening skills. Because we know that our being is fundamentally intersubjective, and tied to not only our relations with others but also to a complex of social, historical, and institutional conditions, we know that we have to work at understanding the mainsprings of feminist politics in specific situations. Here, though, we hit a major problem for feminists who want to also be Hegelian in their understandings—what do we do about his philosophy of history?

BIBLIOGRAPHY

Abrams, Lynn. *The Making of Modern Woman: Europe 1789–1918*. London: Longman/Pearson, 2002.

Anidjar, Gil. *Acts of Religion*. London and New York: Routledge, 2002.

Arendt, Hannah. *The Human Condition*. Chicago: Chicago University Press, 1998.

Aristophanes. "Assemblywomen." In *The Frogs and Other Plays*, translated by David Barrett. London: Penguin Books, 1964.

———. "The Poet and the Women." In *The Birds and Other Plays*, translated by David Barrett and Allan H. Sommerstein. London: Penguin Books, 1978.

———. "Lysistrata." In *Lysistrata and Other Plays*, translated by Allan H. Sommerstein. London: Penguin Books, 2002.

Aristotle. "De Anima." In *The Works of Aristotle*. Vol. 3. Oxford: Clarendon Press, 1931.

———. *Politics*. Translated by H. Rackham. Loeb Classical Library, Aristotle. Vol. 21. Cambridge: Harvard University Press, 2005.

Arthur, Chris. "Hegel's Master-Slave Dialectic and a Myth of Marxology." *New Left Review* No. 143, 1983: 67–75.

Barnett, Stuart. *Hegel after Derrida*. London and New York: Routledge, 1998.

Beardsworth, Richard. *Derrida and the Political*. London: Routledge, 1996.

Beauvoir, Simone de. *Ethics of Ambiguity*. Translated by B. Frechtman. New York: Citadel Press, 1976.

———. *The Second Sex*. Translated by H. M. Parshley. Harmondsworth: Penguin, 1988.

Beiser, Frederick C. "Introduction: Hegel and the Problem of Metaphysics." In *The Cambridge Companion to Hegel*, edited by Frederick C. Beiser. Cambridge: Cambridge University Press, 1993.

———. *The Cambridge Companion to Hegel*. Cambridge: Cambridge University Press, 1993.

———. "Introduction: The Puzzling Hegel Renaissance." In *The Cambridge Companion to Hegel and Nineteenth Century Philosophy*, edited by Frederick C. Beiser. Cambridge: Cambridge University Press, 2008.

———. *The Cambridge Companion to Hegel and Nineteenth Century Philosophy*. Cambridge: Cambridge University Press, 2008.

Benhabib, Seyla. *Situating the Self: Gender, Community and Postmodernism in Contemporary Ethics.* Cambridge: Polity Press, 1992.

———. "On Hegel, Women, and Irony." In *Feminist Interpretations of G. W. F. Hegel,* edited by Patricia Jagentowicz Mills. University Park, PA: Pennsylvania State University Press, 1996.

Benjamin, Jessica. *The Bonds of Love: Psychoanalysis, Feminism and the Problem of Domination.* New York: Pantheon Books, 1988.

———. *Like Subjects, Love Objects: Essays on Recognition and Sexual Difference.* New Haven, CT: Yale University Press, 1995.

———. *The Shadow of the Other: Intersubjectivity and Gender in Psychoanalysis.* New York: Routledge, 1998

———. "'How Was It for You?' How Intersubjective Is Sex?" Division 39 Keynote Address, *American Psychological Association,* Boston, April 1998. On file with author.

———. "Recognition and Destruction." In *Relational Psychoanalysis: The Emergence of a Tradition,* edited by S. A. Mitchell and L. Aron. Hillsdale, NJ: Analytic Press, 1999.

Berghoffen, Debra B. "Irigaray's Couples." In *Returning to Irigaray: Feminist Philosophy, Politics and the Questions of Unity,* edited by Maria C. Cimitile and Elaine P. Miller. Albany: SUNY Press, 2007.

Bernasconi, Robert. "Hegel at the Court of the Ashanti." In *Hegel after Derrida,* edited by Stuart Barnett. London and New York: Routledge, 1998.

———. "With What Must the Philosophy of History Begin? On the Racial Bases of Hegel's Eurocentrism." *Nineteenth Century Contexts* 22 (2000): 171–201.

Bordo, Susan. *The Flight to Objectivity: Essays on Cartesianism and Culture.* Albany: SUNY Press, 1987.

Borsch-Jacobsen, Mikkel. *The Freudian Subject.* Stanford: Stanford University Press, 1988.

Bouton, Christophe. "L'épitaphe et le tombeau." *Philosophie* 52 (1996): 54–76.

Boys Don't Cry. Twentieth Century Fox, Director, Kimberly Peirce, 1999.

Brandom, Robert. *Tales of the Mighty Dead.* Cambridge, MA: Harvard University Press, 2002.

Brod, Harry. *Hegel's Philosophy and Politics: Idealism, Identity and Modernity.* Boulder, CO: Westview Press, 1992.

Buck-Morss, Susan. "Hegel and Haiti." *Critical Inquiry* 26, no. 4 (Summer, 2000): 821–865.

Bull, Malcolm. "Slavery and the Multiple Self," *New Left Review* 231, no.1 (1998): 95–131.

Butler, Judith. *Subjects of Desire: Hegelian Reflections in Twentieth-Century France.* New York: Columbia University Press, 1987, 2nd Edition, 1999.

———. *Bodies that Matter: On the Discursive Limits of "Sex."* New York: Routledge, 1998.

————. *Gender Trouble*, 10th Anniversary Edition. New York and London: Routledge, 1999.

————. *Antigone's Claim. Kinship between Life and Death.* New York: Columbia University Press, 2000.

————. "Restaging the Universal: Hegemony and the Limits of Formalism" and "Competing Universalities." In *Contingency, Hegemony, Universality: Contemporary Dialogues of the Left*, edited by J. Butler, E. Laclau and S. Žižek. London: Verso, 2000.

————. *Undoing Gender.* New York and London: Routledge, 2004.

————. *Precarious Life: The Powers of Mourning and Violence.* London: Verso, 2004

————. *Giving an Account of Oneself.* New York: Fordham University Press, 2005.

————. *Frames of War: When Is Life Grievable?.* London: Verso, 2009.

Caine, Barbara and Sluga, Glenda. *Gendering European History, 1780–1920.* London and New York: Continuum, 2000.

Chanter, Tina. *Ethics of Eros: Irigaray's Rewriting of the Philosophers.* London: Routledge, 1995.

Chodorow, Nancy. "Family Structure and Feminine Personality." In *Women, Culture and Society*, edited by M. R. Zimbalist and L. Lampert. Stanford: Stanford University Press, 1974.

Cimitilie, Maria. C. and Miller, Elaine. P. *Returning to Irigaray: Feminist Philosophy, Politics and the Question of Unity.* Albany: SUNY Press, 2007.

Clarke, Eric O. "Fetal Attraction: Hegel's An-aesthetics of Gender." In *Feminist Interpretations of G. W. F. Hegel*, edited by Patricia J. Mills. University Park, PA: Pennsylvania State University Press, 1996.

Clement, Grace. *Care, Autonomy and Justice: Feminism and the Ethic of Care.* Boulder, CO: Westview Press, 1996.

Coonzt, Stephanie. *Marriage, a History: How Love Conquered Marriage.* London: Penguin, 2005.

Cornell, Drucilla. *The Philosophy of the Limit.* New York: Routledge, 1992.

Cornell, Drucilla, Rosenfeld, Michael and Carlson, David Gray. "Introduction." In *Hegel and Legal Theory*, edited by Cornell, Rosenfeld, and Carlson. London: Routledge, 1991.

De Boer, Karin. "Hegel's Antigone and the Dialectics of Sexual Difference." *Philosophy Today, SPEP Supplement* 47, no. 5 (2003): 140–146.

De Laurentiis, Allegra. *Subjects in the Ancient and Modern World: On Hegel's Theory of Subjectivity.* Basingstoke, UK: Palgrave Macmillan, 2005.

Deligiorgi, Katerina. "Introduction: On Reading Hegel Today." In *Hegel: New Directions*, edited by Katerina Deligiorgi. Chesham: Acumen, 2006.

————. *Hegel: New Directions.* Chesham: Acumen, 2006.

Derrida, Jacques. *Writing and Difference.* Translated by Alan Bass. London: Routledge, 1978.

————. *Marges de la Philosophie.* Paris: Minuit, 1972. Translated by Alan Bass, *Margins of Philosophy.* Chicago: University of Chicago Press, 1985.

Derrida, Jacques. *The Post Card from Socrates to Freud and Beyond.* Translated by Alan Bass. Chicago: University of Chicago Press, 1987.

———. *The Truth in Painting.* Translated by Geoffrey Bennington and Ian McLeod. Chicago: Chicago University Press, 1987.

———. *Glas.* Paris: Galilée, 1974. Translated by John P. Leavey Jr. and Richard Rand under the title *Glas.* Lincoln: University of Nebraska Press, 1990.

———. *Aporias: Dying-Awaiting (One another at) the "Limits of Truth."* Translated by Thomas Dutoit. Stanford: Stanford University Press, 1994.

———. *Specters of Marx: The State of Debt, the Work of Mourning and the New International.* Translated by Peggy Kamuf. New York: Routledge, 1994.

———. *Khôra.* Paris: Galilée, 1993. Translated by David Wood as "Khora" in *On the Name,* edited by Thomas Dutoit. Stanford: Stanford University Press, 1995.

———. *The Politics of Friendship.* Translated by George Collins. London: Verso, 1997.

———. *Le Toucher, Jean Luc Nancy.* Paris: Galilée, 2000.

———. *Rogues: Two Essays on Reason.* Translated by Michael Naas and Pascale Anne Brault. Stanford: Stanford University Press, 2003.

———. *L'Animal Que Donc Je Suis.* Paris: Galilée, 2006.

———. "Geschlecht I: Sexual Difference, Ontological Difference." In *Psyche. Inventions of the Other,* edited by Peggy Kamuf and Elizabeth Rottenberg. Stanford: Stanford University Press, 2008.

Deutscher, Penelope. *A Politics of Impossible Difference: The Later Work of Luce Irigaray.* Ithaca: Cornell University Press, 2002.

———. "Between East and West and the Politics of 'Cultural *Ingénuité*': Irigaray on Cultural Difference." In *Returning to Irigaray: Feminist Philosophy, Politics and the Questions of Unity,* edited by Maria C. Cimitile and Elaine P. Miller. Albany: SUNY Press, 2007.

Diprose, Rosalyn. *The Bodies of Women.* London: Routledge, 1994.

Euripides. *The Bacchae.* Translated by Geoffrey S. Kirk. Englewood Cliffs, NJ: Prentice-Hall, 1970.

Feuerbach, Ludwig. *Principles of the Philosophy of the Future.* Translated by Manfred Vogel. Indianapolis, IN: Hackett Publishing Company, 1986.

Foley, Helene P. "The Conception of Women in Athenian Drama." In *Reflections of Women in Antiquity,* edited by Helene P. Foley. New York: Gordon and Breach, 1981.

———. "The 'Female Intruder' Reconsidered: Women in Aristophanes' Lysistrata and Ecclesiazusae." *Classical Philology* 77, no. 1 (1982): 1–21.

Foucault, Michel and Barbin, Herculine. *I, Herculine Barbin, Being the Recently Discovered Memoires of a Nineteenth Century French Hermaphrodite.* New York: Random House Knopf, 1980.

Franco, Paul. *Hegel's Philosophy of Freedom.* New Haven, CT: Yale University Press, 1999.

Freud, Sigmund "Certain Neurotic Mechanisms in Jealousy, Paranoia and Homosexuality." In *The Standard Edition of the Complete Works of Sigmund Freud*. Vol.18, edited by James Strachey in collaboration with Anna Freud, assisted by Alix Strachey and Alan Tyson. London: Hogarth Press and the Institute of Psychoanalysis, 1953–1974.

Gatens, Moira. *Imaginary Bodies. Ethics, Power and Corporeality*. London and New York: Routledge, 1996.

Gauthier, Jeffrey A. *Hegel and Feminist Social Criticism: Justice, Recognition and the Feminine*. Albany: SUNY Press, 1997.

George, Theodore D. *Tragedies of Spirit. Tracing Finitude in Hegel's Phenomenology*. New York: State University of New York Press, 2006.

Gibbons, Reginald and Segal, Charles. "Antigone." In *The Greek Tragedy in New Translations*, edited by Peter Burian and Alan Shapiro. Oxford: Oxford University Press, 2003.

Gilligan, Carol. *A Different Voice: Psychological Theory and Women's Moral Development*. Cambridge, MA: Harvard University Press, 1982.

Habermas, Jürgen. *The Theory of Communicative Action*. 2 vols. Translated by Thomas McCarthy. Boston: Beacon Press, 1982.

Hadot, Pierre. *The Veil of Isis: An Essay on the History of the Idea of Nature*. Translated by Michael Chase. Cambridge, MA: Harvard University Press, 2006.

Hall, Edith. "Is There a Polis in Aristotle's Poetics?" In *Tragedy and the Tragic: Greek Theatre and Beyond*, edited by M. S. Silk. Oxford: Clarendon Press, 1996.

Hamacher, Werner. *Pleroma: Reading in Hegel*. Translated by Nicholas Walker and Simon Jarvis. 1978. Reprint, London: Athlone Press, 1998.

Hardimon, Michael. *Hegel's Social Philosophy: The Project of Reconciliation*. Cambridge: Cambridge University Press, 1994.

Harris, H. S. *Hegel's Ladder*. Vol. 2, *The Odyssey of Spirit*. Indianapolis, IN: Hackett Publishing Company, 1997.

Hartmann, Klaus. "Hegel: A Non-Metaphysical View." In *Hegel*, edited by Alasdair MacIntyre. New York: Doubleday, 1972.

Hegel. G. W. F. "The Spirit of Christianity and Its Fate." In *Early Theological Writings*. Translated by T. M. Knox, fragments translated by R. Kroner. Chicago: Chicago University Press, 1948.

———. *The Phenomenology of Mind*. Translated by J. B. Baillie. London: George Allen and Unwin Ltd., 1966.

———. *Enzyklopädie der philosophischen Wissenschaften 2, Werke 9*. Frankfurt am Main: Suhrkamp, 1970. Translated by Michael John Petry under the title *Hegel's Philosophy of Nature 3*. London and New York: George Allen and Unwin Ltd. and Humanities Press, 1970.

———. *Vorlesungen über die Ästhetik 3 [1820–1829]*. Suhrkamp Taschenbuch Wissenschaft, b. 13–15. Surhkamp: Frankfurt am Main, 1970. Translated by T. M. Knox under the title *Aesthetics: Lectures on Fine Art*. Vol. 2. 2 vols. Oxford: Oxford University Press, 1975/1988.

Hegel. G. W. F. *Wissenschaft der Logik II, Werke 6.* Frankfurt am Main: Suhrkamp, 1970. Translated by. A. V. Miller under the title *Hegel's Science of Logic.* London and New York: George Allen and Unwin Ltd. and Humanities Press, 1969.

―――. *Phänomenologie des Geistes, Werke 3.* Frankfurt am Main: Suhrkamp, 1970. Translated by. A. V. Miller under the title *Phenomenology of Spirit.* Oxford: Oxford University Press, 1977.

―――. *Enzyklopädie der philosophischen Wissenschaften 3, Werke 10.* Frankfurt am Main: Suhrkamp, 1970. Translated by Michael John Petry under the title *Hegel's Philosophy of Subjective Spirit 1–3.* Dordrecht and Boston: D. Reidel Publishing Company, 1979.

―――. *Hegel's Logic.* Being Part One of the *Encyclopaedia of the Philosophical Sciences* (1830). Translated by William Wallace. Oxford: Oxford University Press, 1975.

―――. "Über die Wissenschaftlichen Behandlungsarten des Naturrechts, seine Stelle in der praktischen Philosophie und sein Verhältnis zu den positiven Rechtswissenschaften." In *Jenaer Schriften 1801–1807, Werke 2.* Frankfurt am Main: Suhrkamp, 1986.

―――. *Vorlesungen über die Geschichte der Philosophie. Einleitung, Orientalische Philosophie. Werke 18.* Frankfurt am Main: Suhrkamp, 1986.

―――. *Vorlesungen über die Ästhetik 2, Werke 14.* Frankfurt am Main: Suhrkamp, 1986. Translated by T. M. Knox under the title *Aesthetics. Lectures on Fine Art 2.* Oxford: Clarendon Press, 1998.

―――. *Vorlesungen über die Philosophie der Geschichte. Werke 12.* Frankfurt am Main: Suhrkamp, 1986. Translated by J. Sibree under the title *The Philosophy of History.* New York: Cosimo Classics, 2007.

―――. Jenaer Systementwürfe 3: Naturphilosophie und Philosophie des Geistes. Edited by Rolf-Peter Horstmann. Hamburg: Felix Meiner, 1987.

―――. *Elements of the Philosophy of Right.* Translated by H. B. Nisbet. Edited by Allen Wood. Cambridge: Cambridge University Press, 1991.

―――. *The Philosophy of History.* Translated by J. Sibree. Buffalo: Prometheus Books, 1991.

―――. *Lectures on the History of Philosophy,* Vol. 2. Translated by E. S. Haldane and Frances H. Simson. Lincoln/London: University of Nebraska Press, 1995.

―――. *Lectures on Natural Right and Political Science: The First Philosophy of Right, Heidelberg 1817–1819, with Additions from the Lectures of 1818–1819.* Translated by J. Michael Stewart and P. C. Hodgson. Berkeley, CA: University of California Press, 1996.

―――. *Vorlesung über Naturphilosophie* Berlin 1823/24, *Nachschrift von K. G. J. v. Griesheim.* Edited by Gilles Marmasse. Frankfurt: Peter Lang, 2000.

―――. *Miscellaneous Writings of G. W. F. Hegel.* Edited by Jon Stewart. Evanston, IL: Northwestern University Press, 2002.

Heinämaa, Sara. *Ele, tyyli ja sukupuoli. Merleau-Pontyn ja Beauvoirin ruumiinfenomenologia ja sen merkitys sukupuolikysymykselle* (Gesture, Style, Sex. Merleau-Ponty's Beauvoir's phenomenology of the body and its meaning for the question of sexual difference). Helsinki: Gaudeamus, 1996.

Held, Virginia. *Feminist Morality: Transforming Culture, Society and Politics.* Chicago: Chicago University Press, 1993.

Heyes, Cressida. *Line Drawings: Defining Women through Feminist Practice.* Ithaca: Cornell University Press, 2000.

Hodge, Joanna. "Why Aesthetics Might Be Multiple; On Jean Luc Nancy." *Angelaki: A Journal for the Theoretical Humanities.* Vol. 7, no. 1 (Spring 2002).

———. "Kant *Par Excellence.*" In *Kant after Derrida.* Edited by Philip Rothfield. Manchester: Clinamen, 2003.

———. *Derrida on Time.* London and New York: Routledge, 2007.

Honneth, Axel. *The Struggle for Recognition: The Moral Grammar of Social Conflicts.* Translated by Joel Anderson. Cambridge, MA: Polity Press, 1995.

Hutchings, Kimberly. *Hegel and Feminist Philosophy.* Cambridge: Polity Press, 2003.

Hyppolite, Jean. *Genesis and Structure of Hegel's "Phenomenology of Spirit."* Translated by Samuel Cherniak and John Heckman. Evanston, IL: Northwestern University Press, 1974.

Inwood, Michael. "Identity, Difference and Otherness." In *A Hegel Dictionary.* Oxford: Blackwell, 1992.

Irigaray, Luce. *Speculum de l'autre femme.* Paris: Minuit, 1974. Translated by Gillian C. Gill under the title *Speculum of the Other Woman.* New York: Cornell University Press, 1985.

———. *This Sex Which Is Not One.* Translated by Catherine Porter. Ithaca: Cornell University Press, 1985.

———. "Sexual Difference." In *The Irigaray Reader: Luce Irigaray,* edited and translated by Margaret Whitford. London: Wiley-Blackwell, 1992.

———. *An Ethics of Sexual Difference.* Translated by C. Burke and G. C. Gill. London: Athlone Press, 1993.

———. *Je, Tu, Nous: Toward a Culture of Sexual Difference.* Translated by A. Martin. New York: Routledge, 1993.

———. *Thinking the Difference: For a Peaceful Revolution.* Translated by K. Montin. London: Athlone Press, 1994.

———. *I Love to You. Sketch for a Felicity within History.* Translated by Alison Martin. New York and London: Routledge, 1996.

———. *The Way of Love.* Translated by H. Bostic and S. Pluhàčhek. London: Continuum, 2000.

———. *Between East and West: From Singularity to Community.* Translated by S. Pluhàčhek. New York: Columbia University Press, 2000.

Just, Roger. *Women in Athenian Law and Life.* New York: Routledge, 1991.

Kant, Immanuel. *Kritik der reinen Vernunft.* Frankfurt am Main: Suhrkamp, 1974. Translated by N. K. Smith under the title *The Critique of Pure Reason.* London: Macmillan, 1952.

———. *Kritik der Urteilskraft.* Frankfurt am Main: Suhrkamp 1974. Translated by J. C. Meredith under the title *The Critique of Judgment.* Oxford: Oxford University Press, 1982.

Knowles, Dudley. *Hegel and the Philosophy of Right.* London: Routledge, 2002.

Kofman, Sarah. "*Ca Cloche.*" In *Derrida and Deconstruction: Continental Philosophy II,* edited by Hugh Silverman. London and New York: Routledge, 1989.

———. *Selected Writings.* Stanford: Stanford University Press, 2005.

Kristeva, Julia. "Women's Time." Translated by Alice Jardine and Harry Blake. *Signs: Journal of Women in Culture and Society* 7, no. 1 (1981): 13–35.

———. "Stabat Mater." In *Feminist Social Thought: A Reader,* edited by Diana T. Meyers. New York and London: Routledge, 1997.

Lacan, Jacques. *Écrits : A Selection.* Translated by Alan Sheridan. New York: Norton and Company, 1977.

Lacoue-Labarthe, Philippe. "Typographie." In *Mimesis des Articulations,* edited by Sylviane Agaçinski, Jacques Derrida, Sarah Kofman, Philippe Lacoue-Labarthe, Jean-Luc Nancy, and Bernard Pautrat. Paris: Flammarion, 1975. Translated by Christopher Fynsk under the title "Typography." In *Typography, Mimesis, Philosophy, Politics.* Cambridge: Harvard University Press, 1989.

———. *Heidegger—la politique du poème.* Paris: Galilée, 2002.

Lane, Warren J. and Lane, Ann M. "The Politics of Antigone." In *Greek Tragedy and Political Theory,* edited by J. Peter Euben. Berkeley and London: University of California Press, 1986.

Laplanche, Jean. *Essays on Otherness,* Translated by John Fletcher. London: Routledge, 1999.

Laqueur, Thomas. *Making Sex. Body and Gender from the Greeks to Freud.* Cambridge, MA and London: Harvard University Press, 1990.

Lebrun, Gérard. *Hegel et la Patience du Concept.* Paris. Gallimard, 1962.

———. *Kant et la fin de la métaphysique. Essai sur la "Critique de la faculté de juger."* Paris: Livre de poche / Armand Colin, 1970.

Levinas, Emmanuel. *Otherwise than Being.* Translated by Alphonso Lingis. Boston: M. Nijhoff, 1981.

———. *Totalité et infini. Essai sur l'extériorité.* La Haye: M. Nijhoff, 1961. Translated by Alphonso Lingis under the title *Totality and Infinity: An Essay on Exteriority.* Pittsburgh, PA: Duquesne University Press, 1998.

Lindberg, Susanna. "Vivant à la limite." *Les Études philosophiques* 76, no. 1 (2006): 107–120.

———. "L'inquiétant Hegel de Nancy." *Europe,* no. 960 (April 2009): 262–268.

————. "Ontorythmie." In Déconstruction Mimétique, edited by M. Guiet, L. Kharlamov, J. Rousseau. Forthcoming.

Lloyd, Genevieve. *The Man of Reason: "Male" and "Female" in Western Philosophy*. London: Routledge, 1984.

Lonzi, Carla. "Let's Spit on Hegel." In *Feminist Interpretations of G. W. F. Hegel*, edited by Patricia Jagentowicz Mills. University Park, PA: Pennsylvania State University Press, 1996.

Loraux, Nicole. *Les mères en deuil*. Paris: Seuil, 1990. Translated by Corinne Pache under the title *Mothers in Mourning*. Ithaca: Cornell University Press, 1998.

Lorenz, Kuno. Identität. In: Historisches Wörterbuch der Philosophie Band 4. Basel: Schwabe and Co., 1976: 144–8.

Malabou, Catherine, "The Future of Hegel: Plasticity, Temporality, Dialectic." *Hypatia*, 15 (4) Fall 2000.

Malabou, Catherine. *L'avenir de Hegel. Plasticité, Temporalité, Dialectique*. Paris: J. Vrin, 1996. Translated by Lisabeth During. *The future of Hegel. Plasticity, Temporality and Dialectic*. New York: Routledge, 2005.

McClure, Laura. *Spoken Like a Woman: Speech and Gender in Athenian Drama*. Princeton: Princeton University Press, 1999.

Mills, Patricia Jagentowicz. "Hegel's Antigone." In *Feminist Interpretations of G. W. F. Hegel*, edited by Patricia J. Mills. University Park, PA: Pennsylvania State University Press, 1996.

————. *Feminist Interpretations of G. W. F. Hegel*. University Park, PA: Pennsylvania State University Press, 1996.

Mitscherlich, Alexander and Mitscherlich, Margaret. *The Inability to Mourn: Principles of Collective Behaviour*. Translated by B. Placzek. New York: Grove Press, 1975.

Murphy, A. V. "Beyond Performativity and against Identification: Gender and Technology in Irigaray." In *Returning to Irigaray: Feminist Philosophy, Politics and the Questions of Unity*, edited by Maria C. Cimitile and Elaine P. Miller. Albany: SUNY Press, 2007.

Myers, Diana T. *Feminist Social Thought*. New York and London: Routledge, 1997.

Nancy, Jean-Luc. *The Experience of Freedom*. Translated by Bridget McDonald. 1988. Reprint, Stanford: Stanford University Press, 1993.

————. "Identité et tremblement." In *Hypnoses*, edited by Mikkel Borch-Jakobsen, Eric Michaud and Jean-Luc Nancy, 13–47. Paris: Galilée, 1994.

————.*La remarque spéculative. Un bon mot de Hegel*. Paris: Galilée, 1973. Translated by Céline Surprenant under the title *The Speculative Remark: One of Hegel's Bons Mots*. Stanford: Stanford University Press, 2001.

————. *Hegel: The Restlessness of the Negative*. Translated by Jason Smith and Steven Miller. Minneapolis and London: University of Minnesota Press, 2002.

Neuhouser, Frederick. *Foundations of Hegel's Social Theory: Actualizing Freedom.* Cambridge, MA: Harvard University Press, 2000.

Noddings, Nel. *Caring: A Feminine Approach to Ethics and Moral Education.* Berkeley, CA: University of California Press, 1984.

Noelle Vahanian. "A Conversation with Catherine Malabou." *Journal for Cultural and Religious Theory,* 9 (1) Winter 2008: 1–13.

Nussbaum, Martha. *Women and Human Development: The Capabilities Approach.* Cambridge: Cambridge University Press, 2000.

Osborne, Peter. *The Politics of Time.* London: Verso, 1995.

Owl of Minerva. Vol. 24 No. 1 (1992).

Pateman, Carole. *The Sexual Contract.* Cambridge, UK: Polity Press, 1988.

Patten, Alan. *Hegel's Idea of Freedom.* Oxford: Oxford University Press, 1999.

Pelczynski, Z. A. "The Hegelian Conception of the State." In *Hegel's Political Philosophy: Problems and Perspectives,* edited by Z. A. Pelczynski. Cambridge: Cambridge University Press, 1971.

Pinkard, Terry. *Hegel Reconsidered.* Dordrecht: Kluwer, 1994.

———. *Hegel's Phenomenology: The Sociality of Reason.* Cambridge: Cambridge University Press, 1996.

Pippin, Robert. *Hegel's Idealism: The Satisfactions of Self-consciousness.* Cambridge: Cambridge University Press, 1989.

———. "You Can't Get There From Here." In *Cambridge Companion to Hegel,* edited by Frederick C. Beiser. Cambridge: Cambridge University Press, 1993.

Plato. "Timaeus." In *Plato in Twelve Volumes 7.* London: Heinemann, 1961.

———. *Timaeus and Critias.* Translated by Desmond Lee. Harmondsworth: Penguin, 1971.

Pulkkinen, Tuija. "Naisyhteisö: Subjektius, identiteetti ja toimijuus" (Women as Community: Subjectivity, Identity, and Agency). In *Yhteisö,* edited by *Jussi Kotkavirta and Arto Laitinen.* Jyväskylä: SoPhi, 1998.

———. "Identiteetti ja ei-identiteetti. Alkuperästä ja ykseydestä moneuteen ja toistoon identiteettipolitiikassa" (Identity and Non-Identity. From Origin and Oneness to Multiplicity and Repetition in Identity Politics). *Ajatus 56* (1999): 213–236.

———. "Political Identity—An Inquiry into the Concept." In *La passió per la llibertat/Passion for Freedom. Action, Passion and Politics—Feminist controversies,* edited by Fina Birulés and Maria Isabel Penã Aguado. Barcelona: University of Barcelona Press, 2004.

———. "The Gendered 'Subjects' of Political Representation." In *The Ashgate Research Companion to the Politics of Democratization in Europe,* edited by K. Palonen, T. Pulkkinen and J. Rosales. Farnham: Ashgate, 2008.

Riley, Denise. *"Am I That Name?" Feminism and the Category of "Women" in History.* Houndmills: Macmillan, 1988.

Ring, Jennifer. *Modern Political Theory and Contemporary Feminism.* Albany: State University of New York Press, 1991.

Rose, Gillian. *The Broken Middle: Out of Our Ancient Society*. Oxford: Blackwell, 1992.

Rosenkranz, Karl. *Georg Wilhelm Friedrich Hegels Leben*. Darmstadt: Wissenschaftliche Buchgesellschaft, 1998.

Rousseau, Jean-Jacques. *Émile*. Translated by P. D. Jimack. London: Phoenix/Everyman, 1993.

Sallis, John. *Force of Imagination. The Sense of the Elemental*. Bloomington: Indiana University Press, 2000.

Sandford, Stella and Stone, Alison. *Hegel and Feminism*. Special Issue of *Women's Philosophy Review*, No. 22, 1999.

Schiebinger, Londa. *The Mind Has No Sex?: Women in the Origins of Modern Science*. Cambridge, MA: Harvard University Press, 1989.

Scott, Joan Wallace. *Gender and the Politics of History*. Rev. edition. New York: Columbia University Press, 1999.

Stern, Robert. *Hegel and the Phenomenology of Spirit*. London: Routledge, 2002.

Storr, F. *Sophocles in Two Volumes*. Vol. 1. The Loeb Classical Library. Cambridge, MA: Harvard University Press, 1981.

Taylor, Charles. "The Opening Arguments of the Phenomenology." In *Hegel: A Collection of Critical Essays*, edited by Alasdair MacIntyre. New York: Anchor Books, 1972.

———. *Hegel*. Cambridge: Cambridge University Press, 1975.

Toews, John. "Transformations of Hegelianism, 1805–1846." In *The Cambridge Companion to Hegel*, edited by Frederick C. Beiser. Cambridge: Cambridge University Press, 1993.

Weil, Eric. *Hegel and the State*. Translated by Mark A. Cohen. 1950. Reprint. Baltimore: Johns Hopkins University Press, 1998.

Werner, Laura. *The Restless Love of Thinking. The Concept Liebe in G. W. F. Hegel's Philosophy*. Helsinki: University of Helsinki Press, 2007.

Wood, Allen. *Hegel's Ethical Thought*. Cambridge: Cambridge University Press, 1990.

Wright, Elizabeth. *Feminism and Psychoanalysis: A Critical Dictionary*. Oxford UK and Massachusetts USA: Blackwell, 1992.

Wyckoff, Elizabeth. "Antigone." In *Sophocles 1*, edited by David Grene. *The Complete Greek Tragedies*. Edited by David Grene and Richmond Lattimore. Chicago: University of Chicago Press, 1954.

Zeitlin, Froma I. "Travesties of Gender and Genre in Aristophanes' Thesmophoriazousae." In *Reflections of Women in Antiquity*, edited by Helene P. Foley. New York: Gordon and Breach, 1981.

Žižek, Slavoj. *Enjoy Your Symptom!* London: Routledge, 1992.

Index